PRAISE FOR LEAPFROGGING THE COMPETITION

"This is not a book to be read once and shelved. It is the essential guide to the future of business. . . . There is a new axiom in business: It's 'leapfrog or languish.' And victory belongs to those who leap."

—From the foreword by Bob Ulrich, chairman
and CEO, Dayton-Hudson Corporation

"This book wisely urges organizations and those who lead them to leave the burdens and risks of conventional thinking behind, and provides a generously detailed and useful roadmap to achieving ongoing organizational success and excellence."

—J.W. Marriott, Jr., chairman, president
and CEO, Marriott International, Inc.

"A refreshingly blunt and no-nonsense book that dispels any sense of complacency about what it will take to be a market leader in the 21st century. Oren Harari gives practical advice and relevant examples of how we can build our own leapfrogging organizations."

—Jinny Goldstein, president and CEO,
PBS The Business Channel

"Fabulous! Oren Harari has distilled all of the latest leadership philosophy into a single, highly readable volume. If you can read only one book to help you lead your company into the 21st century, *Leapfrogging the Competition* is that book."

—Peter Van Nort, senior vice president, Raytheon E & C Co.,
former president and COO, H. B. Zachry Co.

"Practical and surprising thoughts on how to stay ahead of the competition. The end result inspires the reader to come up with big solutions to big problems and stamp out predictable, mediocre strategies."

—Mike Rawlings, president,
Pizza Hut, Inc.

"Harari's call to 'catapult strategy over conventional wisdom' is a must read for every manager who engages in strategic planning."

—Steven J ⁒

D1367777

"Even better than the first edition. This book describes what leaders must do to create a culture of innovation and what organizations must do to excite and amaze customers."

—Kathleen A. Dore, president,
Bravo Networks

"Oren is a man who walks his talk. This is not only a groundbreaking piece of work, but a tool that will empower us to succeed with gratitude and grace. Every entrepreneur should read and follow this book."

—Mitch Schlimer, chairman,
Let's Talk Business Network

"This is a power-packed book. Without platitudes or piety, Oren Harari delivers the essential lessons for smashing through the barriers to excellent performance and market leadership."

—Peter Danis, CEO,
Boise Cascade Office Products Corporation

"This book is the real thing. The insights on global competition, technology, and strategic alliances are right on target. This is a book that every executive, and every aspiring executive, ought to read."

—Jim Hebe, president and CEO,
Freightliner Corporation

"If you've missed Harari, take the time to learn why you need 'bifocal' vision. You won't regret it but your competition will."

—Karen Ignagni, president and CEO,
American Association of Health Plans

"Demonstrates how we can leverage our business opportunities by using information and people as strategic assets."

—Daniel Meyer, chairman and CEO,
Milacron, Inc.

"If you want to transform your company from hardware based to knowledge based, Dr. Harari's book gives great guidance and challenges conventional thinking."

—Lars Nyberg, chairman and CEO,
NCR Corporation

"Gives a genuinely fresh perspective on what customer focus really means."

—Douglas West, senior vice president of Finance, Information,
and Human Resources, Toyota Motor Sales, U.S.A., Inc.

Leapfrogging the Competition

Five Giant Steps to Becoming
a Market Leader

FULLY REVISED 2ND EDITION

OREN HARARI, Ph.D.

PRIMA PUBLISHING

PRIMA PUBLISHING and colophon are registered trademarks of Prima Communications, Inc.

Library of Congress Cataloging-in-Publication Data

Harari, Oren.
   Leapfrogging the competition, fully : five giant steps to becoming a market leader / Oren Harari.   Rev., 2nd ed.
      p.   cm.
   Includes index.
   ISBN 0-7615-1973-4
   1. Organizational change. 2. Strategic planning. 3. Organizational behavior. 4. Corporate culture. I. Title.
   HD58.8.H3637   1999
   658.4   dc21   99-15038
                                                                                    CIP

99 00 01 02 HH 10 9 8 7 6 5 4 3 2
Printed in the United States of America

How to Order
Single copies may be ordered from Prima Publishing, P.O. Box 1260BK, Rocklin, CA 95677; telephone (916) 632-4400. Quantity discounts are also available. On your letterhead, include information concerning the intended use of the books and the number of books you wish to purchase.

Visit us online at www.primalifestyles.com

To Leslie,
with love

CONTENTS

Foreword   ix

Note on the Second Edition   xi

Plan of the Book   xiii

Acknowledgments   xv

Introduction   xviii

GIANT STEP **I**

Catapult Your Strategy over Conventional Wisdom   1

  1. Be First, Be Exceptional   11
  2. Make Yourself Obsolete Before
     Someone Else Does   23
  3. Go Beyond Traditional Competitive Weapons   36
  4. View the World Through Bifocal Lenses   56

GIANT STEP **II**

Flood Your Organization with Knowledge   63

  5. Obliterate Barriers to the Flow of Ideas   79
  6. Don't Empower Your Employees—
     Liberate Them   97

GIANT STEP **III**

Wrap Your Organization Around Each Customer   111

  7. Obsess About Customers, Not Profits   121
  8. Focus on Market Units of One   130

GIANT STEP **IV**

Transform Your Organization into a Web of Relationships   145

  9. Get Real About What It Takes
     to Build a Web Team   161
10. Invite Your Competition In—
     Don't Fence Them Out   169
11. Bless Thy Complaining Customer   177

GIANT STEP **V**

Eat Change for Breakfast— Serve It Up for Every Meal   185

12. Get Honest—Walk the Talk   195
13. Don't Get Snookered by Fads du Jour   206
14. Sponge Up Daily Doses of Reality   225
15. Beware the Danger of Success   232

A Short Epilogue: Putting It into Perspective   241

Index   245

As much as their authors talk about openness to change, most business books are substantially alike. Not this one. With all the energy and frankness of his frequent lectures and his 1994 book coauthored with Nick Imparato, *Jumping the Curve*, Oren Harari practices what he preaches in this latest book, *Leapfrogging the Competition*. His brilliant analogies, astute observations, and cut-to-the-chase analyses leapfrog over the conventional wisdom of theorists who spend little if any time in the trenches.

This book is not for the faint-hearted but for the courageous. It is for managers and executives who are still as excited about being in business now as they were in their first days on the job. It is for those who, as Harari puts it, "eat change for breakfast."

If you're lucky, however, you may find that your organization is already taking some Giant Steps. In that case, this book will help you hone your strategies. If the book helps you recognize that your company has not yet moved itself into leapfrogging position and is merely reacting to customer feedback and competitors' moves, you'll find no better catalyst for springing into action.

In clear, no-nonsense language and with plenty of relevant examples, *Leapfrogging the Competition* demonstrates how companies can "lower the cost of failure while simultaneously boosting the returns on successes." That's why I like this book. Harari doesn't just tell executives *what* we ought to do; he tells us *how*, so that we're not left to reinvent the wheel.

Harari speaks the plain truth about the mistakes corporations are making and about what it takes to avoid playing catch-up and instead surge ahead into the information-intensive, hyper-competitive millennium. Although contrarian—admonishing managers to rely on intuition and judgment rather than market research for strategic decisions and product ideas, for example—

the author's words are weighty and genuine. This is fine-grained wood, not veneer.

"*Exciting, coherent*, and *ever-evolving* are the operative words for describing . . . the leapfrogging organization," says Harari. To my mind, it is the first chapter, or "commitment," and the last that most strongly support that description. Commitment 1: Be First, Be Exceptional might sum up the driving force at Dayton Hudson Corporation, which, today at least, fits the author's definition of a leapfrogging organization. Nevertheless, along with leaders in every other industry, we are susceptible to complacency and must rout out routineness every day. If your company already occupies the leadership position, pay special attention to Commitment 15: Beware the Danger of Success.

Leapfrogging the Competition is the most compelling argument yet written for being first to market with products and services, and for being first on the all-star list with your customers. Harari dispenses with the commonly held belief that market leaders must constantly study their competitors and fight or dodge their every move in an effort to finally "beat" them. Instead, he issues a charge more realistic for today's marketplace: "Leapfrog" over your competitors and literally redefine not only your organization but the marketplace as well.

The author's organization of his material into five Giant Steps makes the book—and the prospect of wholesale change—digestible. It matters little whether you read the chapters in order or at random, so interwoven are the principles of innovation, openness, customer focus, relationship building, and the courage to change. So well told are the stories of failure and success that you are bound to derive value from every page.

This is not a book to be read once and shelved. It is the essential guide to the future of business, in which the concept of permanence is meaningless and in which risk taking is imperative. With the publication of this book, there is a new axiom in business: It's "leapfrog or languish." And victory belongs to those who leap.

Bob Ulrich
Chairman and CEO
Dayton Hudson Corporation

NOTE ON THE SECOND EDITION

Why write a revised version of a book that's just over a year old? After the first edition of *Leapfrogging the Competition* was released in fall of 1997, it received numerous accolades, including a citation from Management General as one of the ten best business books in 1997. So, as the saying goes, why fix it if it ain't broke?

Well, as I tell clients, if it ain't broke, you ain't looking hard enough. In the world of business today, everything is breaking—at an extraordinary pace. A few years ago I spoke with the CEO of a privately held company that develops and manufactures jewelry which is sold in major retailers. "It used to be," she told me, "that if I had a great product idea, I could count on eighteen to twenty-four months to reap the benefits from it. Now, I'm lucky if I have three months."

Three months. I've heard that before. Executives across industries are looking at three months as *the* window of opportunity—which means that one year represents long-term strategic planning. In my business—information and knowledge—one year is an eternity.

Accordingly, I found myself constantly updating and revising my presentations to audiences and clients after the first edition of *Leapfrogging* was published. New Internet opportunities, new technologies, new capital market crises, new mergers and acquisitions, new startups, new customer and employee expectations—they all came fast and furious. This meant that as good as the first edition was, there was a compelling reason to update and revise it.

The result is what you hold in your hand. This next-generation *Leapfrogging the Competition* is about 40 percent new. The foundation of the book—the goal of market leadership and the five Giant Steps necessary to leapfrog the competition—stays intact. The chapter titles and their themes remain the same also.

However, I reckon that nearly every page has something new, different, and provocative in it. Those of you who enjoyed the first edition will find fresh value in reading this revised version. Those who didn't see the first edition will be reading an up-to-date blueprint on what it takes to maintain a sustainable competitive advantage in today's free-market global economy.

I hope you enjoy this book. Let me know what you think of it. Send me an e-mail at oren@harari.com or visit my Web site at www.harari.com. Thanks!

PLAN OF THE BOOK

The basic premise of this book is that the way to leapfrog the competition is to take on five huge strategic steps, and the way to do that is to take on a challenging set of personal and organizational commitments. This process will change the way you and your organization think, act, and do business.

Accordingly, the book is divided into five main parts. Each part introduces a Giant Step, and is followed by a practical set of commitments. These commitments are not "feel-good homilies"—they are not "dare-to-be-great" platitudes. They are tough, rigorous, and ultimately very rewarding, for they serve as the why-and-how blueprint for implementing the Giant Steps. The book presents fifteen vital commitments in all. In fact, since each chapter represents a specific commitment, the book is organized and numbered by "commitments" rather than chapters.

For example, the first four chapters/commitments illustrate the work needed to achieve Giant Step I: Catapult Your Strategy over Conventional Wisdom. First, you'll find an overview and discussion of the Giant Step itself. The next four commitments are relevant to that Giant Step: Commitment 1: Be First, Be Exceptional; Commitment 2: Make Yourself Obsolete Before Someone Else Does; Commitment 3: Go Beyond Traditional Competitive Weapons; Commitment 4: View the World Through Bifocal Lenses. And so on.

Unfortunately, the two-dimensional nature of books requires the commitments to be presented sequentially. However, please keep in mind that in practice, the Giant Steps and the Commitments are not meant to be implemented sequentially, nor are they listed in any particular order of importance. As leaders, we don't have the luxury of doing anything sequentially. If we are to be successful in leapfrogging the competition and establishing market leadership, we must embrace the idea of at least confronting all five Giant Steps and every commitment—during our workday, every day.

The foundation of each chapter/commitment is selectively drawn from a collection of over five years' worth of topical research in articles that I have written for *Management Review*, the flagship publication of the American Management Association. I have significantly integrated, updated, and supplemented that information to fit into the framework of this book. If you approach the material as seriously as I believe you will, I predict that you'll find the content of each chapter to be an important aid in your quest for competitive advantage.

ACKNOWLEDGMENTS

All authors face the temptation to make this section infinitely long by thanking anyone who has ever had any involvement with any part of the book, however minuscule. I'll avoid temptation in this case, but I do want to acknowledge just a few people without whose support this book could not have been completed.

First, I'd like to thank the executives who provided the testimonials you see on the jacket and inside. It's not merely that they took time from their busy schedules to read a draft of this book but, more important, that they did it quickly and graciously to meet a tight publication deadline. I'm very grateful to Bob Ulrich for writing the foreword, and, for their kind endorsements, I sincerely thank Peter Danis, Michael Dell, Kathleen A. Dore, Steven J. Douglass, Jinny Goldstein, Jim Hebe, Karen Ignagni, J.W. Marriott, Daniel Meyer, Lars Nyberg, Tom Peters, Colin Powell, Mike Rawlings, Mitch Schlimer, Scott Shuster, Peter Van Nort, and Douglas West.

At the University of San Francisco, where I am a faculty member, several individuals merit special acknowledgment. My MBA research assistant, Joshua Engel, was invaluable in helping me put together both editions of this book. Whether using the USF library or electronic databases, making phone calls or sending E-mail messages to key individuals, or poring over hard copy documents or Web sites, Josh was exceptional at ferreting out the kind of information I needed—and often did so at a moment's notice.

My students in the strategic management courses that I taught in the MBA and Executive MBA courses in 1997 and 1998 were a joy. I like to think I taught them something, but these sharp professionals taught me a lot by coming up with some terrific insights, data, and anecdotes, which I have included in this book. I cannot list my class rosters, but I would like to acknowledge Colleen Faryabi, a FedEx manager who went beyond the call of duty in ferreting out the FedEx/Fujitsu story which I feature in Giant Step IV.

I'm particularly grateful to Dr. Gary Williams, the dean of the USF McLaren School of Business, where I teach. Over the years, Gary has been extremely supportive of my research efforts. He has provided me with the kind of advice, resources, and encouragement that has made it much easier for me to write this book as well as my other publications.

Among these "other publications" has been my monthly "Cutting Edge"—recently renamed "Harari At Large"—column in *Management Review*. As noted, I drew from some of the research and commentary in those columns in writing this book. For nearly five years, Genevieve Capowski was my very able editor of those columns.

My assistant, Susan Darling, has been wonderful in organizing my life and keeping me in touch with the daily reality of my calendar, including flight schedules, appointments, conference calls, and a mountain of deadlines. Her efficiency, graciousness, and above all, friendship allowed me the time to create and write.

My friend Mike Childs, a successful entrepreneur in his own right, provided me with very practical insights and feedback. I credit his input for my decision to organize the entire book around five giant steps.

Since the first edition was the foundation for the work you hold in your hands, I'd like to acknowledge two individuals. Kristen Stoimenoff of American Century Press, the publisher of the first edition, was exceptional in coordinating the perpetual stream of details and shepherding the entire project to fruition.

Martha H. Peak, currently Director of Publications at the Chicago headquarters of consultancy A.T. Kearny, was my editor for the first edition. I cannot thank her enough for her skills, acumen, dedication, and spirit. She did an outstanding job in helping me shape and develop the final manuscript.

Prima Publishing is the publisher of this second edition, and I cannot say enough good things about the people who worked with me to create this book. Ben Dominitz, president and founder of Prima, was supportive from the beginning, and Steven Martin, Susan Silva, David Richardson, and Andrew

Mitchell were a delight to work with. They—and, it seems, everyone at Prima—were fast, flexible, efficient, responsive, helpful, friendly, and totally professional. Wow! Many thanks!

Finally, and most important, I want to express my profound gratitude to my wife, Leslie, who gave me generous heaps of encouragement and support from the inception of this project. Of course, those are the kinds of words that any author is supposed to write about his or her spouse. But in this case, in view of the fact that our second son was born right in the middle of the writing of the first edition, and in view of the fact that Leslie voluntarily took on the brunt of the child-care responsibilities for both Jordan and Dylan so that I could work on both the first and second edition, I'd say that the laudatory sentiments about her are more than justified. I can't thank her enough, for that and for many other things, and it is to her that I gratefully, and endearingly, dedicate this book.

INTRODUCTION

In the fall of 1998, I had the opportunity to address the annual meeting of the Mortgage Bankers Association of America. Mortgage bankers arrange loans and then sell them to other lenders and investors. The business has been a lucrative one. During my speech, however, I pointed to an article in the trade publication *Real Estate Finance Today* that suggested some interesting, potentially ominous developments brewing. On July 13, 1998, Microsoft entered the electronic mortgage market by launching a Web preview of Microsoft HomeAdvisor. HomeAdvisor offers a rate-shopping menu and a heap of information about the home-buying process in general. It also offers the consumer the capacity to complete a mortgage application on-line by linking up with several participating mortgage companies.

Many other electronic sites already existed before Microsoft's entrée, such as HomeShark, E-Loan, and Intuit's QuickenMortgage. As a whole, these Web sites are extremely popular, receiving millions of "hits," or visits, a month. Their popularity is due to the information they offer: understanding the mortgage process, making sense of the financial picture surrounding a mortgage offer, finding the right home in the right neighborhood, securing the best rates, going through prequalification, and understanding the mechanics of the total package, including the closing process. In effect, these Web sites help empower customers to analyze a situation professionally and make rapid, efficient decisions on their own.

After citing these facts, I asked the audience a simple question: "What exactly do I need you people for?"

It was a half-tongue-in-cheek question, and the audience enjoyed a laugh over it. Certainly, mortgage bankers can provide many services that software alone currently does not, in both primary markets where loans are originated and secondary markets where pools of loans are resold.

Nevertheless, a nerve had been struck. The traditional products and services in the business are steadily becoming low-margin commodities. Many established lenders, from Chase Manhatten to Countrywide Credit Industries, are themselves offering consumers ways to originate and partially execute a mortgage package on-line. However, new Internet companies are coming on board daily, offering consumers user-friendly product that walks them step-by-step toward executing the entire package on-line. As of September 1998, 3,000 mortgage Web sites were operating, up from 60 two years ago.

To differentiate oneself in this world and to avoid the free fall of dog-eat-dog price competition, it becomes clear that mortgage bankers must develop radical new offerings in information, delivery, and customer care. As the president of one new on-line provider noted, "It's going to put pressure on loan officers to one-up what you can get on the Internet site; otherwise, what value do they add to the process?"

Speaking to me privately after my speech, one outside observer of the business added, "Mortgage bankers will have to incorporate the Internet not just as a simple add-on to what they currently do but as a fundamental way of driving the business. They'll use it to create totally new service packages. The smart ones will also use it as a two-way marketing channel—to dialogue with consumers around the world and then customize services to them. I don't know what this is all going to look like—nobody does. But it's pretty clear that computer-literate consumers are going to be fiddling around with more choices than ever before, and vendors had better make sure they're solid players in this new value chain."

As you consider your own business, does any of this sound familiar?

It certainly sounds familiar to those in the music recording industry. If you were a record label that made and sold CDs (compact disks) in the 1980s, you couldn't keep up with all the money flowing in. It was a wonderful, predictable business. Once you signed up an artist and cut the master disk, the marginal cost of production was negligible. You pumped the product through radio for exposure and then sold it through retailers such as Tower Records and Wherehouse, where consumers dutifully ponied up $15 a pop. Nice revenues, nice margins.

But over the past few years, big storm clouds have been forming. First came the rash of new independent record labels, which not only crowded the marketplace with niche-oriented product but also were able to attract artists with better terms because their break-even point was lower. At the same time, the glut of content intensified as further fragmentation hit the entertainment industry as a whole: consumers were overwhelmed with product options, including CDs, cable, video, movies, radio, books, magazines, and computerized games. All this began to adversely impact the record labels' financials.

The problem was exacerbated by the entrée of entirely new players who disrupted the distribution "rules" that everyone in the industry had always followed. "Big-box" retailers such as Wal-Mart and more specialized retailers such as Circuit City began to sell CDs at cost, even below cost. They viewed CDs as loss leaders and were using them to attract buyers into the stores to purchase the bigger-ticket items.

In response to all this, many of the record labels engaged in painful, expensive consolidations as a means of reducing cost and boosting marketing clout. But even as many of these debt-filled deals were (and still are) waiting for the big payoffs, further splintering in the industry occurred as more niche players, unburdened by big overhead, jumped into the enticing entertainment arena.

Then came the most unexpected and powerful blow. New irreverent upstarts such as N2K, Liquid Audio, CDnow, Headspace, EveryCD, ElectricVillage, and GoodNoise have begun to literally rewrite the industry rules with an entirely new business model. This new model asks, first, why a consumer needs to go to a retail outlet at all. Why not use your PC to browse and sample items from a playlist containing ten times the number of selections you could get from a retail outlet—then choose what you want and we'll overnight it to you? Or, you can create your own CD. Pick the songs, we'll cut the disk, and we'll overnight it to you. Or, forget the disk. Using an MP3 data format, go ahead and download your selections directly into your computer and play it off attached speakers with digitized stereo quality—and, if you wish, store your selections permanently right into a little Walkman-size Rio PMP300 portable music player.

Currently, only a small percentage of consumers are fully taking advantage of these options, and the technology is not as user-friendly as it will be—but the trends are clearly looming over the horizon. It's relentless, potentially crushing the carefully developed sales processes, delivery systems, and economies of scale built by the big, established players. New waves of customers, especially the young, are embracing technologies that are alien to many in the established industry. The MP3 format, for example, allows anyone to compress, patch together, copy, and trade songs on the Internet. Suddenly, the whole concept of production, distribution, sales—even piracy and copyright law—undergoes radical revision. N2K founder Larry Rosen told the *Wall St. Journal's* Holman Jenkins, "There's a whole generation that thinks this is how you get music. What are you going to do? Go to the universities and arrest everyone?" Somehow, he argues, record companies will have to figure out a way to open up their archives and new playlists and allow people to sample, rent, and buy in an entirely new open marketplace.

While the big record labels are trying to figure out how to best respond to these developments, the upstarts aren't waiting around. On-line record company GoodNoise, for example, is signing artists to create music that, in addition to traditional avenues, will be distributed via an MP3 format and a Net radio station and sold on a CD-wide or individual song download basis. N2K is developing a new network of strategic partners that are completely out of the industry mainstream: America Online, Netscape, Excite, Infoseek, CBS Cable, and Ticketmaster. Just to remove any doubts that this is a serious phenomenon, a new professional association has been formed—the Digital Media Association (DiMA).

As we consider the stark realities faced by mortgage bankers and record labels, we can ask a reasonable question:

What in the world is going on?

Morgan Stanley executive Barton Biggs summarized the situation with four simple words in an August 1998 letter to his top clients: "The world seems precarious." Indeed it does. Biggs was referring primarily to the volatility in the financial markets, but I believe his words can be applied to every aspect of business today. Every industry I've researched over the past few years is facing radically new challenges and opportunities.

In fact, the world of business today has been described as being in "perpetual white water."

It's a good metaphor. Deregulation, globalization, and technological advances are generating remarkable upheavals in both organizations and products—upheavals that none of us could have imagined even a few years ago. Markets are fragmenting and splintering, becoming less and less predictable. Waves of consolidation are routinely followed by waves of divestitures and restructurings. Barriers to entry in industry after industry are crumbling, and new businesses are bubbling up in market arenas that didn't exist just a few years ago. Small wonder that in many industries, descriptive terms such as *mature market*, *convergence*, *overcapacity*, and *saturation* are becoming the norm rather than the exception.

All this makes it increasingly difficult for any organization to maintain a preeminent position, in terms of either customer loyalty or market share. Yes, one can point to the Intels, Microsofts, and Gillettes as exemplars of domination in their particular industries, but those examples are the exception rather than the rule. (Besides, as we'll discuss later, their success is due to an ever-present healthy paranoia that they'll lose everything tomorrow if they don't act as if they've got nothing today.)

In every sector, competition has intensified exponentially. With up to $2 trillion being exchanged worldwide every twenty-four hours, it's increasingly easy for entrepreneurs to access capital to start a business. Add to that the immense opportunities of global alliances and technologies that allow real-time worldwide linkups, and suddenly everyone—from established behemoth to tiny startup—has the power to be a significant player in any market segment on the planet.

Recently, a World Bank official observed that "your competitor is someone in another part of the planet that you never heard of." With globalization and technological advances, one can also apply that statement to employees, customers, suppliers, and partners. A company in one country can now perform data entry, production, or customer service functions for another company located in another country. Scientists and engineers in one site can work together simultaneously on product development with colleagues in another continent using videoconferencing screens, computer displays, whiteboards, electronic notebooks, and synchronized Web browsers.

The new technologies themselves are becoming potent sources of competition: remote banking software systems threaten conventional retail branches, Electronic Data Interchange (EDI) threatens middlemen in any distribution chain, the interactive potentials of the World Wide Web threaten everyone. Customers, meanwhile, with an increasing number of choices and options available to them, are continuously raising the bar on the kinds of performance they expect from vendors.

To survive in this whirlpool, organizations themselves are becoming leaner, faster, smarter. The only other option is to perish: life cycles of both products and organizations are shrinking rapidly (nearly half of the 1980 Fortune 500 has already disappeared). Even organizations that are prospering today still have the uneasy sense that calamity is right around the corner. It doesn't matter how big your balance sheet or press clippings are. There are no guarantees anymore.

What's happening? Novell CEO Eric Schmidt answers succinctly: "This is just the beginning of a very big deal." Yes, indeed. The players are different. The rules are different. The game itself is different. So much so that Hewlett Packard CEO Lew Platt was moved to tell a number of his colleagues during a speech, "Whatever made you successful in the past won't in the future."

I see the statements of Schmidt and Platt as fundamentally optimistic. They're not saying to throw in the towel. They are saying that it behooves us to recognize that huge impending forces around us can overwhelm us if we ignore them but can enrich us tremendously if we pay attention to them and capitalize on them.

For the past few years, I have been dissecting this message with clients and audiences around the world. I have observed that managers in all segments of the economy have become increasingly receptive to this message and desirous of confronting it head-on. But while doing so, they have brought an important issue to my attention.

Paradoxically, in a world where the forces of change appear overwhelming in number, what practitioners need more than anything are a few precise, reliable, durable, cutting-edge leadership tools. Too many paths and solutions can themselves become overwhelming. When Nicholas Imparato and I wrote *Jumping the Curve: Innovation and Strategic Choice in an Age of Transition* (Jossey-Bass, 1994), we presented many ways for leaders to address the emerging marketplace. But the operative word was *many*. Over the past few years, I have often been asked if it is possible to boil down the blueprint for competitive advantage to a smaller, more manageable set of action steps that could serve as a bold compass for visionary leadership.

This is a very legitimate concern, and in response, I have updated and consolidated the findings of my own research into a set of five steps. I can assure you that these five steps, if diligently and honorably pursued, will most definitely put you in position to leapfrog your competition.

This is why I chose the words for the title of this book carefully. First, consider the word *leapfrog*. An organization that can leapfrog is one that can *bound over* a chaotic terrain, flexibly *bounce off* unanticipated hurdles, and *spring forward* to snare any opportunities that fleetingly appear. Competitors? The leapfrogging organization is not obsessed with either imitating or avoiding them. The leapfrogging organization simply *vaults over* them. It does so with explosive speed and outrageous product-service offerings that simultaneously amaze customers and reshape the industry.

These words may sound overly dramatic, but in the emerging millennium they will be the clues to organizational success. In a business world crowded with throngs of jostling competitors and bursting with advances in technology and science, the winners will be those organizations that have both the commitment and the capacity to zoom ahead of the mob. Managing with "me-too" products, "let's-play-it-safe" strategies, and "at-least-we're-no-worse-than-anyone-else" mind-sets will be the kiss of death.

Simply keeping up with the competition means consigning your organization to mediocrity. There's nothing wrong with mediocrity per se, except that in the emerging marketplace there will be so many mediocre players that ultimately the act of being just another face in a rapidly growing crowd will doom your organization to nonentity and demise.

But *how* does one leapfrog the competition? How does one create an enterprise that can regularly vault over the morass of mediocrity and thus stand out above the fray?

I propose five steps. Radical steps. Giant steps. These words hold significance. Giant steps are not small. They are not easy. They are not tentative. They are not faddish. They are not minor variations of conventional wisdom. They are not tweaky extensions of the status quo.

No, they are big, brassy, bold, and occasionally bizarre. They represent the strategic fundamentals of a select but fast-growing group of organizations that are already in the process of inventing the future.

The five Giant Steps, the meat and potatoes of this book, can be your path to the future as well. Let me briefly summarize them:

GIANT STEP I:
CATAPULT YOUR STRATEGY OVER
CONVENTIONAL WISDOM

Paul Handlery, chairman of the Handlery hotel chain, once commented to me that in business, what is revolutionary today is mundane tomorrow. How true. Likewise, what is labeled conventional wisdom today will become anachronistic tomorrow.

Organizations that leapfrog their competition understand and capitalize on this insight, which is why they insist on doing the unconventional today. They start with the premise that the key to competitive advantage is to gear everything—strategic thinking, decision-making styles, employee development, organizational systems, you name it—toward being first to market with exceptional ideas and exceptional offerings. These organizations then ferret out the ordinary in favor of the extraordinary—be it in product, service delivery, distribution, or after-sale. Anything that smacks of mundane, vanilla, and commonplace is rejected as uninteresting. For leapfrogging organizations, what their competitors are doing today is a quick benchmark to be noted but not a style sheet that imposes limitations to what is possible.

That's why these organizations find the courage to deliberately obsolete their ongoing products and processes (*especially* if those products are currently successes) regardless of what their competitors are doing. That's also why they do not overly rely on traditional tools such as strategic planning, competitive analysis, and market research—all of which reflect today's realities and conventional wisdom, not tomorrow's.

Companies that adhere to this Giant Step are externally focused, constantly scanning the vast terrain ahead and seizing on emerging forces in technology, demographics, and consumer preferences. They use these forces to fuel their obsession with *leading* the market, not just "responding" to it. This is why their actions are often deemed weird or outrageous by those who wear the lenses of traditional management.

Finally, the leaders who pilot these catapulting organizations have developed the capacity to view the world bifocally— that is, not simply with "vision" but with *bifocal vision*. Every day, in every meeting, in every report they simultaneously attend to today's market realities (technology, competition, customers, etc.) while aggressively anticipating and preparing for tomorrow's.

GIANT STEP II:
FLOOD YOUR ORGANIZATION
WITH KNOWLEDGE

In a knowledge-based economy, smart organizations will be the clear winners. Leapfrogging organizations see themselves not as amalgams of bricks and mortar, but as growing, bubbling cauldrons of interesting, exciting ideas—ideas that can be translated into fast action. They see that competitive advantage is no longer a result of balance-sheet size or press clippings but of rapid-fire information, expertise, and networks that allow people to create what currently doesn't exist, in either product or process. Organizations that carry out this Giant Step carefully cultivate an ever-growing pool of knowledge as a dominant strategic weapon, and they ensure that this knowledge is flooded to every corner and every person of the organization.

Unlike many enterprises today, leapfrogging organizations don't drown their people with data, paper, and protocol. Instead, they deliberately smash existing barriers to the flow of information, learning, and communication. They do this so that employees can access the knowledge and the people they need, when they need it, as they need it. In most organizations, barriers to the flow of ideas are numerous. They can be, for example, backward technology, or hierarchical pass-off requirements for even the most mundane decisions, or policies that restrict financial and strategic information to a chosen few, or an "us-versus-them" adversarial relationship with suppliers.

Leapfrogging organizations take pains to weaken—if not obliterate—those barriers so that people in every nook and cranny of the organization can draw upon whatever and whoever they need to make immediate, informed, creative decisions. This means that the culture is marked by openness and accessibility. Information technology becomes an essential tool for everyone, from controller to front-line employee. Computers perform the routine work, provide a medium for expert systems, and allow rapid dissemination of ideas. This free-flooding of knowledge is accompanied by rapid applications, tests, and pilots initiated by a well-trained workforce, the results of which come full circle and wind up flooding the organization with even more knowledge—again accessible to all. All this galvanizes the organization to continually leapfrog its slower, narrow-thinking, idea-restricted competitors.

GIANT STEP III:
WRAP YOUR ORGANIZATION
AROUND EACH CUSTOMER

The winning organizations in the emerging millennium will understand—as some leapfrogging organizations already do—that mass markets are dying. Uniform, standardized products and services are dying. Customer patience and tolerance is dying. Leapfrogging organizations begin by vaulting over the standard lip service of "customer is king" and live instead by two precepts.

First, they adhere to a philosophy that states that we are in business *not* to build profit but to build customers, which means building long-term constructive relationships with customers. If that is done right, the numbers we all seek—earnings, market share, shareholder value, profit—will soar as the scorecard builds for making the right plays.

Certainly, the ability to manage costs, assets, cash flow, and earnings effectively is a vital component of solid management. (In fact, as we shall see in Giant Step II, it ought to be an important part of everyone's job, not just top management's.) The issue, however, is one of priorities. Focusing on the financials at the expense of creating value for customers will concentrate the organization's entrepreneurial efforts on myopic, chess-piece reorganizations and financial sleight of hand, which will ultimately diminish both customer loyalty and stock value in an increasingly fickle marketplace.

Second, leapfrogging organizations commit to tailoring their products and services for each individual customer. They understand that the winning organization will be smart enough, light enough, and fleet enough to wrap itself around the unique needs and desires of each customer. Personalized service, customized products, turn-on-a-dime responsiveness, and solution-based efforts *to each customer's needs*—these are the passwords of organizations that follow this Giant Step. By so doing, they leapfrog over competitors that in effect insist that their customers wrap *themselves* around the standardized products, processes, and time frames of the organization.

GIANT STEP IV:
TRANSFORM YOUR ORGANIZATION
INTO A WEB OF RELATIONSHIPS

To leapfrog, you need allies. Organizations that leapfrog their competitors do so with the assistance of a trusted network all around the world. They seek intimate partnerships constantly, because they do not believe for a minute that they—or anyone else—can magically collect and hoard the best talent within the confines of their four walls. In fact, they don't even view their organizations in terms of four walls. They view their organizations as extensions of other organizations—their allies—all of whom have unique expertise and vital competencies.

Unsurprisingly then, they do not define their business environment in terms of insiders versus outsiders because in their minds there is no "us" or "them." Instead, they view themselves as networks, combinations, clusters, and alliances—all open and permeable, where information is freely shared and where people of all parties freely move in and out of changing boundaries. These "webs" (networks, alliances) are increasingly virtual, usually organically ebbing and flowing, and they hold themselves together by that most intangible of organizational glue: trust.

Visualize the organization not in terms of the traditional heavy, massive, hierarchical pyramid bolted to the ground by the weight of vertical integration. Think of it instead as an ever-multiplying, virtual set of overlapping concentric circles. Visualize an organization that cocontracts (not "subcontracts") every function in which it is not a star player and keeps only that in which it is truly the best. Visualize an organization that looks to any world-class player anywhere—including its competitors and customers—as a potential partner for breakthrough market offerings. Visualize an organization that is unencumbered, perpetually spinning new offspring in new directions in every corner of the world. In fact, visualize an organization that uses alliances to make the planet its playground—and you'll start to envision an organization that perpetually leapfrogs over heavy, turgid competitors that have no comprehension of what's skyrocketing above them.

GIANT STEP V:
EAT CHANGE FOR BREAKFAST—
SERVE IT UP FOR EVERY MEAL

A few years ago, Harry Quadracchi, chairman of Quad/Graphics, explained his company's extraordinary success with a simple statement: "We eat change for breakfast." He meant that his entire company embraces change as a business opportunity and that the organization is managed in such a way to quickly capitalize on it. I like what he said, and I would extend that advice a bit further.

The leapfrogging organization is one that is mobilized not merely to adapt to change but to *cause* it. The charge of creating visible, regular, customer-wowing, market-shaking change becomes the personal priority of leaders who are committed to leapfrog the competition. Hence, preparing change for every meal means that corporate leaders quite literally define their management role as *provocateurs* of change.

As provocateurs of change, they proactively seek opportunities to challenge the process *every day*. They "walk the talk" by altering their personal behaviors and calendars to reflect their new strategic priorities. They constantly seek feedback from customers and employees to monitor their progress toward their chosen path. They don't get snookered by management fads du jour, not even widely accepted ones such as reengineering or TQM. They continuously scan the marketplace with healthy paranoia; that is, they desperately fear the complacency that often follows success. Finally, they understand that this composite of behavior is what really defines leadership, because while everyone loves to talk about change, the fact is that too many people hate the innovator who dares disturb the status quo.

Ultimately, the leapfrogging organization is propelled by individuals who possess the courage and perseverance to confront a new world with a daily serving of meaningful change. These are the leaders who turn their organizations into ones that are so fit and fine-tuned that leapfrogging the competition becomes not just a figure of speech but a real, continuous event.

These are the five Giant Steps, and this book presents the whys and the hows of executing each of them, as well as numerous examples of organizations that are already in the process of vaulting forward. But make no mistake; these are truly giant steps—relatively easy to understand conceptually, but damnably difficult to execute. If you think about it, that's a good thing: if these steps were easy to execute, everyone would be doing it, and that in turn would mean that all of us would be right back in the middle of the pack.

Yet, with commitment and diligence, these five Giant Steps can be successfully accomplished. And when you do so, you will not merely "respond" to the market; you will *lead* it. That is why the subtitle of this book refers to market "leadership." It is market leadership that allows our investors, our customers, and our employees to reap the greatest rewards. It is market leadership that spurs our careers. And it is market leadership that creates—and is created by—an exciting, fun work environment.

Buddy Ryan may not have been a particularly successful head coach in the National Football League, but he was right on target when he described competition in terms of a bunch of dogs hauling a snow sled: "If you ain't the lead dog," he observed, "the scenery never changes." I suspect that you have picked up this book because you're not interested in constantly looking at someone else's backside or, for that matter, constantly feeling the breath of someone else behind you. For you, leapfrogging the competition is the most attractive option—in fact, the only option—and this book will help you attain that goal.

GIANT STEP I

CATAPULT YOUR STRATEGY OVER CONVENTIONAL WISDOM

A few months ago I was asked by the CEO of a large, publicly traded corporation to analyze the company's most recent strategic plan. This I did, and then I addressed the fifteen officers. I commended them for the logic and reasonableness of the plan—and then pointed out that those attributes were its Achilles' heel.

"Your plan is so reasonable that it probably differs little from the plans of every one of your major competitors. But in a crowded marketplace, that's a liability, because the key to competitive advantage is uniqueness: distinguishing oneself from the pack by doing something truly different and inspiring. Bluntly speaking, there's none of that here. After wading through the numbers, the graphs, the jargon, the heuristics—this plan is ordinary and mundane. There's nothing special or exciting about your strategy, which means that the outcomes for your customers—and ultimately your investors—aren't going to be very special or exciting, either. And if that's the case, the difficulties you're currently facing vis-à-vis dwindling margins and earnings will most likely continue."

This was tough talk, and it is to the CEO's credit that he was open to discussing these ideas in depth. Once we did, he agreed with my assessment and committed his team to a complete overhaul of the document they had worked so hard to produce. What finally convinced him was remembering that none of the fifteen officers, including himself, had felt any excitement or exhilaration in developing the plan. It had been a mechanical, analytically detached process, which meant that the plan itself had little "soul."

During our discussions, we came to some interesting conclusions. First, a company must do the unconventional today, before it becomes conventional wisdom that everyone else rushes to emulate. (Have you noticed that many of those rushing to mimic CNN's all-news programming or Dell Computer's path-breaking, direct-sales approach are the same people who derided those business models at their inception?)

Second, we concluded that when you catapult your strategy over conventional wisdom, appealing consequences emerge: a temporary monopoly, a brand imprint on a new market, a head-start learning infrastructure for next-generation products and services, an environment that attracts the best and brightest employees, and, of course, revenue growth and margins that knock the socks off investors.

Third, we reviewed case histories of companies such as CNN, Dell, Schwab, Wal-Mart, Nike, and Amazon.com, and we agreed that because these companies broke and reinvented industry rules, their leaders were initially labeled insane by industry pundits, analysts, competitors, and even customers.

Says Amazon.com's founder Jeff Bezos, "Nobody sane would have predicted that we would be where we are today after a few years." Exactly. I showed the fifteen executives the October 27, 1997, issue of *Fortune* magazine, which highlighted "The World's Most Admired Companies." The one factor that differentiated the most admired from the also-rans was guts. "Their managers are willing to take some risks so bold they may cause shareholders, stock analysts, and employees to seriously question their sanity—at least until they turn out to have been right."

Our little group concluded, in fact, that if their new, revised strategy is not considered somewhat insane by their current competitors and traditional industry observers, they're probably still operating within the dull prison of conventional wisdom.

As the executives prepared to redo their strategy, I challenged the officers to take a hard, fresh look at their business. "Ask yourself, how can we revolutionize our business? How can we rewrite industry rules? How can we amaze today's customers? How can we delight tomorrow's? How can we completely baffle our competitors? These are some of the demanding questions that will excite both you and your stockholders."

As the 1990s end and the next millennium begins to unfold, your company's need to be unique and special becomes especially urgent. The explosion of technological advances, competitor entrants, and global risk capital coupled with the relentless movement toward free trade means that the worldwide arena of products, services, players, partnerships, and ideas is becoming ever more crowded at a frighteningly accelerating pace. The symptoms are clear: glutted, saturated markets; indistinguishable products; image and price convergence.

In this high-pressure arena, tepid, ultracautious, or "me too" strategies are a prescription for uphill struggle at best, outright failure at worst. If customers and investors can't identify what makes your organization and your products unique and special, you're headed for serious trouble.

Why? Because customers are continually raising the bar on what they expect from vendors. They are demanding more, sooner, better, and cheaper—and they expect it all on their own terms and timetables. Think about it: the expectations that you hold today toward telephones, computers, and hotels are logarithmically greater than they were five years ago. Small wonder that marketing guru Regis McKenna says that we are in the age of the "never satisfied customer."

And the most ominous part is the sequel: if customers can't get their fickle, unreasonable demands met from you, they'll get them met somewhere else because they've got an ever-increasing number of choices.

Customers in all fields are being bombarded by vendors, options, ads, and enticements that they never even considered just a few years ago. To survive and thrive in these circumstances, you've got to be special and unique enough to separate yourself from the din of the mob.

As the future unfolds, this need will intensify, because tomorrow's customers will be even more knowledgeable and more aggressive than today's. Already, with consumers able to choose from myriad products and vendors from around the world, and with their ability to use PCs to vastly enhance their options, every organization in every industry is learning a painful fact of life: customers are no longer prisoners to the vendor's strategic plan, production schedule, hours of operation, and product promotion mix.

Savvy investors know this, and they know that future earnings depend on your organization's ability to capitalize on this trend.

Unconventional times call for unconventional strategies. Bold actions aimed at being first and being exceptional—that is, first to market with exceptional ideas and unique product-service offerings—create the capacity to differentiate yourself in the marketplace, which in turn create the kinds of customer loyalty, margins, revenues, and market share you seek. Striving to be first and exceptional also pushes you to innovatively harness today's opportunities for tomorrow's market leadership, rather than relegate you to perpetually playing catch-up to brash, new competitors.

You won't become first and exceptional with hypercautious decisions and bland responses. Nor will you get there with lip-service platitudes that reflect the latest fad or "management speak." Leapfrogging requires daring, *unorthodox* action. Anita Roddick, founder of the Body Shop, and the late Sam Walton, founder of Wal-Mart, represent about as dissimilar a pairing of personalities as I can imagine, but they agreed on at least one thing: to be successful in business, you have to "go in the opposite direction as everyone else" (Roddick), and you have to "swim upstream" (Walton). More recently, Michael Bloomberg, founder of financial information empire Bloomberg LC, echoed this sentiment with another directional metaphor: "If the world is going right, then we will go left."

Consider this example: to the average individual investor in 1982, the very idea of trading securities electronically without human contact would have seemed a scenario straight out of a sci-fi movie. The aggressive, progressive investor at the time used discount brokers, to be sure, but left the computers to the scientists and techno-nerds. Only a small percentage of Americans had a computer on their desks at work, much less in their homes.

But Bill Porter, founder of E*Trade, was attentive to the emerging trend of decentralized information technology. To him, the idea of using the personal computer to manage an investment portfolio seemed a viable means to achieve total control, immediate responsiveness, and save big commission bucks. Accordingly, he persevered in developing and marketing an electronic method of placing trades, and his foresight paid off as PCs and on-line services became commonplace media for commercial transactions.

That's proved to be just the beginning: "E*Trade carved out an early identity," says James Marks, an electronic commerce analyst at CS First Boston. "They're in a good position to take advantage of on-line media—not only in brokerage services, but in a whole range of financial products." Under the leadership of Chairman Porter and CEO Christos Cotsakos, the company's growth rate has been exceptional. During the year following the August 1996 IPO, the company opened a whopping 500 accounts daily, elevated trading volume 120 percent, tripled revenue, and doubled the stock price.

Fast-forward another year: on September 10, 1998, the company surpassed the one-half million mark in account acquisition, while reporting a third-quarter earnings increase of 114 percent on revenue growth of 68 percent. During the quarter, the average value of securities traded electronically through E*Trade was $1.5 billion per week, almost double the $800 million during the same quarter in 1997. According to Media Metrix, a New York–based research firm, E*Trade is one of the top ten financial destination sites of any type, Internet or otherwise—all this within the context of a business model where the fixed cost of brokers and retail offices does not exist.

When Ted Turner talked about launching a twenty-four-hour news and information station in the 1970s, every particle of conventional wisdom—from market researchers to broadcast professionals to industry pundits—agreed that his vision was crazy, bizarre, guaranteed to fail. But as history proved (and as we shall examine in some detail in Commitment 2), Turner's foray (while admittedly audacious) was actually prudent. The only thing that was "bizarre" was that he catapulted his strategy over convention—and in the process created a powerful global brand that has generated 35 percent gross margins.

Nowadays it's riskier to be conventional than unconventional. If you're serious about embarking on a visionary path toward being first and exceptional, this section will be of real use to you. Specifically, this section will present the evidence that the most powerful and enduring results are those that serve to continually create new products, new markets, and new futures. Companies as diverse as CNN, E*Trade, Body Shop, Federal Express, Dell Computer, Home Depot, Netscape, Nike, and Sony did not merely "adapt" to the market. They led it—in fact, they invented it—with breakthrough products, concepts, and business models. They were not market driven. They *drove* the market. They did not respond to customers. They *pulled* them into the future. Moreover, it is important to note that these companies did not and do not rely extensively on traditional management tools such as strategic planning that are considered sacred in many organizations today.

Traditionally, strategy—per formal strategic planning—revolves around consolidating existing heuristics, algorithms, premises, and brilliant thinkers in an attempt to "predict" the market, even though research study after research study shows that the business world today is fundamentally unpredictable. Traditional strategy—per competitor analysis—also revolves around carefully monitoring existing competitors and today's product lines, even though new technologies and unorthodox competitor entrants are being launched daily, out of range of the competitor analysis periscope.

Traditional strategy—per market research—revolves around tracking customers' existing mind-set today, even though customers often have difficulty conceptualizing tomorrow's needs, and even though numerous breakthrough products and concepts (from Post-It notepads to Walkmans to 50-cc motorbikes to twenty-four-hour news programming) initially scored negatives in survey and focus group results.

All these traditional tools are inadequate and often futile in today's madcap economy. Moreover, as this section shows, they place artificial caps on the breakthrough possibilities that any company can enjoy.

The examples in this section will demonstrate that a commitment to aggressive action, aimed at being first and being exceptional, will turbo-charge you to leapfrog the competition. Why? First, because it creates your ability to differentiate yourself in the marketplace; second, because the usual lip service to innovation notwithstanding, many organizations today (including many of your competitors) are preoccupied with maintaining tradition, hypercaution, and routine practice, all of which generate "being the same and being ordinary."

This section also demonstrates that organizations that leapfrog the competition do not flinch from obsolescing themselves because they know if they don't, someone else will. Intel's dramatic decision to abandon the high-volume, low-margin, commodity-like DRAM memory chip business in 1985 in favor of microprocessor chips propelled the company into dominant breakthroughs in both technology and shareholder wealth. Tactically, Intel and other innovators, such as Hewlett-Packard, continue to pursue this planned obsolescence strategy daily by simultaneously improving and cannibalizing their currently successful product lines before they can become commodities amenable to the mass-production economies of scale better left to low-cost competitors.

Yet today, the explosion of sub-$1,000 PCs and non-PC computing alternatives has caused serious concern at Intel. I suspect that Andy Grove's voluntary departure from the CEO position in 1998 was due primarily to his desire to have time, as chairman, to scan the horizon for the next breakthrough paradigm for Intel, which some say might be in networks and "information appliances." As it abandoned DRAM, Intel—a company not afraid of obsolescing itself—may one day abandon the chip business in favor of the next "wave."

This brings up a critical point. Relying *solely* on paradigm creation is unrealistic. On the other hand, as the companies discussed in the following pages demonstrate, sinking most of your capital into improving products that are already conventional or headed toward obsolescence can only lead to corporate demise. Concentrating on improving products and services that are becoming low-cost commodities is no way to generate excitement or loyalty among either customers or investors. Putting your primary attention on improving internal processes and systems that should be eliminated outright is the height of myopia.

Consultant Tom Brown and I recently concluded that many companies today are reminiscent of a high-level task force at the turn of the century holding a top-secret off-site meeting to figure out how to reengineer their premier stagecoach. Those who were not trapped by the horse-and-buggy paradigm—those who had the foresight to challenge convention by exploring new technologies and evolving consumer needs—were the ones who were able to catapult both their thinking and their organizations to both dream and take advantage of RPMs and horseless transportation.

The discussion of Giant Step I ends with a perspective on strategy that I call "bifocal." Here, ironically, is where "continuous improvement" can create some value. Bifocal vision allows a company to straddle the fence between the present and the future, continually improving today's business while investing in the qualitative changes necessary for tomorrow's business.

FedEx, in responding to the steady inroads of competitors as diverse as UPS, the U.S. Postal Service, fax, and E-mail, is providing customers with more diverse time and delivery options, as well as the technological capacity to track their own packages. These are meaningful improvements from the customer's perspective. Still, FDX, the parent company, understands that continuous improvement on its own is a slippery slope. That is why, simultaneously, in a paradigm-catapulting process, the corporation is leveraging its technological expertise to reposition itself as a high-value, outsourced provider of warehousing and information services that can help corporate customers sharply reduce their inventory costs. Further, as more and more companies outsource their transportation function, FDX is positioning itself to be a major player in this fast-growing logistics business by combining an acquisition of trucking company Calipers with FedEx's traditional core transportation and information technology competencies. FedEx approaches its business bifocally, aggressively enhancing its flagship product while reinventing itself with entirely new ones.

This section ends with a personal challenge to leaders: to learn how to "do" bifocal vision—that is, to develop the ability to confront *today's* challenges (payroll, demanding customers, general ledger, quarterly reports) while simultaneously probing *tomorrow's* opportunities, and to do so for every management decision. This doesn't require genetic brilliance. It requires time, practice, and commitment.

Audit most leaders' personal calendars and you'll find more than 90 percent of their time is devoted to "right now" problems and "today's crises" activities. Too many managers don't make the tough choice to spend a minimum of 50 percent of their time scoping what the future holds or projecting how they can leapfrog far ahead of their competitors in that time frame. Nor do they insist that each of today's decisions—in budgeting, personnel, marketing, product development, and so forth—have a bifocal dimension: demonstrating that the decision will both strengthen the company today and prepare it to be strong in the face of tomorrow's challenges. That will change.

In summary, leaders and companies that follow Giant Step I are constantly beating against the walls of conventional wisdom. They know that conventional wisdom mesmerizes companies into staying in the pack and fighting it out with the same old competitors in the same old market using the same old industry rules—which is why so many conventional managers complain about being stuck in a "mature" or "saturated" market.

Instead, leaders who follow Giant Step I focus on perpetually reinventing their product-line and persona in terms of bare-knuckle questions such as "What *will* our customer want?" "What *can* our business be?" and "Whom *could* we serve?" They truly understand Michael Bloomberg's dictum that "any company who offers today what is sold yesterday will be out of business tomorrow." Accordingly, they focus not only on today's market but on the total *possible* market of tomorrow. By truly catapulting over convention, and by insisting that their colleagues do the same, they prepare their organizations to leapfrog the competition.

To catapult your strategy over conventional wisdom, resolve now to make four commitments that will underlie your organizational strategy and your own daily decision making:

- Be first—be exceptional (Commitment 1).
- Obsolete yourself before someone else does (Commitment 2).
- Go beyond traditional competitive weapons of strategic planning, competitive analysis, and market research (Commitment 3).
- Scan the world with bifocal vision (Commitment 4).

Being first and being exceptional is the commitment that must underlie both strategy and operations. Commitment 1 reveals clues as to the whys and hows by following the true story of a company that was working hard to move in the right direction but in fact was mired in the slough of conventional thinking. We can learn a lot from others' mistakes, so see how you and your organization compare with this company.

Commitment 2 introduces the insidious corporate disease I call the "Thomas Lawson Syndrome" and explains how companies that don't obsolete themselves wind up being obsolesced by someone else.

Commitment 3 sounds the clarion call for rejecting an overreliance on so-called sacred tools such as strategic planning, competitive analysis, and market research. The byword on all this: use these tools sparingly to get a quick scan of conventional wisdom, and then concentrate your efforts on leapfrogging by taking advantage of potential alternatives that are much more rewarding.

Commitment 4 calls on you and your organization to develop "bifocal vision"—the capacity and willingness to attack every challenge and every decision with a twin perspective: how the decision impacts today and how it will impact tomorrow.

Be First, Be Exceptional

> BE FOREWARNED: The first story in this chapter is not about how to put on a better corporate retreat. It's about the fact that so many companies come to accept goals, standards, and expectations that are ordinary and mundane. As you read, note that the goals that the company in the story envisioned as groundbreaking were in actuality no more than tepid, same old/same old. My commentary will provide some alternatives that are really "first and exceptional." As you read, ask yourself which better describes the goals your organization is striving to reach.

This is a tale of a company that seemed to do everything right during its annual corporate retreat but in reality did almost everything wrong. As Jack Webb in the old *Dragnet* TV series would say, the story you are about to hear is true; only the names have been changed to protect the innocent.

It all began innocently enough. The $250 million high-tech company—let's call it Ajax—held its two-day retreat in a pleasant resort hotel. The CEO, the president, and the eighty-person management team attended. The company hired a consultant (no, it wasn't me) to facilitate the discussions. For two days the managers discussed issues such as competition, emerging technologies, and the future of their business. They agreed that at the top of their wish list was the desire to triple revenues in five years—that is, to be a $750 million company by 2002. They also listed their operational priorities for the following year, priorities that would be key to moving Ajax toward a tripling of revenues. They were as follows:

1. Meet customer needs.
2. Reduce time to market.
3. Improve communications.
4. Optimize resources.
5. Reduce functional barriers.
6. Change corporate culture.

Sounds good so far, right? There's more. With the help of the consultant, the eighty participants self-selected themselves into six groups, one per priority. They then focused on developing action plans to help deliver each priority back on the job. Each group agreed to get together after the retreat, write up its list of recommendations, and submit it to top management. Top management—in this case, the CEO and the president—agreed to review the recommendations and get back to each group with timely feedback.

Doesn't all this sound eminently reasonable? Doesn't it sound terribly productive? The answer, quite simply, is no, because there was nothing first, nothing exceptional about the new priorities. In fact, I propose that the entire process was an exercise in mediocrity, guaranteed to perpetuate everything that leads to corporate stagnation.

Why? Well, let's examine the six priorities, and then you be the judge:

1. "MEET CUSTOMER NEEDS."

This is one of the surest roads to flat revenues and earnings. Nowadays, "meeting" customer needs merely allows a company to play in the game and possibly survive. But if meeting customer needs is all it can do, it is unlikely to thrive. As noted earlier, customers are more demanding, more aggressive, more impatient, and more astute than ever before—and, worse, they have more choices from competing vendors than ever before. They're increasingly fickle, and they're continually raising the bar. A company that simply "meets" customer needs provides the bare minimum of value to them, which means that it inspires little loyalty.

Less loyalty, as researchers such as James Heskett and Frederick Reichheld have independently demonstrated, yields less repeat business, lower margins, and less word-of-mouth referrals—and, hence, significant reductions in profitability, market share, and "share of customer."

Loyalty and resultant growth in financials emerge when companies *exceed* customer expectations with market-leading concepts, cutting-edge products, and knock-your-socks-off service.

Go through a mental exercise with me: first, think of the business concepts underlying the initial launches of E*Trade and CNN—radically divergent from conventional wisdom at the time. Then, think of Mpath Interactive, today redefining the computer gaming industry by making it possible for customers to interact with one another over the Internet with flight simulations, sports, and war games. Think of Lego introducing the Mindstorms Robotics Invention System, which allows kids to use a computer program to build their own little robots.

Think of ProAir, a Detroit-based startup that offers corporate customers, like GM and Chrysler, unlimited business travel for a flat monthly fee anytime there is space on a flight. Think of Kinko's Copiers introducing on-the-road and SOHO (small-office/home-office) employees to the uncharted possibilities of a virtual, full-service, office-away-from-your-office. Think of First Direct, the first-off-the-block branchless, telephone-only British bank that has fostered a loyal and steadily growing customer base.

Think of FedEx teaching corporate customers to use a self-service Power Ship software system to fix its point-of-sale FedEx terminals. Think of little Natick, Massachusetts–based ScrubaDub Auto Wash Centers, where computer databases on individual customers yield personalized services and regular customers receive a three-day guarantee, complete with the promise of a free rewash even if the weather turns rainy or dusty.

Think of IKEA, creating a new concept of making and selling furniture: "clean" Scandinavian design (1,500 suppliers in fifty countries then build the products), flat packaging (easy to store and transport), easy self-assembly (by customer), and low price. Think of 3Com launching the fastest growing new segment of the computer business—little handheld devices—with its simple, elegant Palm products. Think of the Sabre Group, first to develop and market their on-line reservation software to anyone with a personal computer.

Think of the Century Plaza Hotel in Los Angeles offering guests "cybersuites" with a huge screen Web access, voice-activated electronic butler (who closes curtains and turns out lights), cellular phone in addition to regular phone access, virtual reality games, and teleconferencing capabilities.

Think of American Standard developing a bathtub with features including a touch-tone speaker telephone system, a stereo, and a remote control for household appliances.

Finally, think of fast-growing little Peapod, an on-line grocery service currently serving 100,000 families in seven metropolitan areas, which provided a group of my MBA students a delightful virgin experience:

> On a test drive, we were able to browse the aisles on our computer screen and compare products by price, fat content, calories, and other variables. A running total in the corner of the screen allowed us to constantly view the total cost of our "cyber" market basket. The ordering process is easy to use and provides value-added features such as menu-planning, customer item instructions, and simple cost-saving redemption of product and store saver coupons without using scissors. We could have even ordered a San Francisco Muni bus pass! Viewing package information was accomplished by a double click of the mouse button. To simplify our ordering process, the software made it easy for us to create a repeat order or to modify a previous order.

These are all exceptional companies doing exceptional things, and the list could go on and on, but the punch line of the story remains the same:

All these companies go much, much further than merely meeting customer needs!

Often, in fact, they go so far that they create "needs" that customers didn't even know they had. That's why they engender a strong customer following, often yielding the kinds of returns and growth rate that most organizations merely fantasize about.

2. "REDUCE TIME TO MARKET."

Oh, dear. That's like telling a 400-pound man that he ought to lose some weight. It's grossly insufficient, and it doesn't carry nearly enough urgency or compelling purpose. As already indicated, the real key to competitive success is not simply to "reduce" time to market but to be first to market with something fresh, exceptional, groundbreaking—be it product, services, after-sale processes, distribution, or a basic business model. The company that does so gets to define customer expectations consistent with its own capacities, and it can charge a healthy premium in the process. The company that is first and exceptional also gets a lock on valuable learning, resources, and partnerships that serve as a critical mass for future endeavors. The research is unequivocal: being first, especially with something that violates conventional wisdom, is the most effective path to the profit margins and market share we all crave.

And even when profitability doesn't appear immediately, growth and stock value shoot upward when a company is first to market with a breakthrough idea. McCaw Cellular never declared an operating profit in the ten years prior to its sale to AT&T, yet investors were (rightfully) so impressed with Craig McCaw's breakthrough vision and execution that they kept on bidding the value of his enterprise skyward. On-line retailer Amazon.com has sales of under $300 million and has yet to post a profit, but its market value is $4 billion. How can this be?

The answer is simple: Amazon is a pathbreaking business model, and founder Jeff Bezos is plowing back all revenues into building and extending it further to be able to ultimately peddle any product. Just consider the current numbers:

- Thirty times the number of books, twenty times the number of CDs as in any Borders or Tower Records superstore
- Two percent of Barnes & Noble inventory

- No conventional "receivables" lag, since buyers pay immediately with credit card
- Per-employee sales of $240,000, versus $100,000 at Barnes & Noble
- Automatic database on each customer, allowing suggestions à la "because you bought this book, you might be interested in the following"
- Seventy percent repeat business
- No stores

It took Wal-Mart (itself a breakthrough business model twenty years ago) a dozen years and seventy-eight stores to hit $150 million in sales; it's taken Amazon three years and no stores to hit that milestone.

Amazon won't replace innovative bricks-and-mortar bookstores. A bookstore that is *first and exceptional* in providing consumers a terrific interpersonal and entertainment *experience* will provide something that Amazon is not positioned to do and doesn't want to. Already, savvy companies such as Borders and Barnes & Noble are transforming their properties into arenas that consumers will want to go to simply to "hang out" for the experience: music, entertainment, coffee bars, lounge areas, discussion groups, author lectures, children's programs, self-help classes, and helpful customer service. In this model, the books are the commodity—simply part of the total package.

Again, the key is be first; be exceptional—and continue to stay that way. Not merely for the financials and corporate reputation, but because doing so can also generate a winning learning infrastructure. That is, the pathfinding organization can leverage its premier technologies, people, and systems in a way that perpetuates its position with next-generation breakthroughs, which is the trademark of companies such as Dell Computer, Nokia, the Gap, Cisco Systems, FedEx, Johnson SC, and Gillette.

Dell Computer, for example, having introduced the concept of direct-mail ordering of PCs, is now one of the pioneers perfecting the nuances of customized, direct-sales, direct-service Internet commerce. The company enjoys sales of over $4 billion annually in that medium alone, and it is growing that business rapidly. Finnish telecommunications company Nokia launches new digital handset models every thirty-five days, including, recently, the smallest digital cellular phones to provide weeklong battery life, the ability to surf the Web, and the most powerful roaming capabilities across divergent networks in Europe and Asia.

The preceding point is crucial, because being first to market with one great idea will not sustain competitive advantage in a world where product life cycles are shrinking exponentially. Without an infrastructure and mind-set that allows a firm to be first and exceptional—over and over again—it's likely that the gains of any breakthrough will be short-lived.

For example, Planet Hollywood was initially such an original, sexy concept that it was valued at $3.5 billion when it went public in 1996. Since then, sales and repeat business have nose-dived, and the stock has plummeted by 90 percent. Why? Because after the movie stars left, there was little else left other than high prices, mediocre food, and uncomfortable lighting. Nothing new or inspiring in the concept, food, service, or ambience emerged. It remained the same old/same old atmosphere, and once people tried it out, they looked for another experience.

Remember Hard Candy a few years ago? The product was a first-to-market bright nail polish in nontraditional black, blue, green, and yellow colors, all high priced and sold at exclusive department stores. Sales initially skyrocketed, but there was no follow-up action to enhance product diversification, large-scale distribution, and brand marketing. Hence, cosmetics giants such as Revlon and Maybelline quickly mimicked the concept, undercut Hard Candy prices, and sold their version in drugstores where they reached a much wider consumer market: teenage girls.

The moral of this entire discussion is that consistently being first with something exceptional takes you on the path toward leapfrogging the competition. Ajax managers would have been well advised to concentrate on what they need to do to address this issue vigorously. In a world where the life cycles of information, products, and technologies are compressing dramatically, a company that is satisfied with merely "reducing time to market" is a company that will be playing perpetual catch-up.

We're not finished yet. Remember, there were six goals. The remaining four goals were presumably meant to help Ajax attain the (arguably weak, flaccid) priorities of "meet customer needs" and "reduce time to market." Let's quickly examine them anyway:

3. Improve communications.
4. Optimize resources.
5. Reduce functional barriers.
6. Change corporate culture.

3. "IMPROVE COMMUNICATIONS."

What does this bland motherhood maxim mean? On one hand, it means everything, because in today's information age, everything is communication and communication is everything. But from a practical standpoint, it means nothing at all, because it's such a vague, apple-pie item that everyone can nod their heads without really committing to anything, which is precisely what happened at this retreat. If the Ajax managers had really been serious about this issue, they might have prioritized their goal as something like this: "Develop open-book communication throughout the company." Now that would be something worth talking about. John Case has written eloquently on this subject in his book *The Open Book Experience* (Perseus, 1998). Let me take his ideas a step further to argue that open-book communication means that anyone—regardless of job title— can review sales data, quarterly financials, today's income statement, today's quality data, and so on, in the quest toward adding value to the company. It means that anyone can meet and brainstorm with anyone else in any part of the organization without having to go through myriad preliminary hoops and post hoc interrogations. It means that leaders share strategies, competitive analyses, financial challenges, knotty operational problems, and market opportunities with all hands, both face to face and electronically, on a regular, collaborative problem-solving basis. It means no barriers, no turfs, and no hoarding when it comes to information and "intelligence."

That's the kind of environment that is emerging in successful businesses as diverse as Springfield Remanufacturing (engine overhaul), Manco (industrial tape), VeriFone (credit card authorization), and Oticon (hearing aid products). What these companies are doing is confronting the nanosecond demands for constant innovation in today's business world by obliterating barriers to information exchange. Their open-book efforts represent a helluva lot more than what most companies—including Ajax—refer to when they say they want to "improve communications." (More on this in Giant Step II.)

4. "OPTIMIZE RESOURCES."

This is a bit of a no-brainer, isn't it? Doesn't every manager "get" the idea that his or her job includes efficient allocation of resources? Once again, the goal is reasonable, but in today's madcap economy, "reasonable" is unreasonable.

In their book *Reengineering the Corporation,* Michael Hammer and James Champy were specific: the changes they were calling for were, in their words, "fundamental," "dramatic," and "radical," not gradual or incremental: "Reengineering is about beginning again with a clean sheet of paper . . . about inventing new approaches to process structures that bear little or no resemblance to those of previous eras." Heady words.

But among the hue-and-cry lip service that so many companies give to "reengineering," Hammer and Champy's warnings are often ignored. Instead, "optimizing resources" within the current structure, as was the politically correct goal in the Ajax retreat, passes for real change. Lip service has no impact other than making a few internal people feel good. (More on this in Giant Step V.)

5. "REDUCE FUNCTIONAL BARRIERS."

"Reducing" them means they still exist. How about eliminating them altogether? That would have been a much more valuable goal to discuss at the Ajax retreat. Companies today no longer have the luxury of subsidizing a chain of horizontal pass-offs. They're slow and costly, and they inevitably foster warring fiefdoms.

In contrast, as early as November 1992, Lee Gammill, Jr., executive vice president of New York Life Insurance described in *Management Review* what happens when departmental barriers are eliminated: "Actuaries, lawyers, underwriters, and investment analysts—as well as product, marketing, and sales experts—sit on management teams. *All* work with the understanding that nothing is sacred or taboo, and that no parochial interests are allowed." The results? "We analyze market forces more quickly and deliver more responsive products and services. The time required for many products has been reduced by half."

Amen to that, and if Ajax was really serious, it would have sent its managers to visit successful companies such as Sun Microsystems, Nypro (plastics molding), and Solcetron (electronics contract manufacturing), companies that apply the concept of obliterating barriers to their customers and suppliers. These companies often share production plans and databases with these "outsiders," a practice that puts to shame the typical functional gang warfare among "insiders." (More on this in Giant Steps II, III, and IV.)

6. "CHANGE CORPORATE CULTURE."

Once again, this is too tepid a goal. When applied to corporate culture, the word change implies tweaking, tinkering, and fine-tuning—all mild, timid responses. UCLA's Wellford Wilms and his colleagues attribute the extraordinary success of NUMMI (New United Motor Manufacturing), the Toyota-GM joint venture in Fremont, California, to a virtual "transformation" (their word) in corporate culture. The new culture includes just three job classifications for the entire unionized labor force (a reduction from more than eighty), significant gain-sharing pay plans, heavy investments in cross-training, genuine self-management and peer discipline, and open dialogue between managers and "workers" on production and quality decisions that used to be the sole domain of management.

When Ajax managers blithely talked about "changing" culture during their retreat, were they prepared to take on the magnitude of change that managers at NUMMI did? Wilms quotes NUMMI managers who are frank in admitting that nothing short of a sheer overhaul in corporate culture would have allowed the plant to meet external competitive pressures. I'll wager that the same statement can be applied to most organizations today—Ajax included. (More on this in Giant Steps II and V.)

Now comes the finale of this little tale. If these six priorities are problematic, the very process within the retreat itself compounds Ajax's difficulties. Here's why: First, a once-a-year all-hands discussion of issues such as emerging competition, technologies, and markets is grossly inadequate. When people get back to the job, they get right back to their normal routines. Thinking about the future, and meeting with colleagues to discuss the future, must itself become the daily routine. Most of the time, this sort of activity is absent in management life. Strategy gurus Gary Hamel and C. K. Prahalad argue that this near-absence is striking even within executive circles.

And what about the notion of top management at Ajax receiving the specific action-plan proposals from middle management, and then responding with yea or nay? I can't think of a better way for a company to reinforce a debilitating command-and-control structure and induce passivity among its managers. Suppose that instead, Ajax managers had used the retreat to come to consensus on some broad legal and financial boundaries that would apply to everyone, and then agreed to leave it to the six teams to take full responsibility for both developing action initiatives and executing them. No passive waiting for "approval" required, which, by the way, is what "empowerment" is all about.

Finally, there's this business of tripling revenues in five years as the top organizational priority. What sort of priority is that? Sure, concrete growth objectives are helpful as performance benchmarks, but saying that it's the top priority of an organization is like saying that the primary purpose of your life is to grow your net worth. If that really is your main goal in life, I feel sorry for you. Besides, even in business it's a myopic goal.

CEOs as diverse as Howard Schultz (Starbucks) and Bernard Marcus (Home Depot) have emphasized that the numbers are not the raison d'être of a business but the consequence of doing things right in terms of products and customers. It would have been a lot more productive for Ajax managers to have concentrated on questions such as these: What are we best at? What are we world-class great at? What makes us unique? How are we going to serve today's customers and tomorrow's customers in such a way that nobody else can? What "wow" products and service can we offer? What are we going to do, perhaps in alliance with other world-class greats, that will lead the market? If we can execute the answers to those strategic questions, we'll be successful over the next five years, and maybe we'll even hit that desired $750 million mark as a result of our efforts.

Ajax is a good company. It's staffed by competent, conscientious managers. But as with any company, there's no guaranteeing that it will even be around five years from now. Strategic thinking can move a company toward breakthrough action or toward mediocrity. As you prepare for the future, you may wish to contemplate these things. Let's check in five years to see what has happened to Ajax.

Make Yourself Obsolete
Before Someone Else Does

WHEN A Southwest Airlines executive reckons that in three years more than 50 percent of ticket bookings will take place via the Web, I hear a funeral dirge start to play for conventional travel agents. But Philadelphia-based Rosenbluth Travel is already capitalizing on this relentless technological trend by developing software systems that will allow its corporate clients to surf travel sites on the Web more easily and, in partnership with Rosenbluth, create their own travel deals. Rosenbluth is an exception. Too many companies wind up waiting for someone—or something—to make them obsolete. Don't become a fragment of yesterday's news.

"Toward dawn on Friday, December 13, 1907, the sailing ship *Thomas W. Lawson* sank off the Scilly Isles in the English Channel." So begins McKinsey director Richard Foster's excellent book *Innovation: The Attacker's Advantage* (Summit Books, 1986).

The *Thomas Lawson*, a huge, unwieldy seven-masted ship, was the Rube Goldberg-like product the sailing establishment put forth to compete against the new steam-powered vessels that increasingly had taken cargo business away from sail. The last-gasp effort to deny technological advance was futile, of course, and as Foster observes, "The age of commercial sail ended with the *Thomas Lawson*, and steamships began to rule the seas."

It's been over a decade since Foster wrote his book, yet the *Thomas Lawson* still sails among us. The affliction I call the

23

"Thomas Lawson Syndrome" is the tendency for organizations to tenaciously prop up current products, services, and processes in the face of technological advance that often spells the obsolescence of what the organization is currently protecting. By hindering managers from discarding the old technologies and embracing the new, the Thomas Lawson Syndrome prevents organizations from transcending the status quo and looking ahead to the future.

The syndrome can afflict any firm, but it is especially pernicious among organizations with successful products and enviable balance sheets. Foster describes how Du Pont clung to nylon, its cash cow, in the early 1960s, despite the scientific evidence that a new product—polyester—was superior for tire cords and despite the fact that Goodyear, its leading customer, had publicly come out in favor of polyester. Meanwhile, Celanese, a competitor whose position in the tire industry was small relative to Du Pont's, faced far fewer internal barriers to polyester. Celanese had no nylon investments to protect, no nylon tire-cord facilities whose cost had to be justified. Nor, I suspect, did Celanese have managers and researchers whose career success, reputation, and egos were tied to nylon. While Du Pont poured R&D money into improving nylon, Celanese, unencumbered by its past, began to turn out polyester tire cord. The product was quickly adopted by tire manufacturers, and within five years Celanese had captured more than 75 percent of the market.

Think about this history lesson: the market research was clear, the test data was clear, the technology was available, and Du Pont had the resource base befitting a market leader. Logic would predict that Du Pont would quickly adapt to market realities and blow Celanese out of the water.

But the Thomas Lawson Syndrome is an insidious disease. It blocks both logic and vision. It causes managers to tenaciously cling to the geese that laid yesterday's golden eggs even as the geese are reaching the end of their life cycles. Consistent with the Du Pont–Celanese case, MIT's Jim Utterback found that in thirty-two of thirty-four companies he investigated, the market leader "reduced investment in the new technology in order to pour even more money into buffering up the old."

Even when market leaders are not closed to new advances, the Thomas Lawson Syndrome paralyzes their ability to apply them. Researchers Arnold Cooper of Purdue and Clayton Smith of Notre Dame note that even "where established firms enter threatening young industries, they do not pursue the new product aggressively, and they continue to make substantial commitments to their old product even after its sales begin to decline." Researchers attribute this trend only partially to lack of technical expertise. The more significant causes are internal politics, managers' comfort zones, habit, and the need to justify sunk costs.

Thus, even though Du Pont "explored" the possibilities in polyester, proponents of polyester were placed in a subservient position in the organization's budgeting and political pecking order. The result was inevitable.

More recently, Motorola's stock and reputation have taken a hit because of a failure to capitalize on the rapid development of digital technologies for wireless communication handsets. Motorola knows analog technology; it's built a great reputation on analog technology. So over the past few years, the company has concentrated on improving its analog products despite repeated requests by customers for digital cell phones and despite competitor Nokia's very visible success in slipping the bond of analog obsolescence with the cutting-edge 5100 and 6100 digital handset series.

The Thomas Lawson Syndrome also emerges when managers' comfort with an existing process or technology literally blinds them to new business possibilities. Prior to the Time Warner merger, Time, Inc. was undervalued by $6 billion, a phenomenon that perplexed many Warner people. One Warner executive told me that Time had the infrastructure to dominate the emerging information and entertainment sectors, "but Time management grew up in print and saw the world in print. They didn't understand the revolution in technology."

Unsurprisingly then, the Thomas Lawson Syndrome often causes those who appear to be best positioned to get into a new business actually to be among the worst. This often yields huge opportunities for new-entry competitors and entrepreneurs who are burdened with considerably less old baggage.

Companies such as Apple Computer and Sun Microsystems were born because their founders became frustrated at trying to sell concepts such as personal computers and workstations to established firms whose roots and profit margins were embedded in products of the past. The Chicago upstart CCC Information Services has grown to well over $160 million during the past decade by leapfrogging over existing technologies in the auto collision/estimating market. While much larger established competitors were content to "continuously improve" the traditional print media ("blue book" and "red book" auto value publications) and manual systems (adjusters filling out and mailing spec sheets), CCC introduced a set of entirely different service paradigms. With computerized used car databases and collision/estimating software systems that operate on portable computers, CCC has significantly reduced errors in data transmission, turnaround time, and clients' fixed costs. Accordingly, it has become a dominant player in the computerized total loss evaluation market and the collision/estimating market.

The CCC story is important because it shows that the Thomas Lawson Syndrome is just as applicable to service industries; just ask CCC's competitors. Consider a few of the ominous technological challenges (and opportunities) looming over the horizon for other service companies. Overnight mail deliverers are experiencing painful dents in their revenues because of fax, E-mail, and Web delivery. Insurance brokers, stock brokers, car dealers, and travel agents are realizing that advances in information technology are such that many of their services can be duplicated by smart customers who can access the same database and come to their own informed conclusions. Universities are seeing interactive computer and telecommunication technologies as well as electronic self-paced learning options begin to obsolete much of their traditional class-lecture formats. Airlines are concerned that rapid improvements in teleconferencing capabilities may preclude the need for some current business travel.

Ad agencies' traditional delivery formats in TV commercials and magazine spreads may soon be rendered ineffectual by digital interactivity. Grocers and other retailers are being challenged by new cyberproviders who appeal to consumers' desires not to spend limited free time doing household errands. Middlemen in a wide variety of supply chains are learning that their old-boy connections and customer service skills don't count for much in the face of networked computing and electronic data interchange, which eliminates the need—and expense—of many of their current services.

What all this implies for service providers is a call to abandon the *Thomas Lawson* ship. It is a call to seek and absorb the opportunities inherent in new technologies. This is nothing less than a call to reinvent the business with a combination of cutting-edge technology driven services that really add value to tomorrow's customers.

That is a tough but necessary challenge for any leader in any business. As noted earlier, even when companies are in distress and *know* they must change, the Thomas Lawson Syndrome induces either paralysis or "more of the same" responses. At troubled Eastman Kodak, "continuous improvement" of the core film photography business may be necessary for surviving, but it is surely insufficient for thriving. The company's salvation is much more likely to result from breakthrough applications in digital imaging. The challenge for CEO George Fisher is to scuttle the *Thomas Lawson* and get his crew to focus on the fast-moving technologies in the electronics field while, simultaneously, creating support structures (manufacturing, distribution, marketing) for those efforts. The talent and technology is already within Kodak; the challenge is to overcome—you guessed it—the dreaded syndrome.

On the other hand, if the organization is prosperous, the Thomas Lawson Syndrome can be doubly insidious, for it sabotages even the desire for change. Apple Computer, the company that made computers cool and the term *user-friendly* a nonoxymoron, became fat and happy by the mid-1980s. The snazziest technology, the most recognizable brand name, and the sweetest margins in the microcomputer business all conspired to generate complacency and arrogance.

Accordingly, the operating system went without a major rewrite for years and, in a disastrous decision by then-CEO John Sculley, Apple refused to license its technology to non-Apple clones. Why share the crown jewels? Why fix it if it ain't broke? But had the company done so, Macintosh technology would have become the universal PC standard and Windows 95 would have been stillborn long before reaching market. Instead, Apple's profitability and market share sank, and the post-Sculley era of Michael Spindler and Gilbert Amelio saw a further deterioration.

A lot of energy went into tightening costs, streamlining processes, pruning payroll, and fine-tuning existing products—all within the "reasonable" boundaries of conventional wisdom, but nothing unique, exciting, or inspiring emerged. Customers left for Windows pastures, and a slew of the more innovative, renegade, highly marketable managers and developers left as well. Such is the consequence and legacy of the Thomas Lawson Syndrome.

As a quick postscript, things began to change when Steve Jobs took over as interim CEO in 1997. Eliminating nonstrategic and poorly performing businesses, Jobs focused Apple on its core computer skills and in the process inspired a reinvigorated workforce to launch interesting new variations on the Macintosh, culminating in the multicolored, cool-looking, ultra-user-friendly, Internet-ready iMac. No less an authority than Intel chairman Andy Grove commented that in considering what future computers will look like, "the iMac embodies a lot of the things I'm talking about. Sometimes what Apple does has an electrifying effect on the rest of us." Once again, be first, be exceptional—which helps explain why fourth-quarter 1998 climaxed four straight quarters of healthy profit at Apple. Whether Apple can come back as a serious player remains to be seen, but the company certainly seems to be moving in the right direction.

So is IBM, a company that Apple used to mock in the 1980s. Under Lou Gerstner's helm, IBM's steadily improving health over the past few years can be partially attributed to its willingness to confront the Thomas Lawson Syndrome head-on. No more stuffed-shirt self-importance, no more smugness in responding to small startups and alternative technologies, no more clinging to old habits and past glories. As such, the new "E-commerce" IBM is no accident; in fact, conventional wisdom within pre-Gerstner IBM would have derided it as fool-hardy, if not impossible.

The lesson is clear. When executives get comfortable with the status quo, when they think they are impervious to market real-ities, or when they start believing their own press hype, the emergence of the syndrome is a sure thing. Today's numbers are a reflection of yesterday's decisions; tomorrow's numbers are a reflection of today's decisions. There's always a delay in the marketplace, and actions that led to success today may not lead to success tomorrow. Fighting tomorrow's battles with yes-terday's successful products and services is not a prescription for corporate success, regardless of the organization's size or reputation.

Of the 1980 *Fortune* 500, 230 (46 percent) no longer even exist, in large part because of their anachronistic responses to the pressures of relentless free-market forces. Small wonder that Peter Drucker has argued that one of the deadliest of business sins is "slaughtering tomorrow's opportunity on the altar of yesterday."

So I leave it to you: is your company sailing the *Thomas Lawson*? If so, are you ready to lead the call to abandon ship?

> HINDSIGHT IS 20/20. It's easy to look back and recognize that wooden sailing ships couldn't stand a chance against iron-hulled steamships. But what about the technologies that are sailing along today, unmindful of their nimbler, more futuristic competitors? What follows is a story of a few businesspeople who haven't been afraid to jump ship. Regardless of the indus-try we're operating in, we can learn valuable lessons from them.

"You don't need a weatherman to know which way the wind blows," Bob Dylan sang years ago. The changes in society, eco-nomics, technology, and politics—which seem revolutionary to us when they do happen—are not sudden at all; the forces that caused them existed long before the actual changes occur. Just as we can hear the vibrations on a train track before the train comes into view, the emerging phenomena around us are perceivable to those willing to stretch their comfort zone and step out of the paradigm in which they currently reside.

Consider this example. In the 1970s, three TV networks—CBS, NBC, and ABC—owned nearly 90 percent of the viewing market. The news was delivered at 7 P.M. in half-hour segments by venerable anchormen including Walter Cronkite and David Brinkley. Billboard advertising executive Ted Turner was astute enough to take seriously certain societal changes that those in the television world did not. First, the traditional family unit was fraying. With two parents working to support often-blended families, there was less time to gather dutifully around the TV set to watch the 7 P.M. news. Second, people increasingly wanted more news and information than the half-hour format usually offers.

Third, they wanted news on *their* time schedule and in whatever locale their jobs and interests might take them. In other words, any time, any place. Fourth, the advent of cable was a potentially serious threat to the near-monopoly status enjoyed by the Big Three. One could argue that in view of these demographic and technological changes, Turner's decision to launch CNN in 1980 was a prudent risk, not the insanity that conventional wisdom derisively labeled it at the time.

The real question is, Why didn't the established companies launch these innovations themselves? Why didn't ABC, for example, create a twenty-four-hour news service? Why didn't NBC unroll an all-information alternative viewing option? Why didn't CBS aggressively pursue the cable market? One would assume that the giants could easily have preempted any move by a pesky outsider such as Turner. One would even assume that the big boys, by virtue of their formidable market presence, financial strength, and technical know-how, would have been more likely than any newcomer to pilot a new product in a new delivery system.

In fact, the opposite occurred. In most cases, big market positions yield entrenched thinking, as I noted in describing the Thomas Lawson Syndrome. Big players are no smarter and no dumber than new entrants. The problem is that they are burdened by historical baggage: the psychological comfort of the status quo and the financial necessity to justify sunk costs. Moreover, even though yesterday's market conditions may be entirely different than today's, and even though tomorrow's opportunities may diverge from today's conventions, established companies like to point to (i.e., cling to) prior successes with the current products as a reason for maintaining a dogged commitment to them.

This commitment is so pervasive that even when they do enter young industries, established companies do so almost reluctantly, without a full-court press. IBM labs turned out important breakthroughs in microprocessors, microcomputers, and PC software in the early 1980s, but the company's "soul" remained firmly entrenched in mainframes, allowing feisty newcomers such as Apple, Compaq, and Microsoft to aggressively capitalize on the new developments. Likewise, Smith-Corona's "soul" remained in typewriters, even in the face of a ten-year trend toward computerized word processing. The company eventually came out with a series of computer-like typewriters—curious, clumsy hybrids with limited appeal—thus hastening the demise of that venerable organization.

Back in 1962, Thomas Kuhn predicted this phenomenon in his classic book *The Structure of Scientific Revolutions* (University of Chicago). Kuhn is the scholar who introduced the concept of paradigm shifts to the public consciousness. How and when paradigms change is virtually impossible to predict, Kuhn says, but who changes them is almost invariably the young or newcomers to a field. Why? The young and the new are not burdened by the mental constraints that limit the vision of those whose successes have been built on the past.

Like the child in "The Emperor's New Clothes," it is often the newcomer's innocence that is his or her greatest asset. At Xerox's Palo Alto Research Center in the 1970s, scientists were creating the precursors to today's PC (mouse, icons, minute screens, keyboards) for in-house usage. The corporation higher-ups, applying conventional strategic and financial projections, could not see any commercial application of these contraptions that would justify a capital investment into the unknown. It was young outsiders such as Apple cofounders Steve Jobs and Steve Wozniak who had the passionate vision that these innovations could one day be shaped to form the dominant tool on everyone's desk.

More recently, note that Jeff Bezos, founder of Amazon.com, did not come from the book industry. Perhaps that's why his vision was not blurred by the spectacles of industry conventional wisdom. He paid attention to several trends: the explosive rise of home-based Internet activity, people's increasing desire for more free time and immediacy in service, and the burgeoning "cocooning" trend (let's curl up at home). Bezos is candid about the fact that he had no particular allegiance to selling books; in view of these three trends, he could have peddled any number of products. But he also paid attention to the fact that books are an easy product to move with the right partners (like FedEx and warehouser Ingram) and that even in the age of television and video games, people are buying more books than ever before. Put it all together, and the idea for Amazon is born.

According to Kuhn, decisions on whether to stay or leave a paradigm are usually not based on data per se (or else Xerox would have inaugurated the PC revolution). Furthermore, says Kuhn, choosing how we look at a given paradigm is often not a matter of appealing to deductive proofs and rigorous methods. Instead, our decisions, and how we see a given situation, are based on the weight we place on certain values, or what philosopher Hans Gadamer calls our "prejudgments."

In 1980, the television veterans were not able to transcend the prejudgments that had brought them success. That is why they ridiculed Turner when he launched CNN. They couldn't move beyond the awareness that the forces that brought them to power no longer had monopoly status: divorce rates were up, both parents were working, cable television was diversifying the viewers' choices, people wanted a richer menu of news and information than thirty minutes every twenty-four hours, and they didn't want to wait until 7 P.M. to get it. Of course, all these trends were public knowledge; the TV veterans had access to the same information and technology that Turner did. The difference was the way they saw, interpreted, and acted on the data. As Kuhn notes, by clinging to paradigms that no longer represent reality, defenders of the old are often left to the side.

Like Ted Turner and Steve Jobs, Federal Express founder Fred Smith and McDonald's founder Ray Kroc were able to use existing paradigms as jumping-off places for further progress. Each of these individuals had less commitment to defending the old system than organizations such as CBS, IBM, the U.S. Postal Service, or the old-time funky hamburger joint. They realized it is not by repeating the tried-and-true but by making new choices given all the available knowledge that ensures progress in their field. Choosing and innovating are rational activities that challenge rather than refine an old paradigm.

Naturalists have verified that within any species, certain ambitious animals are constantly roaming from their adapted environment, stretching their comfort zone to take up homes where they don't traditionally reside. Guided by what could be best described as vague desire or curiosity, some coyotes will go too far north, some mockingbirds too far south. They stay, they adapt, and in time a new breed emerges.

Wired magazine editor Kevin Kelley, in his book *Out of Control* (Addison-Wesley, 1994), describes how one species of finch learned to pick up a cactus needle to poke for insects. The finch opened up a new niche for itself and ultimately for its species. Like the coyotes that sniff out new areas to live in or birds who test the limits of new behaviors, business innovators create change that affects a whole population. Kuhn notes that while the aesthetics of a recent development "often attract only a few scientists to a new theory, it is upon those few that its ultimate triumph may depend."

Today, of course, Microsoft has teamed with NBC to create an all-news channel. Welcome to the party, fifteen years late. Even being that late, Bill Gates is worthy of being taken seriously. But not because his company owns 90 percent of the operating system market. (Many companies with a commanding market share have not necessarily been exemplar investment opportunities; witness General Motors and Eastman Kodak as just two examples.) Gates deserves to be taken seriously because he has demonstrated that unlike the Big Three TV networks of 1980 (which, remember, also owned 90 percent of the market at the time), he is capable of changing the direction of a multibillion-dollar company 180 degrees.

Initially, Gates looked at the Internet as simply another product that he could load into his software arsenal. He admitted
being blindsided by new realities such as Web browsers and
open architectures, and he quickly backpedaled from his initial
strategy when Microsoft found itself in a hitherto unthinkable
position of having to play follow-the-leader with the likes of previous unknowns such as Netscape and previous nonfactors such
as Sun Microsystems. In a remarkably rapid, complete corporate
turnaround, Microsoft did a metamorphosis into a company
that approached the Internet as its business, not simply as a
product. And once again, it appears to be a preeminent player.

As this book goes to press, the Justice Department continues
its lawsuit against Microsoft for taking unfair advantage of its
market dominance in the aftermath of this transition. Although
the outcome of the trial is uncertain (especially in view of the
America Online/Netscape marriage), one thing is clear. Microsoft's transformation was remarkable, because as we've seen,
the big players in an old paradigm usually move to defend it
rather than to catapult over it. And that is why many dominant
players in so many industries are struggling today.

In contrast, argues Kuhn, those who succeed re-create their
existing paradigms before somebody else does. In the words of
McKinsey director Richard Foster, the winners challenge and
change the existing order rather than protect the existing cash
flows. Kuhn argues that full commitment to a new way, with a
risk of being wrong, is the price of significant scientific advancement. The more entrenched a company is in old routines, the
harder it will be to take on that full commitment and fully capitalize on new possibilities. The ability even to see the emerging
forces in a field often seems to be inversely proportional to one's
investment in that field.

Ultimately, one must choose, for today's paradigm maps
should not be mistaken for permanent "reality." Any strategy is
temporary. The key for leaders and organizations is to encourage the qualities of flexibility, adaptability, open-ended learning, risk taking, creative thinking, and personal responsibility
so as to capitalize on the forces that are all around us, rather
than staying comfortable with what is familiar.

If any established company can do it, Microsoft has shown that it can. Bill Gates is driven by his acute awareness that no software company in history has ever pioneered two revolutions.

What about CNN, now a part of the Time Warner empire? In the face of new competition from other entertainment, software, and communications titans, will it also be able to reconstruct the paradigm that brought it fame and fortune?

We'll know the answers soon, for in his joint venture with NBC, Gates is formally meeting Turner in the marketplace arena. The software genius who loathes being second in anything will confront the iconoclast who commented on Fox chairman Rupert Murdoch's decision to unroll an all-news channel by saying, "I'm looking forward to squashing Rupert like a bug."

I don't know how the final outcome will pan out, but for us customers at ringside, it'll be a very, very interesting show.

Commitment 3 —————————————————

Go Beyond Traditional
Competitive Weapons

WHERE WOULD Nike be today if, during the 1970s, founder Phil Knight had simply benchmarked the existing "black and white sneakers" competition and developed just a slightly better or cheaper product? And how likely is it that customers at the time would have responded positively to survey and focus group questions such as "If I make multicolored, heavily engineered, athlete-endorsed running shoes, would you buy them at $100 a pair?"

Conventional tools provide a snapshot of conventional wisdom. There's nothing wrong with using them to peruse today's lay of the land, but what your current competitors are doing and what your current customers are accustomed to buying should not put a ceiling on breakthrough possibilities.

In this chapter we'll consider the limitations of three traditional weapons: competitive analysis, market research, and strategic planning. Let's start with competitive analysis. If you truly want to leapfrog the competition, don't rely on your competitors' movements as the cornerstone of your strategy.

Back in the 1960s, American tire companies—all bias-ply producers—concentrated so much on each other that they were blindsided by the powerful left hook coming from Michelin and its radials. A few years ago the Baby Bells, having so carefully analyzed the movement of other local telephone providers, wound up, in the words of one business publication, "shocked" at the first indications of the AT&T–McCaw Cellular merger, a marriage that would allow the steadily increasing number of cellular users to bypass Baby Bell lines (and the $14 billion in access fees) altogether. Meanwhile, AT&T analysts initially had no earthly reason to track oil hauler Williams Company until one day they woke up to learn that Williams had decided to use their pipelines to carry fiber-optic cables, thus immediately becoming an important participant in the phone wars.

Today, anything's possible. The gumption of entrepreneurs, coupled with the twenty-four-hour electronic flow of capital they can access worldwide, means that competitors suddenly turn up out of nowhere, and traditional barriers to entry in any business fall like bricks in an earthquake.

All this is why I confess to a mixture of surprise and amusement when I read reports that conclude, as one did recently, that "competitive analysis is the cornerstone of effective strategy formulation and implementation." It ought to be anything but the cornerstone.

Effective strategy formulation and implementation relies on concepts such as uniqueness, differentiation, and standing out in a very, very crowded marketplace. Ineffective strategy formulation and implementation relies on concepts such as imitation, caution, and blending in with the rest of the pack. Competitive analysis does a great job in fostering the latter.

Let me say right up front that I have no problems in performing a quick, occasional scan of what today's competitors are doing. That is just plain prudent management. It ought to be done sparingly, but, yes, it's a good thing to do. The problem is that executives can easily wind up sinking big resources and becoming hypnotized into tracking the movements of today's "official" competitors, who themselves are often lodged in yesterday's solutions for yesterday's customers. And when all these gyrations start seriously influencing strategy, the end is in sight. New sources of competition (read: opportunities) become slighted (the way Digital Equipment and IBM reacted to microcomputers, software, and related services in the early 1980s), or they become treated with arrogance (the way the Big Three TV networks treated the emergence of the cable companies).

Let's face it: if one assumes that the 1960s and 1970s corporate world of mainframes and centralized MIS will go on forever, then IBM's decision to continue focusing primary attention on the actions of other mainframe providers made perfect sense. And if one assumes that the huge market share held by the Big Three networks in the 1970s would go on forever, then their single-mindedly obsessive concerns with imitating each other's programming and promotions also made sense.

Competitor analysis can provide a quick snapshot of today's obvious competitors, which is useful information. But that snapshot is often shortsighted in depth, range, and possibility. Remember the compact disk companies described earlier? They focused their attention on each other's movements to such an extent that they became oblivious to the possibilities of radical new delivery systems and the innovative movements of nontraditional competitors who were prepared to capitalize on them quickly. "Competitive analysis" of each other's strengths, weaknesses, and management decisions mesmerized the record companies into acting as if the traditional business model was inviolable.

Nowadays, even the identification of a "competitor" becomes problematic. Who should a bank consider as a "competitor"? It used to be, simply, "other banks." But what about brokerage and financial services firms such as Merrill Lynch (which not only offers secured loans but is a giant in the world of mutual funds, money market funds, personalized financial portfolios, and investment banking)? What about companies such as Hartford Insurance, American Express, or the new Citigroup, all of whom now offer a wide range of financial services? What about General Motors, whose GMAC financing division is one of its few consistently profitable entities (leading British philosopher Edward de Bono to comment that General Motors is really a bank that uses cars as incentives)? What about AT&T, whose joint venture with Wells Fargo on the Mondex electronic purse card is aimed at setting the standard for on-line Internet payments? What about companies such as Intuit and E*Trade, which capitalize on disintermediation and provide consumers with PC tools to bypass banks in accessing financial markets? What about currently unknown, totally unanticipated sources of competition?

The answer to all these questions is, of course, *yes*. And, of course, banks are now a source of new competition to nonbank institutions; many banks have entered hitherto alien sectors of brokerage, personalized financial services, mutual funds, and insurance.

Whether it's banking or anything else, how could you possibly analyze all conceivable competitors, even if you actually wanted to? Ex-IBM chairman John Akers once remarked that IBM has about 50,000 competitors. If one considers that IBM has 20,000 partnerships in almost every pocket of the world in the computer electronics-telecommunications-education entertainment arena, 50,000 competitors sounds about right. Conducting and analyzing scans on each one of those competitors sounds suicidal to me, especially when, like weeds, new ones are sprouting as you read these very words.

What all this means is that if you're spending a lot of valuable time tracking your competitors' movements, you're not only running in circles, but you're probably paying too much attention to the wrong guys. It's the folks that you can't track— the ones that don't exist yet either as competitors or even as companies—who are your real problems. That's because they're not worrying about tracking you. They're moving ahead with new offerings, redefining and reinventing the marketplace as they go along.

Glen Tullman, the ex-president of CCC Information Services, which appeared from nowhere in 1980 and revolutionized the auto collision/estimating market, is quite blunt: "We didn't want to imitate our competitors. We wanted to change the rules of the whole game." As described earlier, CCC did, with radical new software, networks, and decentralized technology that upended the traditional manual and mainframe approaches that had been the industry norm for years—and in the process took away significant revenues and market share from venerable established competitors ten times CCC's size.

In summary, seeking future organizational success while wearing the glasses of conventional competitive analysis is, at best, myopic. It is tantamount to driving a car on the highway looking side to side at "competitor" cars while ignoring the road ahead. At worst, it influences an organization to imitate the movements of well-established players that are unknowingly becoming obsolete.

That's why during a recent seminar with managers at the Bravo! division of Cablevision, I agreed that they should certainly keep tabs on what aggressive competitors such as the Sundance Channel are doing. However, I emphasized that while the leapfrogging organization conducts brief periodic environmental scans that include what today's official competitors are doing, the primary attention is on doing something special, something great, to lead the race. The blinders of competitor analysis limit our capacity to capitalize on the vast uncharted terrain before us.

Like the hypnotist who mesmerizes people by having them follow the pendulum-like watch, competitive analysis hypnotizes us to look only side to side, back and forth, and even worse, makes us believe that what lies ahead is the same as what we're looking at back and forth, back and forth, back and forth. . . .

As LONG as we're barbecuing sacred cows, let's look at market research. Just as traditional competitive analysis amounts to studying rivals' cars on the same stretch of road, market research amounts to so much time spent looking in the rearview mirror. Take the case of Mercedes-Benz.

In 1900, Mercedes-Benz completed a market research study that "estimated that worldwide demand for cars would not exceed one million, primarily because of the limitations of available chauffeurs," notes social commentator Stewart Brand. But by 1908, the Model T had democratized the automobile, and by 1920, more than eight million cars were rolling on the roads of America.

Relying on market research for strategic decisions and product ideas is like driving a car while looking only at the rearview mirror. Market research is always a step behind. It provides yesterday's solutions to today's problems and today's responses ("conventional wisdom") to tomorrow's opportunities. This is why Mercedes-Benz came up with the market findings it did and why over the past decade so many companies with huge market (and consumer) research budgets—including Digital Equipment, GM, and Kmart—produced reams of reports and still managed to misread the tea leaves.

The radio and TV industries obsessively fit this description. These brutally competitive businesses are haunted with every nuance of every number. The data of Nielson and Arbitron surveys determine stations' programming, promotions, investments, and people's career prospects. Yet critics, myself included, have argued that these obsessions stifle creativity and perpetuate bland "me too" similarity among stations. Program directors and general managers in radio, for example, are frustrated at having to subjugate their industry experience and creative instincts to a "research-based" playlist that does little but provide a financially unstable, angst-producing, 3 percent market share (the norm) for their stations.

Does this mean I would throw out all market research? No, of course not. But use it cautiously. It should supplement but never replace people's intuitive judgment and sense of creative experimentation. At its best, market research taps into customer preferences and desires given what they *currently* know and expect of the industry. To make business decisions based on market research leaves organizations struggling along with the pack of known competitors, offering variation-on-a-theme products and services. Logic dictates that vendors provide what consumers "want," and consumers "want" what they're accustomed to wanting based on past experiences. It's a self-perpetuating cycle.

The Economist has editorialized that "carmakers are among market research's biggest fans, as the dull similarity of modern cars testifies." Breakthroughs in the auto business have almost uniformly deviated from the conventional wisdom tapped by market research. MIT's Peter Senge quotes one Detroit executive who commented, "You could never produce the Mazda Miata solely from market research. It required a leap of imagination to see what the customer might want."

Similarly, designer Hal Sperlich initially couldn't sell Ford on the concept of the now-wildly successful minivan and thus moved to a more receptive Chrysler. His experience led him to

note a fundamental flaw in Detroit's product development paradigm. Market research probed likes and dislikes among existing
products, hence, executives didn't believe there was a market for
the minivan because the product didn't exist. "In ten years of developing the minivan, we never once got a letter from a house-
wife asking us to invent one. To the skeptics, that proved there
wasn't a market out there," said Sperlich in *Fortune* magazine.

At 3M, one of the major roadblocks to the release of the
Post-It notepad was none other than the marketing department.
Nobody was calling up the company asking for semi-sticky little yellow pieces of paper, and nobody would have known what
to do with them if asked in a research sample. Therefore, there
was no hard data suggesting a viable market for them. Today,
along with paper clips and staples, Post-It notes are one of the
most commonly used office products. 3M's capacity to crank
out new product applications, including Post-It greeting cards,
calendars, stationery, and trainers' sheets, helps the company
generate a cool $700 million in a market they invented and that
nobody asked for.

The movie *M*A*S*H* and the television programs *All in the
Family*, *Hill St. Blues*, *Cheers*, and *Seinfeld* were all characterized by two things: negative initial viewer reactions and a
dogged commitment to those programs by producers Robert
Altman, Norman Lear, Steven Bochco, and Larry David, respectively. (I have always liked business start-up specialist Philipe
Viller's definition of entrepreneurism: "unreasonable conviction
based on inadequate evidence.") *Seinfeld*, for example, was initially perceived during market research as too strange, too New
York, too Jewish. It wouldn't sell.

If one counts the TV spin-off and residuals, *M*A*S*H* made
more money for 20th Century Fox than any other single movie
made for any studio—well over $1 billion. Yet according to
Robert Altman, the only reason the movie wasn't buried at the
outset is because he dragged Richard Zanuck to a sneak preview, where a wildly excited audience of 1,200 people belied the
lukewarm results of the formal market research. Sums up Altman, "I always say that *M*A*S*H* wasn't released. It escaped."

The value of market research, when used cautiously, is that it
can provide a snapshot overview of the current lay of the land,

which can be useful in periodic small dosages. If you're a retailer, assessing the age and income demographics surrounding
a current or potential locale is good common sense. If you're a
ski resort operator concerned about dwindling baby-boomer
visits, tracking the tastes of young snowboarders becomes a
prudent step. If you're a Ben & Jerry's, monitoring the changes
in people's ice cream preferences regarding fat content becomes
essential.

During a visit to Israel a few years ago, I noticed highway
billboards and magazine pages blanketed with Pepsi-Cola ads.
Pepsi was moving aggressively to end Coke's stranglehold on
the Israeli cola market. The ads feature young, virile men and
women in military fatigues, because market research had indicated that Israeli youths admired young, virile soldiers. It made
perfect sense to apply these data in product promotions.

However, there was nothing unique or proprietary about the
data; they were available to Coke and, for that matter, any vendor of any product who did research in Israel. But if everyone is
accessing the same data and if those data are driving the business, then "me too" strategies, promotions, and products are
inevitable. Vendors become indistinguishable from one another,
fighting desperately for ephemeral bits of earnings and market
share, and in the process blinding themselves to breakthrough
possibilities.

Economist Jude Wanniski notes that traditional research endeavors like consumer surveys and that polls ". . . simply re-
discover conventional wisdom, which is a blind alley." An
organization that wants to strategically differentiate itself from
the pack cannot be satisfied with a reliance on conventional
wisdom. It must strike out boldly in uncharted areas—even if
the initial unfamiliarity and discomfort on the part of the consumers yield negative market research results.

With research models and computer technologies becoming
more sophisticated and more readily available, many managers
will be increasingly tempted to base critical decisions on "the
data." Apart from the problems already listed, the danger with
this approach is that one becomes "market driven" and thus
simply reactive. When this occurs, preparing for tomorrow's
opportunities is sabotaged, for as consultant Tom Kelley points

out, "Research can only reveal what people like and dislike today, not what may appeal to them tomorrow."

Even worse, an overreliance on research means that "latent needs" and "deep discovery" don't surface. These are important concepts. Peter Senge argues that for competitive success, "companies need to understand and meet the 'latent needs' of the customer—what customers might truly value but have never experienced or would never think to ask for." Market research simply cannot access these sorts of needs effectively. A related point: customers can tell you what they like and don't like today, and that is useful information. But as strategy experts Gary Hamel and C.K. Prahalad have observed, customers are notoriously lacking in foresight. Quality guru W. Edwards Deming once noted caustically, "No customer ever asked for electric light or photography." And customers didn't line up en masse demanding fully engineered athletic socks and Web browsers, either. Originally, most of today's customers of these products and services didn't even know they "needed" them.

Thus, my advice is simple. Just as you have to look in the rearview mirror occasionally when you drive, so do occasional market research as you feel you must. Analyze the data quickly. Discuss aggregate trends quickly. And don't take the findings too seriously. Concentrate instead on the vast uncharted road ahead. Concentrate on tapping into "latent" opportunities and offering exciting products and services that exceed customers' expectations. Concentrate on moving ahead of the pack and defining the market-to-be. Concentrate not on reacting to markets but on creating them. This means don't be led by customers; lead them. It means don't be market driven; drive the market.

Here are three points to ponder if you're serious about vaulting over the potential pothole of market research:

1. Use research primarily to monitor people's reactions to your innovative actions *after the fact*, not as a means to determine what products and services you should launch. GTE and TCI first develop new digital formats, then test-market them in selected venues. Makes sense. Similarly, executives at Benetton,

MCA Music, Rubbermaid, and Seiko solicit quick consumer feedback on merchandise and features that they have already introduced. The feedback allows them to make revisions in product features quickly and provides valuable information to move to the next step.

The advice, therefore, is this: concentrate less on market research and more on factors such as quick flexible design and manufacturing and on corporate cultures where pilots replace proposals and action replaces hyper-analysis. Within that context, some *quick, post hoc* market research—short feedback loops—can be very helpful as a means to monitor progress. Keep in mind that at Seiko and GTE, not all launches are successful, but their systems and cultures have dramatically lowered the cost of failure while simultaneously boosting the returns on successes. It's all a question of getting your organization focused on tries—more tries, more successes.

2. Insist that everyone on the payroll get involved with lots of "naive listening" to customers as an official part of their job requirements. Then provide mechanisms—from open dialogue to newsletters to groupware—that allow people to share their impressions and come up with ideas for product and service innovations. The key to naive listening is not to ask customers, "Would you buy this?" or "Would you buy that?" The key is to hang out with them—on project teams, during on-site visits, or in bars, if that's where you'll find them, listening to their issues and problems, noticing what frustrates them on the job, staying alert to what they get excited about, and observing what they wish they had to make their lives easier. By doing this, you'll get plenty of food for fresh creative ideas, and you'll know what they'll respond to before they themselves do. Companies as diverse as Interim Services (health care), Intuit (software), and Weaver (popcorn) function this way.

3. Significantly elevate the use of "intuition based on trend sniffing." A few years ago, I asked Tom Peters about his thoughts on market research. Here's what he said: "John Sculley came to Apple after having the job of president of Pepsi-Cola. [Pepsi-Cola] is absolutely driven by the most infinitely minute market research. Yet Sculley's comment was, looking

back at his career at Pepsi-Cola, that he had never seen a good marketing decision that was made based on the data. Sure, you need the data. Sure, you read the data from the systemic market research. But at the end of the day it is a very, very healthy dose of intuition that leads you to invent something that's a little bit special. . . . You have to have the guts to try things that are a little bit different."

Neither Peters nor I are suggesting blind intuition. I'm suggesting intuition based on strategic trend sniffing. When people focus on the market, not on market research, their intuition generates interesting ideas. The *Miami Herald*'s successful Spanish-language spin-off *El Nuevo Herald* emerged as a result of sniffing clues about demographic shifts in southern Florida, not because market research told managers that subscribers would buy a sister newspaper.

The key is to get everyone on your team to look outside to scrutinize and make sense of market displacements that regularly appear on the horizon—all in the public domain. And then do something with that information, like the folks at the *Miami Herald* did, or like Ted Turner and Jeff Bezos did.

Or like Phil Knight did. Prior to launching Nike, Knight paid attention to several emerging trends: the rapidly growing interest in sports, both as a participatory and viewing event; the sharply increasing adulation shown to top athletes; the obsession of baby boomers with health and physical activity; the centrality of sports among teenagers' lives; and the increased "fashionizing" of products. All that was the raw material to which he could apply a new shoe technology and some creative marketing.

Over the past few years, he's paid attention to the rapid globalization of these trends, generating increased international forays. And in the case of women's footwear and women's basketball sponsorship, he paid attention to simple demographics: women were becoming as sports-conscious as men, and in sheer number they comprise more than 50 percent of the potential market. More recently, in the face of the temporary stall of the Nike juggernaut, he's paid attention to the overexposure of the "swoosh" design, and the potential in new products such as All Condition Gear and radically different athletic equipment (e.g., non-leather baseball gloves). This is the kind of trend sniffing that is likely to keep Nike's competitive batteries charged.

At the same time Knight was nurturing Nike in the 1970s, Monsanto chairman Richard Mahoney was doing some serious trend sniffing in his own business. He was impressed with the rapid advances in cloning and techniques to move genes between species. He began pouring money into biotechnology with the conviction, says current CEO Bob Shapiro, "that the fundamental technology would succeed and the rest would fall into place." Further trend sniffing revealed a heightened consumer interest in nutrition, health, and longevity. Monsanto's strategy eventually began to integrate the possibilities inherent in these trends. The company ultimately repositioned itself as a leader of an exciting new market called "life sciences," an amalgam of biotechnology, pharmacology, agriculture, genetics, and nutrition. Monsanto's strategic moves were not predicated on market research or competitor analysis, for this new market did not even exist yet. The strategy evolved from paying attention to trends and events in the public domain—and then acting on them.

In short, remember that market research, like competitor analysis, is at best simply one of many tools in the arsenal of an effective manager. Don't ever let the numbers replace entrepreneurship based on a hands-on feel for the market. If numbers alone were adequate for business decisions, software would replace leadership. Thank goodness that's not the case.

NOW LET'S look at that sacred cow of management, strategic planning, which provides neither steak nor sizzle. How can we set the table in anticipation of a tomorrow unlike anything we've swallowed thus far in our history? One solution may be the most radical step of all: replace traditional strategic planning with high-precision strategic conversation.

Let's start with the bad news. Read it and weep:

- "No battle plan survives contact with the enemy." (General Colin Powell)
- "A good deal of corporate planning . . . is like a ritual rain dance. It has no effect on the weather that follows, but those who engage in it think it does." (Brian Quinn, professor of business at Dartmouth)
- "Strategic plans are forecasts of historical trends and rarely anticipate new opportunities." (an Arthur Andersen director)
- "If you start planning, you blind yourself to opportunity." (Harry Quadracchi, Quad/Graphics)
- "Business plans may be great for bankers and investors, but if companies really followed them, you might never have heard of Compaq, Lotus, or Ben & Jerry's." (*Inc.* magazine)
- "There is no foundation beneath the multibillion-dollar strategy industry. Strategy is lucky foresight. It comes from a serendipitous cocktail." (Gary Hamel, strategy expert and coauthor of *Competing for the Future*)
- "Tonight, I'd like to tell you about strategic planning at General Electric or, more specifically, why we no longer do strategic planning." (Lawrence Bossidy, at the time a senior vice president at GE)

You get the drift. Increasingly, the rap on strategic planning is that it's either irrelevant or harmful. The conventional wisdom is that smart, degree-studded people armed with software and algorithms can forecast the nonlinear discontinuities of the future in a linear systematic manner. But as Nokia vice president Martin Sandelin confessed to an executive audience in San Francisco recently, "Forecasting is difficult, especially if it's about the future." Nobel laureate Frederich Hayek was more blunt, calling the traditional forecasting assumptions "the fatal conceit" of managers. Writing in the *American Economic Review*, Hayek argued that "economists must understand that the complex phenomena of the market will hardly ever be fully known or measurable, unlike most of the factors that determine events observed in the physical sciences."

Most managers will ruefully agree with corporate intelligence expert Herbert Meyer, who notes that "no sooner do you conclude what the prevailing circumstances are than your conclusions begin to lose their validity." The reason is simple: the planning process relies on certain premises about technology, capital markets, competitors, customers, cash flow, inflation, market value, sales, and geopolitics—all of which may be appropriate today but irrelevant tomorrow.

That, by the way, is why another pet premise of strategic planning is false: the idea that endless analysis of current data will somehow yield brilliant predictive insights and groundbreaking decisions. In fact, the opposite occurs: the mountain of analysis invariably yields vanilla "me too" strategies. Analysis is a useful tool for any rational manager, to be sure, but researchers such as McGill University's Henry Mintzberg have persuasively argued that it is creative synthesis—of information, resources, people's creativity, and commitment—that makes the difference in terms of successful strategic action. In other words, it is collaboration, teamwork, and collective entrepreneurship that generates business success.

As flawed as strategic planning is, its execution is frequently worse. Planning is often done by one of three groups: corporate staff groups who are out of touch with the fluid, day-to-day realities faced by line managers; top managers who themselves are out of touch with the prevailing realities faced by "real people" in the trenches; or conventional assembly line consulting firms that are out of touch with everyone but still manage to crank out a pseudo-customized boilerplate, which guarantees that the client's strategy will be basically the same as everyone else's. Regardless of the source, the final "plan" is then hierarchically imposed on everyone else, generating neither commitment nor understanding within the organization. It soon gathers cobwebs on a shelf anyway.

But the damage it does before it hits the shelf can be mind-boggling. Writing in the November 1993 issue of *Fast Company*, Mark Fuller notes, "Think of it as Joe Stalin visits corporate America." Once the ringing commitment to meet the goals of "the plan" are heralded, the fun begins. Continues Fuller, "Companies then decompose pieces of their strategy into separate projects and assign them out to different people in different places—people who have never worked together, never even met each other. In fact, these people were hired, promoted, motivated, and rewarded in ways that trained them not to like each other, not to trust each other, not to help each other, not to speak to each other. They were trained not to work together."

Is all this depressing enough? It ought to be. Strategic planning as we know it is as sacred a management cow as one can imagine, and it can be downright dangerous to your company's health. Well, never fear, because the good news is right around the corner.

Back in 1985, McKinsey's Frederick Gluck showed prescience: "Management by remoteness, management by the numbers, and management by exception are dead. Management by involvement is in," he wrote in the *Journal of Business Strategy.*

Why involvement? Because the primary driver of competitive advantage nowadays is how innovative can you be. And innovation does not come from any one "plan" or solely from a few people sitting in top management suites. Innovation is an all-hands, everyday effort, regardless of whether the boss is around or not.

So while top management may set broad strategic parameters, a dynamic culture of constant innovation is necessary to give those parameters vitality, uniqueness, momentum, and constant adaptation. A true culture of innovation occurs when every person on the payroll transcends his or her current role to assume the role of "businessperson" or "owner." This means that people approach their work activities as if they owned the business. Which, in turn, means that every person takes on the strategic responsibility not of performing a fixed, static job but of adding value to the organization.

Thus, strategic planning done by a select few is yesterday's paradigm. In the new paradigm, strategic thinking and execution become the job expectations of everyone. Each individual comes to work with the goal of thinking of opportunities, and seizing opportunities, in the arenas of cost reduction and revenue enhancement—and then working collaboratively with like-minded souls to develop ideas and take action. The question now is: how do you create such an environment?

My suggestion: First and foremost, start visualizing strategy as *conversation*. Imagine strategy not as a plan but as a process—a perpetual set of conversations aimed at developing an exciting, coherent, ever-evolving "motion picture" of the organization and the business. *Exciting, coherent,* and *ever-evolving* are the operative words for describing the strategy of the leapfrogging organization:

1. *Exciting*, as in, What can we do that's world-class and market dazzling? How can we execute it in such a way that we "knock the socks off" of customers and investors?
2. *Coherent*, as in, How do we maintain clarity, commitment, and consensus among all hands as to our priorities, values, and directions?
3. *Ever-evolving*, as in, How do we ensure that our priorities and so forth do not stagnate? How do we ensure that we move and change as quickly as the marketplace does?

The answers to these three questions reside not in a strategic plan but in *strategic conversation*.

Your conversation is your picture, your picture is your strategy, and it's never complete. To do this, you'll need to address three issues with your team(s): purpose, uniqueness, and values. The list on the following pages encompasses some questions that you can draw on to stimulate the discussions you will hold.

AMMUNITION FOR LEAPFROGGERS

Purpose

1. Why do we exist? Why should we?
2. What is our purpose?
3. What exactly is the business we're in? Now and three years from now?
4. Who exactly are our customers or intended beneficiaries? Now and three years from now?
5. Who are our competitors?
6. What, specifically, are the changes (domestic and global) in technology, consumer choices, capital structures, demographics, sociopolitical trends, and science that we must be especially attentive to?
7. What are we doing to stay abreast of and capitalize on these changes?
8. How do we define "success?" Now and in the future?
9. How will we know we are succeeding or failing over the next three years?
10. What, if anything (our structure, our culture, our habits), is preventing us from moving in the right direction? What do we need to do to change?

Uniqueness

1. How are we different from any other organization?
2. What's unique and special about our organization?
3. In what unique way do we add value to our customers? How do we amaze them? How do we dazzle them? What benefits can we offer them that will allow us to boost our share and returns sharply in the future?
4. Why should customers come to us rather than to anyone else?
5. What are we better at than anyone else? What skills and resources do we have that nobody else has?
6. What are we doing today to ensure that we remain better and unique?

7. What, if anything (our structure, our culture, our habits), is preventing us from moving in the right direction? What do we need to do to change?

Values

1. What do we stand for? What is our philosophy?
2. What are the values we will live by?
3. What do we really care about? What excites us?
4. What are we striving for? Who do we serve?
5. How do we define success? How *should* we?
6. How will we behave toward one another and toward our customers and partners?
7. What do we need to do to ensure that we can all rally around a common purpose and common values?
8. What are we doing to ensure that our behavior, systems, and processes are aligned with our values and ideals?
9. How have we changed our roles and behaviors as a result of this process? How should we change them?
10. What, if anything (our structure, our culture, our habits), is preventing us from moving in the right direction? What do we need to do to change?

These questions are meant to fuel problem-solving strategic conversations that you—the leader—drive and orchestrate. The discussions are open and freewheeling, but you're at the helm. You push and direct the process. You demand commitments and accountability. Your priorities are coherence, excitement, and evolvement vis-à-vis the big goal lines (strategic priorities, business imperatives, corporate philosophy) and the broad sidelines (financial, legal, ethical, cultural) that everyone plays in. The discussions define the "business game," which means that your people must be fully aware, and involved, in the financial, strategic, and ethical "rules of the game" (more on this in Commitments 5 and 6). The discussions are a mixture of pragmatism and business theory. They instill in people a common purpose, language, and viewpoint.

Furthermore, the conversations are not limited to a select group of people, such as the people who report to you. The more you can expand the scope of the conversation to include relevant people in other departments and other organizations (e.g., lead users and key suppliers), the richer the insights, data, and commitments that will emerge.

As Arie de Geus, former chief planner at Royal Dutch/Shell has noted, the real purpose of effective strategy is not to make plans but to change people's "mental models." The conversations I suggest can provide a framework to evaluate alternatives and make the strategically "right" choices every day as they quickly create and capitalize on new opportunities.

Most important, these discussions are not a one-shot deal. They're ongoing. You do them again and again. You insist that your direct reports follow your lead. This is crucial because, as a group, you constantly need to refine your direction, address problems, and build ongoing consensus so that people's every-day thinking and entrepreneurial action are in alignment with the strategic "motion picture."

"What?" you say. "Repeat the same discussion over and over?" No, I mean you initiate strategic conversations over and over, not the "same" conversation repeatedly. Create your own questions. Choose among the questions from the list as appropriate. Adapt them to your needs; for example, perhaps your concern is two to three months ahead, not years. Use the conversations as a vehicle to explore business issues, generate "best bets," probe alternatives, applaud commitments, review trends, analyze data, critique decisions, bless new initiatives, share learning, and address implementation problems. If, after all this, you find yourself having the "same" discussions, you know nothing new or interesting is happening in your organization. Which means you're in deep trouble. You want your organization bubbling with audacious ideas and creative pilots.

If this process generates a charter, a mission, a vision statement, or even a rough document called a "plan," well and good. But these things are not end products in themselves because there is no end product. They are simply temporary by-products of a never-ending chain of conversations.

Keep in mind that I am not calling for "democracy." Conversation is not an excuse for putting strategic options up for ballot box voting. Nor is it another word for "employee involvement," though, clearly, involvement is central to any legitimate dialogue. Leaders must still lead. You, the leader, have the responsibility to drive the conversation and focus people's mind-set. What conversation allows is to generate reality checks on everyone's thinking (including yours), collectively ponder alternatives, clarify ambiguities, confront inconsistencies, gather ideas for execution, challenge the process, pinpoint accountability, heighten excitement, and perpetually raise the ante. In short, the leader creates a living, vibrant environment that allows employees to put on a strategist's hat and come up with innovative decisions daily.

Some will find it difficult to accept this idea. They are still wedded to the notion that strategy is a document or that strategy formulation is somehow their private fiefdom. To them, I say, Change or perish. Other doubters will insist that, at the least, big-ticket corporate strategy-like acquisitions, alliances, and asset management must remain a top-level domain.

Why? If you can't talk about—and justify—big-ticket corporate strategy with your general managers (and their direct reports) using the Ammunition for Leapfroggers questions as a reference guide, then I am frankly suspicious about your company's use of shareholder investment. (More on the dangers of merger and acquisition mania in Giant Step V.)

In sum, your job as a manager and executive is to initiate perpetual conversations about strategy, which then create the arena for people to implement the fruits of their discussions proactively. Strategy is exciting, dynamic, and organic, just like business. And if you want people to act as businesspeople and think strategically every day, you drive the conversations in that spirit. Do it with sincerity and persistence, and, trust me, your payback will be huge: a wealth of ideas, opportunities, and initiatives that will yield organizational transformation and market leadership.

Commitment 4 ─────────────────

View the World
Through Bifocal Lenses

> EVER WONDER why otherwise well-meaning managers focus
> on quarterly results to the exclusion of tomorrow's needs? Ever
> wonder why everyone is in favor of vision exercises, but noth-
> ing new ever seems to get accomplished? Maybe the reason is a
> lack of "bifocal" vision.

My colleague Chip Bell tells me that when he was growing up on
a Georgia dairy farm, one of his chores was to herd the cattle in
the evening. To be successful at this, he had to learn bifocal vision; that is, he had to acquire the capacity to monitor each and
every one of the cows while in the midst of them and simultaneously look ahead to where he needed to move them next.

The young farmboy can teach us a lot. Management gurus
tout the importance of vision for leadership, and one cannot
argue with that. But vision as it's usually presented—unidimen-
sional, static, overgeneralized—is not enough. To really help the
organization meet today's business requirements and prepare
for tomorrow's, vision must be pragmatically and unabashedly
bifocal: it must simultaneously paint a picture of the opportunities today and the "best bets" of tomorrow, and, when push
comes to shove, it must prioritize the latter.

In *Jumping the Curve*, Nicholas Imparato and I briefly intro-
duce the concept of bifocal vision. Since then, I've come to realize that it's a much more vital tool than we initially thought.
Here's why:

To meet responsibilities to today's customers and investors,
the leader must insist that today's products and services be con-

tinually improved and perfected. At the same time, to prepare successfully for responsibilities to tomorrow's customers and investors, the leader must insist that the company aggressively pursue the development of tomorrow's products and services, which means investing in riskier ventures that draw budget away from, and may ultimately obsolesce, existing procedures and cash-cow outputs. It is a simultaneous process: building on the status quo while catapulting over it in pursuit of bigger opportunities.

This is an important point both strategically and tactically. Unless we are a brand new start-up, we have an already-existing business to run, with numerous demands. When we arrive at work, we have to deal with today's customers, today's employees, today's suppliers, today's general ledger, and today's crisis, all for starters. As Intel's Andy Grove warns, "We don't want to fall into a hole while gazing at the stars."

Nevertheless, it's precisely our ability to head for the stars that will allow us to leapfrog the competition. Hence, we've got to deal with the present and the future simultaneously.

It sounds paradoxical, if not schizophrenic, but the symptoms of bifocal vision are demonstrated in a number of successful companies. The $4 billion Rosenbluth International (4,000 employees, 1,250 offices in twenty-five countries) improves today's travel agency business with better telecommunications processes and customer service. Simultaneously, it is fast-forwarding into tomorrow's travel business, where customers will do much of their own bookings via the Internet. Rosenbluth has already taken the lead in developing cutting-edge software and Web-based tools that allow corporate and individual customers to create—alone and in tandem with Rosenbluth's organizational support systems—the most comprehensive and most customized travel packages on a real-time basis.

MCI/WorldCom continually improves its long-distance voice service via aggressive upgrades in technology, customer service, marketing, global expansion, and penetration into local markets. Yet even as the company improves this primary source of today's revenue, it recognizes that on its own it is becoming a low-margin commodity. The future of the business is in high-speed high-bandwidth digital network products that can blend voice, data, and image. The future is in applications that can synthesize the output of the most advanced PCs, phones, pagers, conferencing tools, and wireless communication systems. The future is in network management services that can be totally customized. That's where the leaps over current competition and the breakthroughs in growth and earnings will come. That's where the serious capital and attention is now concentrated. MCI/WorldCom chairman Bernard Ebbers has gone on record as predicting that the percentage of his market that will be solely voice transmission in the year 2002 will be all of 1 percent.

Walt Disney Co. invests in improving and expanding its flagship theme park business. Simultaneously, the company is relentlessly applying its core skills in entertainment to a broad array of integrated niches, including movies, athletics, children's on-line software and services, TV, cable, and video entertainment, arenas that Disney executives expect will offer even greater opportunities tomorrow. Indeed, it turns out that the all-sports channel ESPN has become the jewel in the portfolio. At a time when other profit centers (including the theme parks) are flat, ESPN accounted for 15 percent of Disney's total operating profit in 1998 and was one of its fastest-growing assets. In fact, with current and planned ESPN spin-offs (other cable niches, radio, sports magazine, Web sites, theme stores, restaurants), the business might be worth $14 billion on its own. Once again, bifocal vision has helped position Disney for tomorrow today.

Personally, I find the idea of bifocal vision appealing. I'm skeptical of all the hype about "vision" and the mega-consulting industry it has spawned. All too often, *vision* becomes a chic buzzword that leads to pleasant corporate retreats facilitated by nice consultants, resulting in fluffy overgeneralized statements that adorn company walls and have little impact on management decision making.

Bifocal vision is more gutsy, earthy, dynamic, and utilitarian. It's more strategic. It requires managers to address today's business realities while they position themselves for tomorrow's. It requires daily discipline in looking at the present and looking ahead at the same time, at interpreting events, choices, and decisions in terms of their impact on today's prerequisites and tomorrow's bigger-picture expectations. So Casio improves its digital watch and electronic calculator business even as it transfers its core skills into the emerging, potentially huge digital camera market. Merck improves its efforts in pharmaceutical R&D for blockbuster drugs even as it builds its health information services and managed care drug distribution business. IBM reinforces its hardware business even as it redefines itself as a significant source of software, servers, and services. General Electric upgrades its product lines even as it aggressively positions itself as a high-margin provider of tailored services around those products. Microsoft beefs up its Windows products while making the acquisitions and alliances necessary for rapid integration of computers and television. Bifocalism is an active, everyday, non-static process rather than a one-shot deal.

A bifocal approach to strategy is a very practical tool, for it allows you to hedge a bit, to straddle the fence rather than immediately abandon your current business. But bifocal vision is not an excuse to perpetuate the old with lip service to the new. The thing that makes bifocal vision vibrant in companies such as Rosenbluth, Disney, GE, and IBM is that they're deadly serious with their future orientation, and it's very visible in their *significant* allocation of capital budgets, time, and senior management attention—often to products and markets that today offer less in the way of income than do the standard, flagship businesses. But today's financials are not as salient as tomorrow's. As one IBM executive told me, "Obviously, our numbers are huge when we sell mainframes, but that's no longer a growth business. The growth is in the e-business."

There's an interesting corollary to all this. Bifocalism allows companies to enjoy some crossover synergies between today's business and tomorrow's, as IBM and Merck have found. Bifocalism also allows companies some breathing room to explore tomorrow's markets while living on the revenues of today's as Rosenbluth has found. But straddling today's and tomorrow's reality is a tricky business. If you're exploring the potential of the Internet for direct customer contact, for example, what do you do with your brokers, distributors, retailers, and salespeople? Companies as diverse as AMR and Levi Strauss are struggling with that issue right now.

Furthermore, at some point, straddling the fence may not be a tenable strategy. Remember our earlier discussion of Monsanto. Monsanto was acting bifocally for nearly two decades, carrying its traditional bulk chemicals business while investigating, and investing in, the new possibilities in biotechnology. A few years ago, it concluded that their flagship business was going to remain a low-margin commodity, and it dropped it to concentrate on leading the new life sciences industry. Similarly, Cincinnati Milacron exploited its brand name in machine tool manufacturing even as it got into new less bulky, faster-growing businesses such as lubricants, coolants, disposable cutting tools, plastics technology, and chemical management. Like Monsanto, Milacron eventually decided that its flagship business was becoming a low-margin, price-sensitive commodity—and highly cyclical to boot. Accordingly, as of October 1, 1998, it sold off its machine tool business. The company, now named simply Milacron, is focusing its resources on the plastics technology, disposable products, and related services cited earlier.

In both cases, a bifocal strategy allowed the companies to pick the time and place to make a 100 percent commitment to tomorrow's business. Obviously, if they are to continue to prosper, the next stage, a new wave of bifocal vision, will have to emerge. Even as these companies build on their new business, they'll need to be looking at the horizon for tomorrow's. It never ends.

In practical terms this means that you—the leader—should insist that every important meeting agenda, document, and decision should explicitly consider dual impacts: on today's marketplace and also on tomorrow's. Whether it's product development, marketing, personnel, or capital budgeting, you should approach all bifocally. Before you hire or promote that individual or spend the money on that particular project or acquisition, make sure you can justify how the decision helps you succeed today and—even more important—how it will help you succeed given tomorrow's realities.

At first, your people will complain: "How am I supposed to know how decision XYZ will impact tomorrow's customer?" Insist, then, that they do over-the-horizon due diligence beforehand. Insist that they pay attention to what Gary Hamel calls the "discontinuities in technology, lifestyles, work habits, or geopolitics that might create opportunities to rewrite the industries' rules." And then—and only then—come to a decision today.

This is not easy stuff. It requires a great deal of practice. The paradox of bifocal vision is that it requires attention to the "now" and the "later" at the same time. It can be done, but it is a competency that does not occur naturally; it must be learned as a discipline. The micro-dynamics of bifocal vision are akin to what professional foreign language interpreters call "shadowing," the skill necessary to listen to a speaker's comments and translate them right now while simultaneously listening to what he or she is saying a few sentences ahead. Interpreters have to master this challenge by initially learning to shadow another speaker's comments in their very own language even before attempting to do it with two languages in play. Try it, and you'll see that the skill is devilishly tough to learn. Unsurprisingly, shadowing demands lots and lots of practice. So does bifocal visioning.

Wayne Gretzky was not the biggest, strongest, or fastest player in the National Hockey League, but he is arguably its greatest player ever. According to consultant William Carey, Gretzky was once asked the reason for his success. Here is a player who obviously must concentrate on the rapid movement of the puck every moment of the game, yet he replied, "When I get on the ice and play begins, everyone else on the ice goes where the puck is. Me? I go where the puck is going to be."

In an eerie parallel to that sentiment, a newspaper story recently described Microsoft's Bill Gates as someone who not only administers a business efficiently but, more important, "is a master at knowing where the market is going and getting there first." Whether it's hockey or software, those who view vision and strategy through bifocal lenses strike gold.

I predict that leaders who intend to leapfrog their competition will find the practice of bifocal vision more relevant than vision alone. It won't be easy. It's much easier to participate in a one-shot vision exercise. It's much harder to do daily bifocal visioning. But if a hockey player and a Georgia farmboy can learn to do it, I think the rest of us can too.

GIANT STEP II

FLOOD YOUR ORGANIZATION WITH KNOWLEDGE

Imagine this: you're a contractor who has purchased a load of mixed concrete and asphalt for a major road-building project, and upon delivery of the product, you receive an invoice with the following note attached:

> If you are not satisfied for any reason, don't pay us for it. This means if any part of this invoice is incorrect or if you were unhappy with the products or service received from this transaction, let us know right now. Simply scratch out the stated line item, write a brief note about the problem, and return a copy of this invoice along with your check for the remaining balance. Someone will contact you immediately to resolve the problem.

Yes, you read that correctly. If you feel, for example, that a botched delivery cost you about $1,000 in labor time, materials, and general hassle, simply deduct it from the invoice. If you're really upset, don't write a check at all. And, by the way, no matter what you pay us, we're going to make things right for you right away.

Sounds insane, but (per the "insanity" described in Giant Step I) this is precisely how the 1992 Malcolm Baldrige Award winning $110 million Granite Rock company in little Watsonville, California, has thrived—building fanatical customer loyalty while charging premium prices relative to its competitors—

since Bruce Woolpert took over the privately held, family business in 1987.

Granite Rock doesn't make many mistakes, or else it would simply go out of business in complying with their pledge to customers.

How is this possible in a company with 500 people (primarily unionized) that supports the northern California area with gravel aggregates, asphaltic concrete, ready-mix concrete, and services such as truck deliveries and building materials retailing? Well, imagine a company:

- where an obsession with the customer results in numerous detailed surveys and analyses monthly, immediate follow-up to the tiniest complaints, and a documented cost in resolving complaints that is equivalent to 0.2 percent of sales, as compared with the industry average of 2 percent;
- where employee expertise and electronically sophisticated systems have allowed a six-sigma quality reliability standard (defect rate of 3.4 per million) on numerous key processes;
- where employees are part of more than 100 highly focused interdisciplinary quality teams and are involved as in-house consultants on issues ranging from production efficiency to purchasing of major equipment;
- where employees are cross-trained, continually educated on matters such as technology, statistical process control, and human relations, and fully reimbursed for any outside (even out-of-state) seminars and university tuition fees.

Imagine a company, further, that has developed new products such as Construction Calculators, a collection of advanced online tools using JavaScript technology that help the customer estimate the amount of concrete or road materials needed for a particular construction job. Or GraniteXpress, a larger-scale innovation in response to its customers' needs for speed. GraniteXpress is the construction industry's equivalent of an automatic teller machine. A driver inserts the equivalent of a credit card into a terminal, types in the kind and amount of aggregate desired, and proceeds to the loading facility where the truck is accurately filled over an electronic scale. Like an ATM machine, the service operates twenty-four hours a day, seven days a week, and has cut the time a trucker spends at the quarry by over 50 percent.

Innovations like this from a gravel and concrete company? Yes, indeed; this isn't a Fred Flintstone cartoon show. In fact, this gravel company received an award in 1997 from *CIO* magazine as one of the top 100 information technology performers nationwide. It received a citation by *Fortune* magazine in 1998 as one of the "100 Best Companies to Work For in America."

What conclusions can we draw from this tale? First of all, you don't have to be a sexy Internet startup to be successful. Secondly, per Giant Step I, any company in any industry (including concrete) that wants to thrive must do something unique and exciting to differentiate itself from the rest of the pack. Thirdly, in order to be unique and exciting, aggressive and creative applications of information technology are absolutely necessary. Fourth, the technology is only as useful as the brains and the talent of the people using it. Competitive advantage lies in attracting the best people, training the dickens out of them, working with them as "partners" in strategy development and execution, and rewarding them handsomely for improvements in corporate performance.

All this is a manifestation of knowledge. I don't use the word *knowledge* like philosophers do. I use it to refer to an organization that is bursting with cutting-edge skills, state-of-the-art tools, creative freedom, business accountability for employees, and speed and intelligence in everything—all aimed at doing something truly special that amazes customers. Granite Rock is not successful because it sells a tangible commodity called concrete. Its competitors sell concrete. Granite Rock is successful because it sells an intangible non-commodity called knowledge.

Put another way, Granite Rock survives because it sells concrete. It thrives because it wraps heaps of knowledge around the concrete. To those who seek clues for leapfrogging their competitors, I suggest they'd be wise to look to Granite Rock as a role model.

Are you a bit skeptical? Okay, stay with me, and consider something even more bizarre.

Go 1,500 miles southwest of Watsonville to Monterrey, Mexico, and visit the world headquarters of Cemex. Over the past twelve years, CEO Lorenzo Zambrano has transformed Cemex from a mid-sized Mexican firm to the third-largest cement company in the world with annual revenues of nearly $4 billion and operations in twenty-two countries, with fast-growing emerging markets accounting for two-thirds of Cemex sales. Even more important than impressive size is the fact that Cemex is the most profitable cement company in the world. Cash flow was 31 percent of revenues last year, and operating margins were 25 percent, twice the industry average.

How do you create such a successful global brand out of cement? And how can you ensure a thriving business with 60 percent market share in your own country—Mexico—when you have to deliver a highly perishable product in totally chaotic circumstances, including inclement weather, traffic gridlock, labor strife, arbitrary government inspections, and up to a 50 percent change rate on customer orders?

Here's how. You not only ensure top-quality product, but you guarantee that, notwithstanding any changes to the order, distance, weather, traffic, and so forth, you will make deliveries within twenty minutes of schedule. If the delivery is late, the customer receives a discount of roughly 5 percent. Cemex's future plans are to guarantee a delivery window of ten minutes and follow up by guaranteeing that late loads will simply be free.

If the Cemex guarantee was simply a typical marketing ploy (the way so many "pseudo-guarantees" are these days), the company would bleed to death in payoffs on these pledges. The key to the guarantee is that on time delivery is an important issue for customers, and the company has innovatively integrated systems and people to deliver on it. And that's no small feat in a company with over 8,000 products, 1,500 vehicles, and 175 mixing plants in Mexico alone.

After studying firsthand the rapid-deployment capabilities of Federal Express in Memphis and the Houston Fire Department's 911 Dispatch Center in 1993, here's what the company accomplished in Mexico in less than two years:

1. A reorganization of the truck pool under central control, but such that each ready-mix delivery truck is equipped with a dashboard computer linked to satellite communication systems so as to constantly report its location and status.

2. A creation of a new operations center with an expert system designed to attend to orders immediately. The system, run by central dispatchers, chooses the optimal combination of trucks and mixing plants to fill (and even predict) each order, based on a constant, real-time flow of information regarding traffic conditions, available inventory, customer location, order specifications, and order history.

3. Comprehensive, weekly training of dispatchers and drivers (many of whom have only a sixth-grade education) in computer and customer service skills, so they could fully access and contribute to the system. Regular training and development continues (Cemex devotes a minimum of 8 percent of total work time to training), resulting in the trucks now functioning as self-organizing business units run by their drivers, all linked to a common database.

In addition to building customer loyalty, Cemex has found that its new flexible systems have boosted efficiencies to the point that mobile equipment productivity has increased 30 percent, while fuel consumption and equipment maintenance costs have dropped significantly.

Cemex has recently expanded the scale of its operating system to its facilities abroad. A strategic alliance with AT&T has enabled the company to develop an integrated information processing and transmission system that not only creates short, flexible responses on a global scale but also allows quick capitalization on potential business opportunities. The new communications network combines wireless and fiber optic technologies so effectively that no computer application in any of the company's worldwide locations has more than a four-second response time on any window. The system is also flexible enough to vary by region and enables Cemex not only to respond quickly to last-moment customer requests but also to anticipate them.

More recently, Cemex has made the Internet the focal point of communication, using it to link the sales, human resources, finance, and other functions with each other and directly with the customer. Gelacio Iniguez, the director of information technology, gives this example in *LatinFinance* magazine to show how it works: "Say if you are in Venezuela and you have questions about the shelf life or maintenance of certain equipment, you can enter the network and post a request or a question. Someone, say, in Spain who is part of that network can enter and give you an answer. If the guy from Spain is traveling, it is not a problem because he has his laptop and he will see the request."

Finally, Cemex recognized that all these breakthroughs were attracting intense scrutiny and admiration in the industry—and hence a potentially lucrative sales opportunity. Accordingly, the company outsourced its "here's-how-we-do-it" teaching to a wholly owned subsidiary called Centech, which now offers training, service, and consulting to customers—and even competitors!

That's how you decommoditize a hopelessly mundane commodity such as cement. That's how you stay on *Industry Week*'s short list of the world's 100 best-managed companies for the last three years. That's how you are cited as the most admired company in Mexico by *Expansion* magazine in 1997.

Granite Rock and Cemex offer valuable lessons. There is nothing more solid and tangible than concrete and cement. Yet the success of these two companies has little to do with concrete and cement. As noted, it's the knowledge they wrap around these products that makes the difference—knowledge as in exceptionally well-trained employees who think like businesspeople, state-of-the-art technology that allows employees to quickly access anyone or any data, and an obsession with creating an extraordinary experience for customers.

Knowledge is becoming the key differentiator in every business. As strategy expert Stan Davis points out, things you can touch and smell (equipment, materials, hardware, etc.) are less important than things you can't touch and smell (customer service, innovation, speed, etc.). In business today, it's the "intangibles" that are paramount in leapfrogging the competition, not the tangible assets that you can accumulate on a balance sheet. It's a lesson that many still haven't learned, because it violates conventional economic wisdom.

The classical building blocks of economic analysis revolve primarily around land, labor, and capital. But these tangible factors become less salient in a business world that can best be described as brain-based. Today, knowledge—or, more colloquially, expertise, intelligence, imagination, and ingenuity—is the key determinant for economic success.

This is as true for the individual company as for a nation's economy. Today, the key success factor of an individual business enterprise is no longer its sheer size or the number of tangible assets it controls. The critical factor is knowledge.

Still the concept of *knowledge* leaves many managers uninspired. It's a very intangible, soft concept, and conventional thinking in economics, accounting, and finance emphasizes the hard, tangible "stuff": size, physical assets, balance sheets—all variations of the land, labor, and capital theme.

Of course, for years we have seen evidence that undermines the premises of conventional thinking. We've seen, for example, a stampede away from vertical integration in favor of downsizing, outsourcing, and partnering. We've seen small underfunded, resource-deficient companies significantly outperforming venerable giant firms on any yardstick (compare returns and growth rates of the *Fortune* 500 with those on the *Inc.* 500 and the *Forbes* 200). We've seen small countries with few natural resources outperforming big resource-rich countries (compare the fortunes of Singapore, Taiwan, and Hong Kong to those of Nigeria, Russia, and Bolivia).

We've seen the market valuation of well-managed companies grow to a significant multiple of their book value because of soft, intangible reasons variously defined as goodwill, brand equity, corporate reputation, market potential, quality of management, and so on. We've seen Microsoft—asset-tiny (i.e., tangible-asset-tiny) compared with the industrial behemoths in the *Fortune* 500 list—attain a market value that exceeds and often dwarfs every one of them. We've seen that the extraordinary market value placed on small, pathbreaking, assetless Internet companies such as Yahoo! and Amazon.com means that the investment community instinctively understands that the knowledge to transform markets is more important than the capacity to simply be big in them. We've seen consolidations among (tangible) asset-meager companies such as America Online and Netscape generate more press and overall business impact than mergers among asset-rich industrial giants such as Boeing/McDonnell Douglas and International Paper/Federal Paper.

Meanwhile, we've seen big companies such as Disney, GE, Sony, and Asea Brown Boveri grow their stock value not because of their size per se (after all, equally large, even larger, companies have ceased to exist over the past two decades). Rather, it's because they're still doing something exciting, unique, interesting—despite their size—that their knowledge is still evolving. Disney, for example, seems to innovate steadily on the extraordinary customer experience provided in its theme parks even as the empire as a whole cranks out a new product (movie, video, game, software, toy, etc.) every five minutes. That, within the context of an immense size, makes Disney quite formidable. But the actual stock value appreciation is based on the non-see, non-touch intangibles.

For the organization that leapfrogs the competition, this entire discussion is crucial. As Thomas Stewart notes in his book *Intellectual Capital* (Doubleday, 1997), it is people's capacity to excel in tasks such as sensing, judging, creating, and building relationships that define the most valuable assets of the organization.

Writing in the *New York Times* on February 12, 1997, Thomas Friedman captures the spirit of this discussion: "As globalization gives everyone the same information, resources, technology, and markets, a society's [or organization's] particular ability to put those pieces together in the fastest and most innovative manner increasingly separates winners from losers in the global economy."

All this has significant implications for your organization, for the question now becomes: how do you create an organization that is characterized by the kind of knowledge-richness and knowledge-in-action that will provide the fuel to leapfrog the competition?

First, as Nick Imparato and I pointed out in *Jumping the Curve*, consider that the size of your organization's "body"—its tangible assets, its personnel size—is less important for competitive advantage than the size of its "brain"—its collective value-adding intelligence and expertise.

This is, parenthetically, very good news for small companies that have great ideas and execution, which is why so many of them have become significant competitors in their industries despite their size. It also places new challenges on large companies, for all other things being equal, the laws of basic physics would suggest that the bigger an organization's body size, the less likely the possibility that it can leapfrog *anything*. The priority for any huge organization (even a currently successful one) ought to be perpetual weight loss coupled with brain gain. That is, smart big companies are continually pruning down their sheer mass by dynamiting crusty hierarchical structures and functional walls. At the same time, they are continually expanding their knowledge base the way Cemex is doing. I find it noteworthy that Bill Gates recently stated that one of his top strategic priorities for Microsoft is to ensure that the company doesn't become bureaucratic as it continues to grow.

So what does a knowledge-based company look like? Visualize an organization with a steadily growing "brain," with a body structure so light and fluid that it is no longer constrained from jumping over competitors whose bodies are encumbered by the weight of fixed assets and sunk costs. The leapfrogging organization obsoletes the traditional model of organization, which revolves around the premise of big body/little brain.

The conventional big body/little brain premise is represented in the omnipresent organizational pyramid, including all of its current "progressive" variations. When all is said and done, knowledge is still primarily concentrated at top management levels and hoarded among specialized professional staff. Think about where expertise (high-end technical, functional, strategic thinking) and information (profit-and-loss data, policy and systems analysis, strategy and business development) really resides. Think about where the decision-making authority and accountability for initiating innovative decisions really reside. You know the answers, and I've illustrated them, and the alternative, as follows:

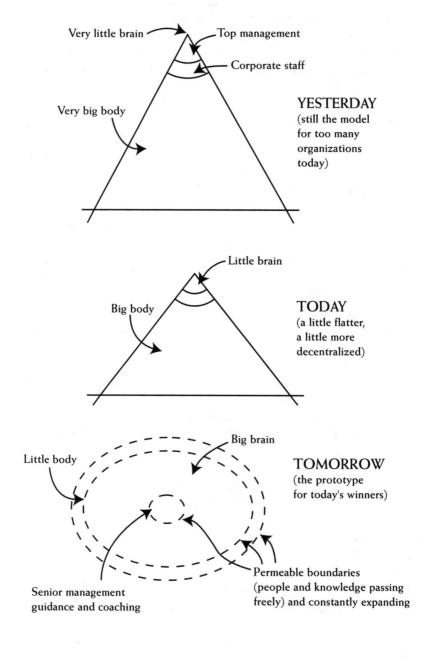

Obviously, these three models represent gross stereotypes, but the point they make is real. Leapfrogging organizations, large and small, move away from big body/little brain and toward big brain/little body.

In the race for market share and profitability, there is an increasing awareness that these "smart organizations" are the horses to bet on. Companies as diverse as Granite Rock, Cemex, Buckman Labs, Chaparral Steel, Oticon, Physician Sales & Service, Quad/Graphics, Springfield Remanufacturing, Sun Microsystems, and VeriFone instinctively connect to this big-brain metaphor. That's why for them, training and job enlargement is de rigueur, because everyone on the payroll continually expands their skills, contributions, and responsibilities to help the organization attain its mission and goals.

Everyone has access to information, expertise, learning opportunities, fast decision-making authority, and accountability. Information and data that were previously hoarded now become dispersed; people with ideas freely cross permeable boundaries within and beyond the organization. Expert systems, electronic databases, and open telecommunication systems proliferate.

Whoever or whatever function is in the organization is part of the big brain—the core competency, knowledge-growing, value-adding part. Otherwise, it is sourced to outside partners or eliminated entirely as value detracting. Nonbrain body weight is kept to a bare minimum.

The manager in this kind of organization is no longer a "boss"—it is self-defeating to put an artificial cap on knowledge. Nor is he or she an "organizer"—knowledge changes so rapidly that it quickly obsoletes any structure or system that has the slightest whiff of permanence. Nor is he or she an empire builder—in a hierarchy-less, demassed organization, playing power politics or even attempting to hoard talent and information for self-aggrandizement become downright absurd.

Likewise, employees are no longer order takers who expect good things to occur if they keep their noses clean. In fact, those sorts of people are the first ones downsized in a brain-based organization because, as Xerox executive Barry Rand declared to his people, "if you've got a yes-man or yes-woman working for you, one of you is redundant."

This orientation is part of a much deeper, more profound perspective: that employees and their brains not only are the most valuable organizational assets but should be treated as *perpetually appreciating assets*. Consider these examples:

- At fast-growing $200 million Sheboygan, Wisconsin-based Johnsonville Foods, cross-functional teams (many staffed by employees with initially no more than a high school education) do all recruiting, hiring, performance evaluation, and termination. They formulate, track, and amend budgets. They make capital investment proposals, and they do necessary research and analysis. They are fully responsible for quality, including control and correction. They develop product prototypes and packaging. They develop and monitor productivity improvement measures. They interface with vendors, suppliers, and customers as necessary. A few specialty teams are now involved in the strategic planning and positioning of the entire company. All this in a corporate environment that is fully supportive of team-based activities, as evidenced by the autonomy, resource accessibility, and continual training opportunities that the teams enjoy.

- PE Biosystems is a Foster City, California, division of Perkin Elmer that develops and manufactures consumable products for biotechnology companies. As reported in the November 1998 issue of *Management Review*, the $925 million division has enjoyed a 20 percent annual growth rate for sixteen years and is known for continual fast-to-market innovations. The company's strategy revolves not around a brilliant, grand "plan" but around the personal initiatives of engineers, scientists, and marketers. Their efforts result in a large number of projects going on simultaneously and semichaotically at any given time, none of which requires any initial approval from top management. Lots of pilots, lots of tests, and as soon as a promising concept emerges from the hubbub, PE Biosystems quickly galvanizes the resources to rush it to market. (By the way, per our discussion in Giant Step I, the company buzzes with strategic conversations, primarily face-to-face, as a vehicle to keep people informed about the present and focused on the future.)

- Nypro is an industry-acclaimed, $433 million plastics manufacturer based in Clinton, Massachusetts. The general manager of each Nypro plant reports to an eight-person board of directors. The board, which meets four times a year, consists of one general manager from another facility and up to eight employees from other facilities. For example, the board of one plant includes a general manager, an automation engineer, a salesperson, an accountant, a human resource person, and corporate quality managers—each one from a different facility. All are volunteers for one to three years, and all exercise careful oversight over strategy, productivity, and financials the way any good board would. Says CEO Gordon Lankton, "It really has been a marvelous system for Nypro and a terrific management development technique."

These three vignettes suggest that leapfrogging organizations no longer view people as a "cost," a "factor of production," an "entry" in a financial statement, or even a "human resource" department issue. Instead, people are "it." Executives in the most successful companies I have researched all agree that one of their most pressing *strategic* concerns is attracting and retaining the best people. Hire the best people, let them loose, and they'll figure out ways of boosting your company's fortunes in ways you and your strategic plans never imagined. Great people working together will capitalize on and further grow the flow of organizational knowledge that will propel you over your competitors. Consequently, these companies go to extraordinary lengths in recruiting, developing, and, as we shall see, unleashing and compensating talent.

An article in the October 21, 1998, *Wall Street Journal* described how Sprint is attempting to lure talent to its Kansas City hub by building a 200-acre campus with training facilities, a technology center, a child care center, athletic fields, jogging trails, an 8-acre lake, and its own conveniences such as banks, dry cleaners, and restaurants. In justifying these expenditures, a statement by the vice president of real estate, Faye Manker, is a superb cap to this chapter's discussion thus far: "The cost of people is greater than the cost of real estate."

In the following sections, we will see that organizations that leapfrog their competition use knowledge in two ways. First, they understand that a perpetual flow of great ideas depends on people's capacity to access knowledge freely. Hence, they deliberately smash barriers to the free flow of knowledge—barriers such as multiple management layers, narrowly focused functional silos, rigid job descriptions, numerous sign-off requirements, obsolete technologies, meager training, and corporate cultures marked by secrecy and one-upmanship. Second, they liberate employees to harness and use knowledge to take action—that is, to create fresh value for customers and shareholders. In this environment, employees continually grow their skills, use state-of-the-art information technologies as their servants, take on an attitude of "How would I act if I owned this business?" and take full accountability for the rapid decisions they're encouraged to make at all times.

Flooding the organization does not mean drowning people with paper and data. It means having an enormous wealth of knowledge for people to access as they see fit. Flooding the organization with knowledge gives people the fodder to use intelligence to transform corporate processes and products—and thus transform organizations in such a way that they can leapfrog the competition.

Flooding your organization with knowledge means that you turn your organization into a big brain/little body entity that can more easily vault over heavier competitors. In short, it means creating an organization where, more than anything else, *mind* matters. To achieve this Giant Step, you'll want to make two crucial commitments:

- Obliterate current barriers to the flow of ideas (Commitment 5).
- Don't empower your employees; liberate them (Commitment 6).

Obliterating current barriers to the flow of ideas will require courage and persistence, for these barriers are the sacred cows of many organizations. Commitment 5 tells how to do it: first, by carrying out several specific actions that will turn your organization into a hotbed of exciting, value-adding ideas; second, by creating a corporate culture of openness, such that opening the doors and sharing the truth becomes a business necessity, not merely the subject of Sunday morning sermons.

When barriers are obliterated, decisions are made faster, better, and more creatively. But there's even greater payoff: employees become more powerful. Knowledge is power. More knowledgeable employees are more powerful employees. More powerful employees make for a more powerful organization.

Accordingly, Commitment 6 challenges you to go well beyond traditional notions of "empowerment." First, via a "Dear Abby" response I gave to a question posed to me by a reader of my monthly column in *Management Review*, I argue that in the new economy, it's inappropriate to "empower" employees, because that retains the hierarchical mode that serves best to control passive underlings. The trick is to create an environment in which employees make *themselves* more powerful by freely taking hold of knowledge to make the cutting-edge decisions that will allow you their enterprise to leapfrog the competition.

This approach requires big shifts in how most organizations deal with their people. As we will see, it also requires big shifts in how most organizations implement their technology. The trick is to let the computers—not the people—be the bureaucrats. When computers are bureaucrats, routine gets accomplished faster and without error, leaving people's minds free to perpetually figure out ways to help the organization spring forward, and over, today's competition.

As you will see, there is extraordinary power to this Giant Step. In fact, each time you turn the spigot further to increase the flood of knowledge in your organization, the impact is leveraged logarithmically in the marketplace. Humans and great apes share 98 percent commonality in their DNA structures. It's that little 2 percent of intelligence that creates that enormous separation between us and them—that cavernous difference in competitive advantage, if you will. Imagine, then, the impact of a 2 percent, or 4 percent, or 20 percent knowledge difference between you and your competitors. Imagine the potentially huge boost in competitive advantage that you could enjoy.

Obliterate Barriers to
the Flow of Ideas

THERE ARE many reasons to obliterate barriers in organizations, but the main one is that by doing so, you morph your organization from a hotbed of internal politics to a hotbed of ideas. Knowledge is power, and people who share knowledge can create incredible things. With that precept in mind, here's how to create a "power-full" organization.

Business is about products and services. Competitive advantage, on the other hand, is about great ideas. When he was chief financial officer at ARCO, Ron Arnault delivered the following challenge to a group of fast-track managers: "The challenge is to do something different. What are the new value-creating ideas? All I can tell you is, if we don't come up with them, the competition is going to get nastier."

Arnault was absolutely right—only he didn't go far enough. It is no longer enough to think of organizations as an amalgam of bricks, capital, and bodies but rather as a perpetually growing reservoir of ideas. In a brain-based economy, the leapfrogging organizations will be those that can generate the greatest number of interesting and compelling ideas, take rapid-fire action on them, and then disseminate immediate feedback to everyone so as to generate yet more ideas. By repeating this cycle over and over and over, throughout every nook and cranny of the organization, the organization's intelligence grows, and thus its efficiency, creativity, and competitive vigor increase as well.

I propose that the best predictor of a company's future earnings is its capacity to generate, consolidate, and use ideas from

every possible source: employees, customers, suppliers, partners, outside experts, and myriad databases.

As the most powerful economies in the world today fuel a free
movement of goods and services, the most powerful companies
fuel a free movement of information and ideas. To flood your organization with knowledge, the first step is to systematically,
ruthlessly obliterate barriers to the flow of ideas. One can do
this—and thereby transform your organization into a bubbling,
churning cauldron of ideas—by applying five basic principles:

1. SPREAD INFORMATION EVERYWHERE.

In the Arnold Schwarzenegger movie *Total Recall*, when one of
the characters begins to tell his superior, "Well, I think . . . ,"
the latter brusquely interrupts with "Who told you to think? I
don't give you enough information to think." Crudely stated,
but unfortunately all too often an accurate description of what
occurs in many organizations today.

The goal of Principle 1 is to create an environment where
everyone can quickly access any information needed for rapid,
creative decision making. Immediate availability is essential.
The charge for you, the manager, is not to filter out information
carefully and benevolently to people. Nor is it to overwhelm
people in a deluge of paper and data. Rather, the key is to create
an environment where a huge wealth of knowledge and information exists and is available for people to draw on, and add
to, as they see fit.

Consistent with the notion of "open-book" management,
everyone must have immediate access to "real" information:
strategy updates, income statements, balance sheets, sales and
quality data, consumer profiles, marketing trends, and current
status of suppliers and partners. The quicker that people can access critical information on their own, without having to depend on the goodwill of others, the faster they can add to the
idea pool, and the more innovative their decisions will be.

Companies that spread information everywhere draw from a
wide range of both high-tech methods (group software, local
area networks, expert systems, etc.) and low-tech methods (interactive newsletters, bulletin boards, face-to-face interchanges,

etc.). These provide employees the tools, resources, and authority necessary to obtain and use information effectively.

Information equals power. When information is spread everywhere, people become more powerful, which means the organization becomes more powerful. It should not be surprising that at a successful, high-technology firm such as Sun Microsystems, all information (on products, on R&D, on customers, on financials, etc.) is on the company's intranet and internal Web sites and available to any Sun employee.

But I'm more intrigued with Springfield Remanufacturing Corporation, an engine rebuilder staffed primarily by what are traditionally termed "blue-collar workers." CEO Jack Stack's candid goal is to create an organization in which everyone thinks and acts like a CEO. That is why open information is a fundamental strategic priority at the company. Everyone learns to dissect a financial statement that sometimes exceeds 100 pages. Daily operations numbers, weekly income statements, and regular cash flow reports are shared and openly discussed. Work teams analyze variances and determine production plans and schedules. The result is that in a "mature" industry, Springfield Remanufacturing has turned its balance sheet around, grown to over $150 million, and been consistently profitable.

An important postscript: spreading information everywhere is only secondarily a technological issue. The hardware, software, and network tools now exist to allow anyone in your organization access to anyone else and to any piece of information. Yes, the selection and implementation of the right technology is always an important consideration, but the primary barrier to spreading information is almost invariably due to personal ego or organizational culture. Bluntly, if information is power, many insecure managers don't want to release it—even though by doing so they increase everyone's power, including their own. There are always self-serving rationales to justify a trickle-down control of information. There are always "yeah, but" reasons to block someone from the information that you define as proprietary. It takes a visionary approach to leadership to understand that nowadays information becomes obsolete so quickly that hoarding it is self-defeating—whereas sharing it becomes a catalyst for cross-pollination of ideas, faster more innovative response, and greater accountability in execution. As one exec-utive pointed out during a seminar discussion on this issue, "We have the tools to do this, but do we have the will?"

2. CHALLENGE SACRED COWS IN PURSUIT OF BOLD GOALS.

The goal is to create a corporate culture that is characterized by two attributes:

- There are no sacred cows other than the most fundamen-tal of corporate mission and values (and even those are examined periodically).
- Everyone on board sees their charge as continually chal-lenging the existing process to strive for quantum leaps in performance.

Dramatic upheavals outside the organization call for radical changes inside. Tweaking and improving the current systems and processes is no longer enough. A "no sacred cows" culture treats everything that is currently done (policies, procedures, structures, methods, meeting agendas, etc.) as an experiment. This means that everything is open to challenge, testing, and renewal.

Pewaukee, Wisconsin-based printer Quad/Graphics is a good example of Principle 2. A $1.2 billion privately held company that has an annual growth rate of 10 to 15 percent, Quad is honored throughout the industry as a cutting-edge benchmark of quality and innovation. As chairman Harry Quadracchi puts it, "Change is our bread and butter. We see change as our job security. That's why in almost every department of our printing operation, there is virtually no similarity to the way things were running six months ago." Can you say the same about your or-ganization?

To foster this sort of atmosphere, companies that challenge sacred cows follow four "to-do's." First, they encourage every-one to ask "why" questions. Why are we doing things this way? Why are we doing this at all? Would a customer pay us to do what we are doing? Would a customer prefer that we automate it, delegate it, outsource it, or eliminate it entirely? What currently prevents us from doing things that we know we ought to—listening to our customer, collaborating with people in other divisions and other world-class companies, starting a project team, making a decision quickly, and then holding people accountable for results?

Second, they constantly shed old goals and set new extraordinary ones. Leaders in these companies set broad decision boundaries (financial, strategic, ethical "rules of the game," etc.); then, within those boundaries, they insist that people regularly set new goals and standards that are bold—even impossible—by current standards. As divisions in companies as diverse as Motorola, Nellcor Puritan Bennett, Johnsonville Foods, and, of course, Quad/Graphics have found, letting people set "impossible" goals (e.g., a 70 percent reduction in cycle time) becomes possible only if they are allowed the freedom and accountability to revamp existing systems so as to attain those goals. Ordinary goals produce ordinary efforts and ordinary results—a kiss of death in a frenetically competitive world economy.

Third, companies that challenge sacred cows liberate people to take action. Liberating people means enabling them to act, which means getting out of the way and, when necessary, helping people overcome organizational hurdles that currently prevent them from taking immediate action. If employees lack the power to ask tough questions, form an exploratory task force, or visit outside the organization for more facts, the idea pool shrinks. Companies that liberate try to get people to adopt a start-up, entrepreneurial mentality when they look at the business, asking themselves, "What would I do if this were my business?" (As we shall shortly see, training is essential in preparing people to adopt this role.)

Finally, companies that expect people to challenge sacred cows on behalf of bold goals make certain, in return, to challenge their own sacred cows of conventional compensation. Brain-based organizations do not simply pay people to come to work in exchange for a set wage or salary. Here is why: companies that are positioning to leapfrog the competition make far greater demands on employees and managers than simply "do your job." They expect them to think like businesspeople and act with the responsibility of owners. Consequently, these companies make enormous efforts to create a culture that will stimulate this state of affairs and will attract the best minds to jump into it. Compensation is part of the culture, and in an organization that expects people to use and contribute knowledge, significant performance-based variable pay—gain sharing, profit sharing, equity ownership—becomes a key part of compensation. The reasoning is simple: If we are raising the bar on our expectations of you, if we expect you to think and act like a businessperson-owner, then we expect to pay you accordingly. At Chaparral Steel, where productivity is triple the worldwide industry norms, gain sharing is universal and stock ownership is nearly so (over 90 percent), while two-thirds of employees voluntarily opt to allocate portions of their paychecks to buy additional shares each month.

All this makes a lot of sense tactically, and psychologically. James Champy, coauthor of *Reengineering the Corporation*, advises *Forbes* magazine readers to tie a "significant" portion of incentive compensation to factors that are crucial to long-term organizational health, such as product quality and customer satisfaction. "Those are the kinds of things that will build a great company over the long run no matter what the stock market or the economy does," he says.

In addition to this sensible advice, I predict that, increasingly, the path to attract and retain the best people will also have to be lined with some form of equity ownership. At companies such as Chaparral, Microsoft, Dell Computer, Physician Sales & Service, GE, AlliedSignal, and Starbucks, the generous stock plans not only attract and keep talent but also create a slew of wealthy employees, from software engineers to truck drivers. At Microsoft, one in twenty employees is a millionaire, and at Physician Sales & Service (a $700 million medical supply company that has maintained a 43 percent annual growth rate over fifteen years), the ratio is one in ten. In Austin, Texas, hordes of "Dellionaires" have been at the forefront in transforming the entire area into what *Fortune* magazine heralded as the "Most Desirable Place to Do Business in America" in 1998.

AlliedSignal chairman Lawrence Bossidy proudly asserts that "our largest shareholder is our employees. We have terminals in the lobby where they check the stock price every day." When asked by a reporter, "Can a company really make employees think and act like owners by giving them stock?" his response is quick: "It sure helps." In other words, none of this is about altruism. It's about providing incentives and rewards for people who continually challenge sacred cows and achieve bold goals—and thus grow the company at a pace far greater than if their pay was conventional.

Whether it's options or 401(k)s (Bossidy believes older employees prefer the latter), the key is to share the wealth so that employees can participate in the value that they helped create. Starbucks CEO Howard Schultz is so adamant on this point that when Starbucks was privately held, he insisted that both full- and part-time employees have access to a phantom stock option plan that would immediately transfer to real stock when the company ultimately went public. Since 1991, a standard percentage of between 10 percent and 14 percent of employees' earnings are allocated as options, depending on the company's performance. The options vest at a rate of 20 percent per year over a five-year period.

GE chairman Jack Welch is considered by some a cold heart who only cares about corporate-wide financials. Well, here is what a *Business Week* reporter observed in the June 8, 1998, issue:

> Combing through the names [of employees who have exercised options], Welch can hardly contain his enthusiasm—not for how well his company's stock has performed, but for the wealth he has put into the hands of people whose names are unfamiliar to him. In the first quarter of [1998] alone, some 3900 employees exercised 8.7 million options with a net value of $520 million. "It means that everyone is getting the rewards, not just a few of us," he says. "That's a big deal. We're changing their game and their lives. They've got their kids' tuition or they've got a second house. That's a real kick. We've all got plenty."

Leaders such as Welch, Bossidy, Schultz, Dell, Gates, and others fully understand that ideas will continue to flourish if employees who invest their brain capital into the company are rewarded with the same spirit as are the outsiders who invest their financial capital.

3. CREATE A PERMEABLE ORGANIZATION.

In June 1994, Bob Ulrich, CEO of Dayton Hudson Corporation, sent a memo to the heads of the company's operating divisions and staff groups. In it, he reminded everyone of a primary goal of the corporation, to wit, "to create a boundary-less organization where the divisions constantly benchmark each other and encourage the sharing of ideas, successes, resources, and people from one operating division to another. I believe that to make our corporation a truly world-class structure, we need to aggressively break down any barriers among divisions, and to create an organization without boundaries." I submit that this commitment to permeability—the easy, smooth in-and-out flow of information, expertise, and minds throughout any organizational boundaries—is one of the main factors underlying Dayton Hudson's successes under Ulrich's helm.

Permeable organizations try to minimize boundaries in the first place. They understand that if employees must butt heads against vertical ceilings or functional walls, then information can't easily spread, and the idea pool stagnates. Even those boundaries that remain are not taken too seriously because results are more important than turf or ego. Companies such as Chaparral Steel, Bloomberg LP, VeriFone, and Sun Microsystems are particularly aggressive exemplars of permeability because they put into action four important prescriptions.

First, they break down adversarial relationships among colleagues and partners into ones based on trust, openness, collaboration, and mutual problem solving. Second, they aggressively flatten the organizational structure because they know that each layer of management simply allows someone to delay, distort, and politically massage information before passing it on. Third, they crush functional turfs by redesigning work so that it can be done by interdisciplinary work groups. Fourth, they create an environment where insiders are outside (say, engineers working with customers at a customer site) and outsiders are inside (say, suppliers are invited to work with in-house folks in solving a knotty operational problem). With permeability, traditional concerns such as rank, hierarchy, and turf become quaint anachronisms. Traditional barriers to information flow become irrelevant. Permeability turns on the spigot to a rapid sharing and cultivation of ideas.

Look at the company structure of financial multimedia powerhouse Bloomberg LP and you'll see, for example, an organization so permeable as to be transparent. No walled offices, no job titles, no dress code, no executive dining rooms. Everyone—regardless of function or status—works together in large rooms solving moment-to-moment problems. Reporters huddle with salespeople, salespeople huddle with analysts, and analysts huddle with systems people; everyone huddles with outsiders, be they traders, issuers, institutional investors, or whomever. People zip in and out; information flows in and out. No barriers to the free movement of ideas.

In terms of our discussions thus far, Bloomberg makes and sells the ultimate intangible: information—in fact, financial information that becomes irrelevant and obsolete very, very quickly. As an organization that must constantly analyze and replenish information at a real-time pace, Bloomberg functions as an exceptional illustration of permeability—because it has to. Michael Bloomberg himself says there's no alternative. His company can serve as a role model for leapfrogging organizations in all industries that will increasingly add value to their own services by augmenting state-of-the-art information.

4. CULTIVATE A CULTURE OF CURIOSITY.

In the conventional paradigm, people are hired based on their specific technical skills and experiences. They are expected to contribute within the narrow scope of their job definition and within the even narrower scope of "here's how we do things around here." Ideas they might develop outside their particular "jobs" are discounted or are plain unwelcome.

In the new paradigm, the charge for the leader is markedly different: to cultivate an organizational culture that supports all-hands universal curiosity. Southwest Airlines, Manco (adhesives),

Chaparral Steel, and Quad/Graphics have found that the most effective way of doing this is to start right at the beginning: hire curious people—that is, hire eager-to-learn people, adventurous people, people who question things, people who want to understand, people who aren't afraid to stumble or take risks. Then create a curious culture around them.

Curious people don't tolerate mediocrity or dull routine. That's why, argues Southwest Airlines CEO Herb Kelleher, one should make curiosity and related attitudes a more important criterion for hiring and promotion than length of résumé or service. One of the key credos at Southwest is "Hire for attitude; train for skills."

Physician Sales & Service (PSS) CEO Pat Kelly agrees fully. As lucrative as the compensation rewards are at PSS, Kelly is clear about who he recruits: "The kid who's hung up on the dollars he's going to get right out the door isn't the kid we want. We look for the ones who want to stretch—and be given management opportunities soon." It's not uncommon for exceptional "kids" in their early to mid-twenties to be given profit-and-loss leadership responsibilities for an entire sales region.

At PSS, simply "doing your job" is a sign of mediocrity. If you're not challenging the process, you're not demonstrating curiosity, and your employment is probably on the skids. For the same reason, it's also not uncommon for employees to terminate their boss. If a boss isn't inspiring employees to challenge the process and go beyond mediocrity, says Kelly, "employees are allowed to fire [him or her]."

In sum, these companies seek curious people, and once they get them, they create a culture that keeps them curious. They support and reward those who are willing to challenge, experiment, stretch boundaries, share learning in teams, and take responsibility for actions. They view curiosity as an appreciating asset.

To further shape a curious culture, these companies teach everyone business literacy. They do so by making serious investments in training, education, and development. Chaparral Steel, Physician Sales & Service, Quad/Graphics, and Springfield Remanufacturing teach people how to "keep score." Employees throughout these companies learn the fundamentals of running a business: strategy, cost accounting, systems applications, computers, income statements, market research, statistical process control, and how to run a meeting. Whatever the organization's purpose and vision, people must have the skills and expertise necessary to move it toward that end. This is why organizations that try to live Giant Step II place few caps on their investment for brainpower. And that's why Quad/Graphics' employees take classroom education weekly (literally) and why Chaparral Steel workers have the opportunity to take educational sabbaticals to augment extensive in-house training.

At Granite Rock and Manco, employees can enroll in any outside course—business or basket weaving—and be fully reimbursed as long as they pass. Manco CEO Jack Kahl's rationale is revealing: "It lets people know . . . that one of the highest values in Manco is to be curious and allow curiosity to take place."

Companies that cultivate curiosity make sure *fail* is no longer a four-letter word. They protect curious people. More important, they encourage mistakes as an important part of competitive advantage. Wood Dickinson, CEO of the Kansas-based Dickinson Theatre chain, tells his property managers that he wants to see them making "intelligent failures" in the pursuit of service excellence. Not thoughtless, sloppy mistakes, but the kind of stumbles that occur in the pursuit of innovative "stretch" goals. This philosophy is shared by Stan Shih, CEO of Taiwan-based Acer, the seventh largest computer company in the world. If a manager at Acer takes an "intelligent" risk and makes even a costly mistake, Shih is prepared to write the loss off as tuition payment for the manager's education. Both Shih and Dickinson emphasize the educational element of error. That is why Dickinson argues that it is essential to share the learning points that emerge from the stumbles, so that everyone can benefit. At Buckman Labs and VeriFone, the learning by-product of errors is welcomed and disseminated electronically. The presence of thoughtful mistakes suggests that people are experimenting with, and learning from, new ideas.

5. INSIST ON PERPETUAL LEARNING.

Arie de Geus of Royal Dutch/Shell once sagely observed, "The ability to learn faster than our competitors may be our only sustainable competitive weapon." In an organization committed to Principle 5, the expectation in the air is that everyone, up to and including the person behind the CEO's desk, takes part in continuous learning so as to augment skills and expand thinking—and hence grow the reservoir of ideas.

Obviously, per Principle 4, the organization must do a big part by providing opportunities for learning. But the key to Principle 5 is that perpetual learning is an individual responsibility. Ultimately, the onus falls on the individual to seek out opportunities for continuous evolvement of the mind.

The advice is basically this: don't wait for someone else to hand you education. In the emerging world of flattened, shrunken organizations, career mobility will no longer be found in vertical promotion. Reengineering guru Michael Hammer correctly observes that it will be found in "mastery." I suggest that those who continually master new skills necessary to add value in new ways will have more freedom, more interesting work, and better pay than those who simply do a routine set of tasks well. They will also have more marketability should they decide to move on.

The "masters," therefore, will pursue learning. They will enroll in courses. They will volunteer for task forces and project teams to build their skills. They will seek new responsibilities, and they will form new networks with people who have different competencies. They will learn from diverse sources—from on-line services to their own mistakes. They will do this without reservation, because intuitively they understand that career growth will depend on their capacity to be a major contributor in a perpetual chain of new ideas. They are determined never to be obsolete, never to rust. An organization that can fan the flames to this sentiment will be the one to bet on in the future.

To view organizations in terms of ideas rather than bricks and mortar is a big challenge. All the companies mentioned earlier are in various stages of development in trying to meet that challenge. But trying they are, because, to paraphrase ARCO's Ron

Arnault, it's the value-adding ideas that will separate the also-rans from those who leapfrog over them. It's safe to say that in the emerging economy of brains, mind does indeed matter.

> THE BEST intentions, the most sophisticated technology, and the biggest training budget in town will have only marginal impact if your organization's culture sanctions secrecy, distrust, and closed-door decision making. If you want to flood your organization with knowledge, you'll need to create a culture marked by candor and straight talk. Consider the decision makers described in the following pages who did just that.

I fly a lot in my work. Over the years I've learned to work on airplanes, sleep on them, even enjoy the edited movies on them. But I've got a confession to make. I'm one of the first to get white-knuckled when the plane starts going through what the pilots euphemistically call "turbulence." And therein lies a story with, I hope, some important implications for leaders who are themselves trying to navigate through the turbulence in their own businesses.

Three years ago I left Copenhagen on an SAS flight to Newark. A few minutes after takeoff, at about 17,000 feet, something interesting happened—"interesting" as in the Chinese curse "May you live in interesting times." Rather than use my own layman's terms to describe the experience, let me quote from an in-house SAS bulletin. This document describes an event that had occurred on another, earlier SAS flight, but it was similar to what happened during my flight. "Just after liftoff . . . the right engine stalled twice with a very loud bang and the aircraft yawed violently. . . . An EGT overtemp warning was displaced. . . . A mayday call was sent and after a short circuit a single engine overweight landing was made."

The bulletin even had a thoughtful sidebar called "What Is an Engine Stall?" Quoth the bulletin, "An engine stall occurs if, for some reason, the engine is unable to 'swallow' the air it has ingested. The pressure buildup through the compressor collapses and air is expelled with a pressure wave the 'wrong' way out of the compressor. This is accompanied with a bang and sometimes also with spectacular flames."

I can do without all that.

But you know what was truly exceptional about this little experience? During the twenty-five minutes it took us to get back to friendly earth, I was quite alert—to say the least—but, surprisingly, I was not nearly as anxious as I have been about a jillion other times on flights that were frightfully choppy but nevertheless completely safe. What made the difference?

The difference was the Danish captain, Ebbe Starcke, who did something unique: during our descent, he never stopped talking to us (in both Danish and English, by the way), never stopped informing us about what was happening. He didn't sugarcoat our predicament but gave us reassurance that he had things under control. His voice was not detached and mechanical either; it was genuine and conversational. His demeanor was focused but not panicked. For twenty-five minutes, until our touchdown, he never stopped communicating: what was happening, what probably had caused the problem (he described and explained every possibility from ice and lags in vane system functions to birds being sucked into the turbines), what he was doing step-by-step ("You'll notice that I'm banking off to the right; the reason is . . ."). Step-by-step: "Eight more minutes, folks. . . . Four more minutes, folks. . . ."

By the time we landed, that pilot was our hero. And get this: when we arrived at the terminal, he actually came out to greet us. In fact, he waved us in for a huddle, and a big bunch of grateful travelers crowded around this man, who continued to amaze us.

First, he was genuine. His first words: "Boy, I need a cigarette." Even the hard-core nonsmokers urged him on. Then he told us that the phone calls he had just completed confirmed that over the past few months SAS and other European carriers had experienced some problems with a Pratt & Whitney 4000 model engine that was being overhauled by a certain shop in Zurich. In fact, he observed that similar incidents had occurred twice before (as noted earlier in the SAS bulletin that he was kind enough to share with me when I talked to him privately thereafter). He told us that SAS had just grounded all 767s like the plane we were on until the problem was fully rectified. In an industry notorious for outright lying to its customers (any business traveler will know exactly what I mean), Captain Starcke's honesty was a stunning breath of fresh air.

In contrast, I can't tell you how often on other flights I have wished that the captain, silently entombed behind closed doors in an aircraft being tossed and plummeted by fierce winds and lightning, would do what Captain Starcke did—even a little bit. And that made me think. What exactly did Captain Starcke do? Not much, really, except that he opened the doors and told the truth. I felt included; I felt like a partner; I felt "empowered" with information; I felt—strangely enough—loyal to him.

I won't bore you with more of the details, nor will I use more space justifying my decision to fly SAS whenever I have the chance from now on. The point is that the reason I was calm and focused in a dangerous situation is that the leader of our "organization," the airplane, kept all of us informed and involved.

And therein lies the lesson for those of us who want to leapfrog the competition. I believe that one of the most self-defeating actions managers can take these days is to work behind closed doors—literally and figuratively. Closed doors inevitably yield a culture of secrecy, "for your eyes only" information hoarding, and sugar-coated, partially true communication to those outside.

Among the "insiders," closed doors create the delusion that they are in control and in the know and that their decisions will be quickly understood and eagerly endorsed by those outside. Among the "outsiders," closed doors generate the kind of paranoid fantasies that can paralyze an organization. How often have managers and staff anxiously wondered about the discussions and goings-on behind closed doors: "What are they talking about?" or "What do you think they will decide about the budget, the product, the pay scale, the downsizing, et cetera, et cetera?" Closed doors, not surprisingly, create a workforce that feels powerless, alienated from the ultimate decisions, and skeptical about the veracity of the communications and the communicator thereafter.

I submit that in a brain-based global economy, where competitive advantage results from an organization's ability to gather, spread, and exploit knowledge, behind-the-door behavior—literally or figuratively—is flat-out destructive. It delays, distorts, and hence corrupts information and the decisions that are based on it. Whereas decentralized information technology should allow everyone on your payroll to communicate immediately with everyone else and to quickly access unfiltered information for rapid-fire decision making, closed-door behavior creates barriers that diminish decision efficiency, accuracy, and speed.

In a marketplace where your greatest assets are human beings who can take on the mantle of proactive businesspeople concerned with the fate of the entire organization (not just with their job description or their department), a behind-the-door culture diminishes personal accountability in favor of passivity, dependence, and a cover-thy-butt mentality. In an environment where collaboration and shared expertise become crucial for market leadership, behind-the-door thinking generates a culture of turfism and egocentric self-aggrandizement. And in a corporate world where credibility is fast becoming both the glue and fuel for the success of any important intervention, be it a product launch, process reengineering, or organizational restructuring, a behind-the-door culture diminishes trust and makes a mockery out of words such as "empowerment" and "teamwork."

After my experience with Ebbe Starcke, I can't say whether Danes have a genetic predisposition to openness and honesty, but I find it ironic that the reason I had been in Copenhagen in the first place was to learn more about an extraordinary company called Oticon. This $200 million company has revolutionized the hearing aid industry and is two years ahead of its competitors, including multibillion-dollar giants Panasonic and Siemens, in product development. With its first-to-market obsession and its cutting-edge product line, which combines state-of-the-art digital technology with fashionlike, multihued designs, Oticon boasts more than a doubling of revenues since 1991 and a tenfold increase in operating profits.

For a company such as Oticon, ex-CEO Lars Kolind (he retired in December 1997) sees little value in mass production of conventional, low-margin, commodity-like hearing aids ("let the big companies do that," he says). Rather, he sees Oticon's competitive edge as "fast and creative integration of all existing expertise in the field," including chip development, circuitry, anatomics, and audiology. Accordingly, under his helm, the sharing and exploitation of knowledge and information became vital. That is why the company still organizes itself around multidisciplinary project teams that are so egalitarian and intertwined that Kolind describes Oticon's organization as a "spaghetti structure."

Unsurprisingly, barriers to open communication are nonexistent—literally. For starters, it's not merely that people don't have offices to close doors to; they don't even have desks to hide behind. Yes, desks do exist and each is equipped with necessary materials such as a computer and telephone, but a desk can be and is commandeered by anyone who needs it. Instead of a permanent office, each employee—including Kolind—has a personal caddie cart, which is basically a little file cabinet on wheels. One wheels one's cart to wherever one is working that day, usually where one's project team is gathered, and takes over a desk as needed.

On the day I first met Kolind, he had just returned from a two-week business trip, and he was informed by a clerical person that her team had moved his cart to another floor. Apparently, her team had required the desk he had been using. Kolind shrugged. Business as usual. No closed doors. No hierarchical power trips. No barriers.

Kolind told me that as a result of a joint software development project with Hewlett-Packard and Andersen Consulting, all incoming mail was scanned into a computer and, with few exceptions, anyone could access anyone else's mail, including Kolind's. His calendar was also accessible to anyone; the software allows an individual to seek an appropriate block of time, which Kolind designated as available. It's not just mail; any document is accessible to anyone. In fact, project teams are encouraged to tap into each other's files whenever possible. Expertise that flows and grows is the key to Oticon's creativity, and Kolind made sure to nourish and reinforce that process. In his most recent letter to me describing Oticon's progress, he jotted this note on the cover of the annual report: "Don't be surprised. Knowledge-based organizations do work!"

So as I tip my hat to the Great Danes Starcke and Kolind, I wonder why the rest of us don't get it. We're all in constant turbulence and choppy air in our businesses. If we want to leapfrog the competition, that's all the more reason to open the doors and tell the truth. People in your organizations can cope with the truth, however unpleasant. In fact, they hunger for honesty and inclusion. It you're straight with them, they'll help you fix the problem or help you take advantage of an opportunity. It's not the turbulence that upsets people; it's the feeling of helplessness—of not knowing what's going on behind the closed doors.

So let's stop treating people with condescension. Smash down the barriers, and make a vow that there will be no more secrets. Join with Starcke and Kolind and others who seem instinctively to understand that a commitment to openness and truth is not just the morally right thing to do, but, when advances in technology ultimately render secrecy a futile prospect, it's a savvy business thing to do as well.

Don't Empower Your
Employees—Liberate Them

FLOODING YOUR organization with knowledge makes sense
only if your people have the capacity to absorb it and the capa-
bility to do something with it. Otherwise, your efforts at flooding will simply overwhelm and drown them. What's the
leader's task, then? As this open letter shows, it's not to "empower" people. The challenge is much more dramatic—and
powerful—than that.

Dear Dr. Harari:

I recently received a promotion to be
general manager of a radio station. In
many ways, it's my first real management
position. I find your opinions very
helpful in challenging my own thinking
about management, but as I take over
this new position, I am worried about
something. I want to empower my people,
but how can I be sure that the decisions they make are the right ones? I
can't be looking over their shoulders
all the time. What should I do?

Sincerely,
Joe Jones
(name changed)

Dear Mr. Jones:

Your questions are so reasonable that you may be shocked when I tell you if you don't change your thinking right away, you'll be out of a job soon and your station's ratings will be plunging south all the sooner.

There is more to this than meets the eye. For example, what exactly do you mean by the "right" decisions? Do you mean the decisions you would yourself make if you were in their positions? Do you simply want clones of yourself? The right decision made by someone else may be different than the one you would make. It may be more innovative, more up-to-date, more appropriate to the current situation (not the situations you previously dealt with), and more appropriate to the style and capabilities of the decision maker. Giving your people the message that the right decision is your decision, or the one *you* would make, is a surefire way to diminish motivation, creativity, accountability, and morale.

Let's take it a step further. You're absolutely right that you can't be looking over their shoulders all the time. Would you want to even if you could? For one thing, your people not only have a more intimate bird's-eye view of their immediate environment, but they're also probably smarter than you. After all, if you're hiring the best and brightest, as you should be, they are by definition experts in programming, disc jockeying, sales, administration, and so on. Why put a leash on their talents? Intel chairman and cofounder Andrew Grove, a brilliant engineer himself in the 1950s, has freely admitted that, given the explosive advances in science, today's twenty-one-year-old engineering graduate knows a lot more than he does. He's happy to hire these young upstarts and set them free to experiment. Not a bad role model if you know anything about Intel's track record over the past few years.

In fact, to be an effective leader, you don't have to be a hero with all the answers, and you don't have to be a cop overseeing clones of yourself. Instead, imagine that your job is to create an environment where your people take on the responsibility to work productively in self-managed, self-starting teams that identify and solve complex problems on their own. If you concentrate on doing this, you'll find that your people will need you only for periodic guidance and inspiration, which frees you to spend your time confronting big-picture, common-fate sorts of strategic and organizational issues. Can you see the opportunities in that scenario?

With all this as a background, let's now get down to the nitty-gritty: the "empowerment" thing. Look in the mirror, and ask yourself how sincere you really are. Can you see that your comment, "I want to empower my people, *but* . . ." is a self-canceling phrase? I hear that big *but* all the time, and that *but* is why the word *empowerment* has turned into a slick, glib, hypocritical concept in many organizations: managers say they're committed to empowering people, but the people who are supposedly empowered know it's a con.

I'll wager, Mr. Jones, that you are a responsible adult who raises kids, pays the mortgage or rent on time, buys clothes and food and other consumer goods, participates in community affairs, plans vacations, and in general is a responsible, productive citizen. And somehow you manage to accomplish all this without the help of a supervisor. Yet, when you go to work, someone immediately insists that you "report" to someone else—and then starts talking about "empowering" you! Doesn't that strike you as somewhat contradictory?

I confess that I have always failed to understand the pseudo-complexity of empowerment. Why is it so difficult to allow rational, well-trained adult human beings to make their own decisions without being second-guessed and yanked around, possibly by someone who feels a need to justify his or her own position? In too many organizations I've found an inverse relationship between the amount of talk about empowerment (hot-air memos, splashy empowerment leadership sessions) and the amount of empowerment that actually goes on. It's really not all that complicated. Consider Peter Drucker's cogent observation that "much of what we call management is making it very difficult for people to do their jobs."

OK, I suspect you're still a little skeptical. Fair enough. Hopefully you're willing to consider the possibility that you don't want clones, you don't want to play hero or cop, and, therefore, you no longer want to play the "empowerment, *but . . ."* scam. On the other hand, you don't want to adopt a laissez-faire attitude that simply tells your people to do whatever the hell they want to do, purpose and consequences notwithstanding. So what can you do? As a reward for stoically tolerating my abuse, I will now share three secrets with you.

Secret 1 While waiting for my appointment with a particular manager, I became impressed by what two of her young clerical assistants were doing. Periodically, one of them would pick up the phone and call a customer and ask how the customer liked the company's product, and then jot down the response. I nodded in approval; no wonder this manager had such a good reputation. When I finally met with her I offered congratulations on her ability to delegate the customer service task to her staff.

"What are you talking about?" she asked, bewildered.

"Why, your secretaries are calling up customers on their own," I replied.

"Oh, really? Is that what they're doing?" she said, laughing.

Now I was the bewildered one. "You mean you didn't delegate that task to them?"

"No," she said. "I didn't even know they were doing it. Oren, my job is to get everyone on my team to think creatively in pursuit of the same goal. What I do is talk to them regularly about why we exist as a company and as a team. That means we talk straight about our common purpose and the high standards we want to achieve. I call these our goal lines. Then we talk regularly about some broad limits we have to work within, like budgets, ethics, policies, and legalities. Those are our sidelines. Once we agree on the goal lines and sidelines, I leave it to them to figure out how to best get from here to there. I am available and attentive when they need feedback. Sometimes I praise; sometimes I criticize, but always constructively, I hope. We get together periodically and talk about who's been trying what, and we all give constructive feedback to one another. I know that sounds overly simplistic, but I assure you it is my basic management philosophy.

"And that's why I don't know what my assistants are doing, because it's obviously something they decided to try for the first time this week. I happen to think it's a great idea because it's within the playing field and it'll help us keep high standards for being number one in our industry. I'll tell you something else: I don't even know what they intend to do with the data they're collecting, but I know they'll do the right thing."

She leaned forward and, with a little smile, continued. "Here's my secret: I don't know what my people are doing, but because I work face to face with them as a coach, *I know that whatever it is they're doing is exactly what I'd want them to be doing if I knew what they were doing!*"

How's that for a statement of trust? I recommend that every manager paste it on his or her bathroom mirror and repeat it three times before going to work each day. And if you buy it but you're still worrying about exactly how you'll be able to "let go" effectively, listen to the second secret.

Secret 2 While working with an agricultural laboratory client, I witnessed a fascinating story unfold. A director of one small division became enamored with the idea of empowerment. He read articles on empowerment, he talked about it frequently, and, by George, the man wanted to empower like crazy. But despite his noble intentions, he simply couldn't "let go." Although he and I agreed fully about the futility of creating clones, cops, and "empowerment, but," he agreed only in theory. Bottom line: he couldn't walk his talk.

One day, he sadly told his boss that he would have to leave the company because serious family matters required him and his wife to move to another state in six months. His boss, in the spirit of flattening the organization, decided not to replace him. The director was thus given the task of organizing the four functional groups that reported to him in such a way that they could fully take over his job. So for the next four months this man worked with the four group heads in reorganizing, stream-lining, and leading his shop. He did one-on-one coaching, he hired trainers, and he helped his direct reports revamp the processes and systems. And after only four months he told me proudly that his direct reports and the newly reengineered division were now able to successfully take on all the tasks and responsibilities that he once used to grapple with on his own. (To tell the truth, I found out that the new four-person management team of the division was able to perform much better than he did under the old system.)

A few days later, this director came to the office in a state of shock. He had just found out that he didn't have to leave town after all. He wanted to stay on with the company, but as what? He had effectively worked himself out of a job. I told him that he had done the company a great service, and it was now up to him to create a new job for himself, one that would truly add fresh value. The company needed his experience and expertise, but it was up to him to figure out where.

After a little hand-holding and reassurance from his boss, this man rose to the challenge. He started a new division to tackle a niche market he felt that the company had neglected in the past. As it turns out, he was delighted with the move, as was his boss once the revenues began to roll in. Finally, his brainpower was being put to optimal use.

The only reason that this director was able to "let go" was that he knew he was going to leave. Just knowing that neither he nor anyone else was going to be around to supervise led to the kinds of actions that all the prior platitudes about empowerment had failed to engender. So here's the second secret: *Pretend you are leaving the company in six months with no replacement, overhaul your organization and train your people to take over your job, and then find a new way to add value.* And be prepared to repeat the cycle, over and over again (maybe with different employers) until you retire.

Secret 3 Mr. Jones, I'll now share with you the last and most important secret of all: *Your goal is not to empower but to liberate.* Liberation involves freeing people from the organizational constraints (including you) that inhibit their willingness to take proactive action and accountability. Power is a feeling, an experience. It is the consequence of liberation. To put it succinctly, one successful manager was quoted as follows: "You know what good leadership is? *Tell 'em the rules of the game, train the dickens out of them, and then get the hell out of the way.*" That's liberation. Feelings of power follow.

All this empowerment stuff is a con because you cannot confer power on human beings. You cannot make anyone powerful. What you can do is create a condition where people will feel powerful, a condition where people choose to create power for themselves.

In short, as you get ready to face an unforgiving business world, please stop trying to empower people. It's a demeaning and futile task. Concentrate on offering your people the gift of liberation from the shackles of the organizational bureaucracy and from your own "helpful" intrusions. Liberate them from the protectors of the old guard. Do that and those delicious feelings of power will emerge among your people, as will productivity and organizational success. I can also assure you that you won't have to look over anyone's shoulders or worry about their making the "right" decisions. Perhaps the nicest thing of all is that you'll never have to use that condescending word *empowerment* ever again.

Best of luck,
Oren Harari

To LEAPFROG the competition, liberated employees need technology to be their servant, not their master. Technology can take over the routine as the organization is flooded with knowledge; technology can help unleash people's initiative and brainpower. But beware: just as a real deluge changes the landscape of a flooded valley forever, technology, if used properly, will also change the landscape of your organization forever.

Your job is dying. All the eleventh-hour, mouth-to-mouth resuscitation of restructuring and "empowerment" won't save it. It's doomed because the economy of the emerging millennium has no room for it. Your only hope is that you can hold off the inevitable until you retire—a rather forlorn wish. Or you can start confronting the future today by preparing to obsolete your current work before it obsoletes you—and then reinventing it.

As noted, we are moving from an economy where intangibles like speed, flexibility, and imagination are more important predictors of business success than tangibles such as mass, size, and physical assets. Accordingly, hitherto sacred principles such as volume, economies of scale, experience curves, mass production, and mass marketing are becoming less and less useful if we're interested in competitive edge. Rapid collaborative application of intelligence is where it's at.

To say, for example, that the success of companies such as Cemex or Dell Computer is due to economies of scale and mass marketing is myopic. Certainly, these companies flex their muscle size in spreading costs and getting the best purchasing deals. And certainly they try to get their brand name exposed to a "mass" market as much as possible. But they know that their real value, the real root of their competitive advantage, is in their ability to put together heaps of intangibles on behalf of customers: speed, imagination, expertise, ingenuity, flexibility, responsiveness, personalized care, and the like. In fact, I did a recent random sampling of pundits' comments on the roots of competitive advantage, and the consensus was words like "breakthroughs," "exploration," "mental flexibility," "production of ideas," and "curiosity as deep as it is boundless."

Now, let's take this a step further. Where do all these intangibles—imagination, expertise, breakthroughs, exploration, ideas, and so forth—come from? Who's going to supply them? Who'll take responsibility for seeing them to fruition? In the old big body/little brain hierarchical model (i.e., the one most corporations are still comfortable with), the answer is clear: a few smart people, such as senior managers, staff experts, and consultants. Everyone else, by and large, executes. It's a nice neat process: logical, sensible, practical—and ultimately suicidal.

In yesterday's economy, hierarchy and centralization worked fine. In the new economy of intangibles, the old way of management is a monumental barrier to information flow, initiative, collaboration, creativity, and speed. And the worst of it—and underlying every symptom listed earlier—is that the old way of management is fundamentally evil. It's evil in that it coarsens people's humanity by robbing them of their imagination and curiosity and turning them into bureaucrats. In a brain-based economy, bureaucracy kills.

Now we get to the crux of the matter. Yes, lots of routine work in organizations exists. Thus, there is a big place for bureaucracy in any organization. However, in the successful organizations of the future, those that leapfrog successfully, bureaucracy will be nonhuman. Specifically, it will be your information systems, and the bureaucrats will be your computers.

Right now, computers have the capacity to do almost every routine task you can do: they can check, monitor, search, scan, view, review, request, locate, list, gather, record, retrieve, edit, transfer, store, access, select, replicate, duplicate, assemble, combine, file, categorize, mail, dispatch, and, of course, compute. In a narrower sense, they can organize, allocate, and project. And they can do it a lot better, a lot cheaper, and a lot faster than people can.

Yet these tasks are precisely the tasks that define many people's jobs. These are the tasks that people spend much of their daily calendar time doing at their desks or on the shop floor. This fits nicely into the hierarchical model, but when people spend much of their time doing routine (including the routine of waiting for directives), there is not much time (or initiative) for ingenuity and unconventional thinking. There is not much time to provide customers with personal attention and imaginative solutions. There is not much time for learning, either, even though in the new knowledge economy, working and learning are equivalent. In short, there is not much time to figure out how to leapfrog the competition.

This brings us to consultant Harry Dent, who makes a provocative point: "Computers can now do the analytically detached, bureaucratic routine at lightning speed. If computers are thus the ultimate bureaucrats, why use people for that sort of work at all?" (Even if you're smart enough to outsource such work, the question can still be aimed at the supplier). Asks Dent, "Why not use the computer to do the bureaucratese to free people to think, to imagine, to create, and to serve customers in a breakthrough manner?"

It's a very valid question. In the emerging economy, there will be less and less space available for bureaucracy in jobs. Yes, there'll always be a need for a travel agent or an insurance broker, but if they're simply providing routine, commodity-like services, they'll be obsoleted by computers. Likewise, looking inside our organizations, we need to ask how we can afford to carry the overhead of bureaucratic jobs if competitive advantage results from the intangibles. Even now, cutting-edge companies are discovering that giving frontline people the technology, the training, and the authority to make decisions without the need for further hand-offs dramatically reduces cycle time, quality problems, and the need for supervision. Bureaucratic conduit jobs, those that are based on pass-offs and reviews of passed-off work, are rapidly disappearing.

The trends are quickly accelerating for a simple reason: information is power, and technology democratizes and universalizes the availability of information. Hence, organizations will no longer be able to subsidize processes and jobs that glorify hierarchical control but turn off the spigot on knowledge flow.

In a world where information is already accessible to everyone and where less and less is secret or proprietary, the only players who will thrive are those who can quickly wade into the water, harness what they need, and then add value to it through speedy, innovative business decisions.

The *1995 White Paper of the World Gold Council* put it nicely:

> In tomorrow's marketplace, information—gathered and transmitted through a vast network of interconnected computers—will be the most valuable currency of business. The companies that win will be those who most efficiently collect and use information to rapidly test new products, identify best-selling items, replenish stock and match marketing efforts to new consumer demands.

There's no place for human bureaucracy in this scenario. The sheer volume of information and knowledge available to any individual (and any competitor) will mean that talent, resourcefulness, energy, and ingenuity will necessarily become an all-hands, collaborative affair—the responsibility of everyone on board. Bureaucracy will thus fill the job description of the computer, not the human being.

Some social thinkers view this trend with alarm. They point to factories where robotics has replaced mind-numbing manual labor. They point to offices where telecommunication systems eliminate the need for people who mechanically take messages. And instead of feeling hope, they despair, painting a picture of a world where only a few human beings have jobs at all. Jeremy Rifkin, in his book ominously entitled *The End of Work* (Putnam, 1995), writes, "We are entering into a new period in history where machines will increasingly replace human labor in the production of goods and services. Although timetables are difficult to predict, we are set on a firm course to an automated future and will likely approach a near-workerless era, at least in manufacturing, by the early decades of the coming century."

I respect Rifkin, but in this case he's only half-right. We'll see not a decline of jobs in general but a decline of bureaucratic jobs. At the last turn of the century, anxiety was expressed about all the farming jobs that were going to be lost. And indeed, they were lost; the industry which accounted for 85 percent of the jobs in 1900 today accounts for about 5 percent of them, and the industry is so productive that it can still feed the world. Likewise, 50 percent of the jobs that existed in 1955 no longer exist. So what? Just as new jobs (and new industries) were born then, new ones are being born as we enter the next millennium. Some projections suggest that the majority of jobs in the early twenty-first century have not yet been invented. Whatever they are, these new jobs will be more fulfilling and more rewarding, because the beasts of mental burden will be the computers.

Parenthetically, the number of computers currently in your organization says nothing about whether your organization is currently preparing for success. Yes, you need the computers, the pagers, the cell phones, the satellites, the videoconferencing systems, the networks, and related technologies. Without them, you run a grave risk of falling behind precipitously. In 1996, when Quaker Oats' mismanagement of Snapple beverage was bleeding the company profusely (this was prior to the sell-off), a Snapple sales manager requested laptops for his team. With laptops, he argued, his team could better communicate with each other, tap into marketing databases more quickly, and prepare professional sales presentations to potential clients using tools such as Excel and PowerPoint. The response of his boss at

Quaker headquarters: "Your salespeople don't need computers. I don't want them sitting on their asses behind their desks all day. I want you guys to sell cases!"

Enough said. That little vignette is a good synopsis of the Quaker-Snapple debacle. You need the computers, and, in contrast to the Snapple vignette, the worm is turning the other direction in many companies. Investment in computing and related technology is the fastest-growing segment of business fixed investment.

But although computers are ubiquitous, they are, in most organizations, not used to flood the organization with knowledge the way Giant Step II suggests. The vertical, functional, and cultural barriers still exist. Rigid job descriptions and thick policy manuals still exist. A byzantine array of passoffs and sign-offs still exist. Hoarding and "for your eyes only" mind-sets still exist. Punishment of curious people still exists. As Paul Saffo of the Institute for the Future observes, most of the time they are used in a way that merely "paves the cowpaths." Or, as futurist George Gilder says, today's computers are like a car stuck in the middle of a jungle. In other words, computers are not fully integrated into the new market realities that I've described. They are adjuncts to the conventional routine work that people continue to do. In fact, argues Carol Bartz, CEO of Autodesk, computers simply perpetuate old hierarchical processes in many organizations.

The challenge, therefore, is to create an organizational infrastructure that attaches routine and hierarchy to technology, not to human beings. This requires a new social order within organizations, a new definition of what jobs are and what people do. You won't give people computers and then continue to restrict information à la "for-top-management-eyes-only" or "go-through-me-before-you-can-talk-to-her." You give people computers and expect them to access anything and anyone, period. Likewise, you don't give people computers and then tell them what to use them for; you give them computers and let them devise the applications necessary to add value to the organization.

I began by arguing that your job is dying. I mean that much of what many of us do is still bureaucratic. This, I suspect, helps explain why studies of both Price Waterhouse and the Boston Consulting Group have suggested that 75 to 95 percent of steps and processes that currently go on in organizations add little or no value to the customer. People are doing the tasks that computers can do better. Even worse, they are fighting the computer by spending their time delaying, distorting, and hoarding information. That's human bureaucracy in action.

In the organization that floods itself with knowledge, there is no place for these activities. To those who are serious about leapfrogging the competition, a major corporate challenge today is to prepare our organizations in such a way that the technologies do the bureaucracy and the people do the creating. Our personal challenge is to prepare ourselves to fit into that reality and, if we're not CEOs, to lobby for it with our current employer or to move to an organization that is heeding the wake-up call. Do we have the managerial courage to face these challenges?

GIANT STEP III

WRAP YOUR ORGANIZATION AROUND EACH CUSTOMER

In the last seven years, Solectron Corporation has enjoyed a compound annual sales growth rate of 53 percent, picking up rabidly loyal customers in the process. Giant Step III is the main reason why.

The $5.3 billion Solectron is a provider of electronics manufacturing services (including printed circuit board assembly, production planning, production design, and systems support) to leading OEMs (original equipment manufacturers) around the world. Corporate customers—primarily from the computer, telecommunications, networking, and medical electronics industries—are those who have seen fit to outsource many aspects of the manufacturing process. Although contract manufacturing is a strategy that many companies are now embracing (it was a $78 billion industry in 1997, up from $46 billion in 1995), this trend hardly explains Solectron's exceptional growth rate, because competition for the business is fierce.

One clue to Solectron's success is found in the fact that it is the only two-time Malcolm Baldrige Award recipient (in 1991 and 1997) in the ten-year history of the customer service award. Another clue is the fact that of the seven core beliefs that founder Winston Chen set for the company more than ten years ago, "Customer First" is first, while "Shareholder Value" is sixth, behind factors such as "Quality," "Supplier Relationships," and "Business Ethics." Yet another clue is in the 1996 annual report: "We strive to give our customers the time and cost advantages they need to stay a step ahead in *their* ever-more competitive markets."

In short, what we see is a company whose corporate philosophy revolves primarily around its customers and, further, a company whose goal to help its customers gain competitive advantage—which means that it is committed to knowing and understanding each customer individually. Consistent with this strategic philosophy, a Solectron manufacturing facility is itself organized as a microcosm of its customers. A facility might be the size of two football fields, and it is divided into more than twenty "production lines," each one helping a different company build a different product—say, a Hewlett Packard laser scanner, a Canon color copier, or an IBM motherboard. Not only are these "production lines" involved in building the product; they are also performing tests and engineering activities on ancillary products.

Each Solectron work team is organized not as a functional or manufacturing group but as a dedicated interdisciplinary team focused on an individual OEM customer. Each work team includes all the roles and activities necessary to run a minifactory, such as production, materials management, program management, engineering, and quality. The charge of the team is to work collaboratively with the customer in identifying needs, understanding expectations, targeting opportunities, and then executing with numerous feedback dialogues with the customer. In addition to helping build product, the work team assists the customer in design, engineering, cost minimization, technology improvement, and forecasting. The giant plant, therefore, is a collage of twenty-some minifactories, each wrapped entirely around their respective client.

Solectron's business model is so powerful and attractive to customers that the company was chosen by IBM to literally take over IBM's electronic card assembly and test operations in IBM's Austin, Texas facilities. But regardless of whether the work is done on Solectron or client sites, Solectron operates as if it was an extension of each unique customer. The company's outstanding growth and financials are a consequence of these interventions.

There are several lessons in all this: first, if you give them the opportunity, customers will gladly provide you the clues and the means as to how to leapfrog your competition. Thus, first and foremost, leapfrogging organizations are genuinely obsessed with customers. Managers in these organizations are, like Winston Chen, fanatics when it comes to really trying to understand their customers: their needs, wants, lives, experiences, challenges, businesses, etc. They do this not only to provide customers with outrageous service now but also to get important insights about what they might want in the future.

Managers in leapfrogging organizations are preoccupied with collecting and disseminating customer anecdotes, warehousing and scrutinizing customer data, talking about customers extensively in management meetings, overresponding fanatically to their complaints, allocating significant capital toward addressing emerging trends that might be of interest to customers, working collaboratively with customers on projects, and "hanging out" with them to learn one-on-one what makes them tick today . . . and tomorrow.

As Solectron demonstrates, customer obsession has a literal physical dimension as well. The success of companies such as EDS and the architectural firm CRSS is in no small means due to their willingness to send small teams to actually camp out and "live" with customers at their businesses, working jointly on customer problems. In the health care arena, Baxter and Interim Services often locate their people in offices situated right in hospital customer sites.

These sorts of healthy preoccupations are, first of all, quite different in tone and integrity from the empty "customer is king" lip service that accompanies everyday customer neglect in so many organizations. Second, they lead managers in any company to the next level—which is the main lesson of Solectron: the realization that each customer is unique and that nowadays, the smart, knowledge-rich, technology-loaded organization can address the unique needs of every single one of them. Hence, the next stage in this process is that the thriving organization is one that can wrap itself not merely around collective customers but around *each individual customer*. Competitive advantage in the emerging knowledge-based economy is no longer primarily dependent on mass production, mass marketing, mass distribution, uniform policies, and economies of scale.

That's because the keys to business success lie in addressing each customer's unique idiosyncrasies. It's a fundamental way to differentiate yourself from competitors, to forge relationships and thus engender customer loyalty, and to transform commodity products and services into genuine value-adds.

Customers themselves are increasingly defining "quality" as the ability of the vendor to provide high-level solutions. Hence, the quality value of a vendor's output will be directly proportional to the extent to which it alleviates or solves the unique problems that each customer faces.

It makes sense to capitalize on economies of scale whenever you can get them. But as markets become more splintered and customers become more demanding, strategies that generate standardized products and services within uniform delivery systems are strategies that will inevitably generate flat earnings—even if the output is efficiently produced and certifiably TQM defect-free.

Remember Cemex? For years it tried to force predictability and uniformity by requiring from customers twenty-four hours advance notice on both orders and changes to orders, even to the point of imposing price penalties on any order changes that did not meet this standard. The results? Lost business, angry customers, discarded product, and costly rework.

What Cemex tried to do in the past is what so many organizations still attempt to do today, which is to make customers wrap themselves around the needs and timetables of the organization. But as Cemex learned, the problem was that those darned customers weren't cooperating. For some odd reason they felt that their own needs and timetables were more important than those of the vendor's. It was only when Cemex made a serious commitment toward flipping the equation around—that is, wrapping its business around each individual customer—that the company began seriously to investigate new organizational structures, alliances, and technologies that could make that happen.

Companies that grudgingly offer customers a few options in products and services still miss the point. The challenge today is to focus on market units of one and to create flexible responses to each customer's unique needs. Last year, the Toronto-based Canadian Pacific Hotel chain enjoyed a record year in operational income ($148 million), and saw its share of the lucrative, high-end business traveler market increase by 16 percent, relative to an industry growth rate of 3 percent. How? Through the Canadian Pacific Club, which frequent travelers are invited to join. The CP Club offers a number of attractive features, such as instant check-in and checkout, 3 P.M. checkout, access to special Business Services and Work Centers rooms, discounts on hotel store products, and exclusive customer service numbers. But even more compelling is the detailed database created for each customer-member, a database that is rapidly becoming accessible in every one of CP's 65 properties. The database catalogs personal hotel preferences, such as smoking versus non-smoking room, bed type and pillow preference, preferred floor level, proximity to elevator, and any special needs or requests.

The goal is twofold: (1) to make frequent guests as a whole feel like they are being appreciated and rewarded, not merely taken for granted by being treated as simply "customers," and (2) to make each individual frequent guest feel like he or she is known, understood, and recognized. It's the latter piece that drives the point home for many of CP's loyal customers: they know me, they care about me, they appreciate my business, and I'm not just another renter of a bed.

It's that second point that is also the most difficult to execute. Hotels are very effective in dealing with groups of business travelers, à la "We've got the Amalgamated Asphalt convention coming in next week." But organizing around each individual traveler is another story altogether. The company is implementing new technologies for data sharing and fast communication among personnel. It is also shaping new organizational forms (e.g., cross-disciplinary teams led by team champions) for rapid response to individual needs.

The Atlanta-based luxury Ritz-Carlton Hotel Company is moving in a similar direction. Each employee is trained to note guest likes and dislikes, and this data is entered in a

computerized guest history profile that provides information on
the preferences of 240,000 repeat Ritz-Carlton guests. The
COVIA/Encore information system allows Ritz-Carlton to give
each customer an electronic identity. The hotel then records information about a customer's preferences and service history in
a company-wide database, which any employee can access.
Peter Kolesar, Garrett van Rysin, and Wayne Cutler, writing in
a 1996 Booz, Allen, & Hamilton report, argue that even the
reservation process becomes vastly different using this approach: "Thank you for calling Ritz-Carlton. Do you have a
membership number? Thank you. Yes, it's good to hear from
you again, Ms. Johnson. How can we help you today? When
and where will you be traveling? Do you want your usual room
profile: nonsmoking, deluxe room with king-sized bed, breakfast package and 6:00 P.M. hold? Very good. We'll make sure
that you have extra towels as usual as well. Will that be charged
to your corporate or personal charge card?"

Kolesar and his colleagues argue that having detailed knowledge of the particular customer enhances the value and efficiency of delivery. Information technologies can be used to
absorb frontliners' daily knowledge and experiences with individual customers (usually this knowledge is ignored or wasted),
so that services can be tailored, each customer's needs can be
foreseen, recovery can be improved, and unnecessary, redundant, and bureaucratic work can be eliminated.

The goal, as with Canadian Pacific, is customized service for
each guest, not simply very good service for "the" (impersonal)
customer.

Already, companies such as General Electric and San Jose–
based Cadence Design (electronic design tools) are determining
that the products they make are only one element of a total
package they offer and that steep rises in both margins and
earnings will come from selling the organization's *expertise* to
individual customers' specific problems. The $916 million Ca-
dence has shaken up the industry with its Spectrum Services operation, which concentrates on contract design services. With
its 300 percent growth since 1995, Spectrum has moved the entire company's business philosophy from selling product to developing solutions and cultivating one-on-one relationships

with customers. Rita Glover, president of EDA Today, a market research company with strong ties to the industry, says that Cadence's services strategy is a "brilliant idea" that turns the company into a "proving ground" not merely for customer loyalty but for new design tool development.

At General Electric, Jack Welch has determined that the future of the company lies not in price-sensitive product but in high-margin services wrapped around it. That is, as with Spectrum, the products themselves are only one element of a total package that GE can offer, and steep rises in growth curves will come from selling the company's expertise to individual customers' specific problems. For example, GE sees its future not solely in selling mass-market medical equipment but in servicing and repairing each hospital customer's medical equipment (including competitors' products), helping hospitals finance their purchases, and working with the hospitals to improve services in, say, X-ray imaging technology.

In the early 1990s, GE's power systems unit was facing significant price pressure in the newly deregulated utility industry it sells to. Rather than aiming for bigger market share by slashing prices, the company shifted its strategy toward gaining more "share of customer"—that is, a larger percentage of each customer's expenditures. As reported in the *Harvard Business Review*, the division not only improved customer response time in general (e.g., slashing order turnaround time on parts by 50 percent) but, more significantly, began a process of customized plant maintenance, thus lowering the need for utilities to keep their own people on staff year around. Toward that end, the company moved a third of its engineers from product development to new service development.

As a result, GE has signed new long-term service contracts with revenue commitments of $1.4 billion over the next five to twelve years. But even more important, says president Robert Nardelli, "If we hadn't reshaped the business, we would still be facing commodity pricing and would have fallen prey to downward spiraling margins. But we've actually been able to generate bigger margins."

Even the products themselves are moving toward this model. In the PC world, the success of Gateway and the *phenomenal* success of Dell over the last decade (growth rates of up to 20 percent a month; stock value appreciation of 29,000 percent since 1990) is due to these companies' capacity to customize each product for each customer. Each customer's demands drive the production and delivery process. No finished product inventory is carried. Whether you're a purchasing manager E-mailing a company order to Dell, for example (very likely on a customized Web site built by Dell for your company alone) or a grandparent calling your own order in, you the customer specify the features, the options, and the kind of computer you want for your particular needs. If you need help, the individual database the company keeps on your prior purchases will help the Dell service person on the other end of the phone line help walk you through the options you might take for your particular needs. Once your order is received, the systems and organization at Dell are so tight that you receive a confirmation within minutes and *your* finished machine within days.

In a similar vein, Andersen Windows is leapfrogging the very notion of just-in-time inventory management because ultimately it may have no real product inventory to manage! The "inventory" will be listed in an electronic catalog that customers (contractors and homeowners) will use to customize their desired window products. Andersen provides each of its dealers with an opportunity to co-invest in a PC, Oracle database, and proprietary software (about a $4,000 price tag). Then, once the customer delineates his or her specs, the computer checks them for structural soundness and feasibility and generates a price. State-of-the-art flexible manufacturing and electronic linkages allow Andersen to respond to each request without having to keep countless variations of windows in stock. Last year, Andersen generated over 350,000 different products this way with minimum inventory.

This section will show that in today's knowledge-based economy, organizations that can wrap themselves around each of their customers will be able to vault over their competitors by sharply redefining the whole notion of "customer service," by snaring new niches, and by perpetually reinventing their businesses. To effectively leave the paradigm of mass markets for that of market units of one, organizations have to be incredibly smart and agile—precisely the qualities needed for leapfrogging competitors.

The days of a vendor offering products with limited features and service marked by uniform procedures at designated hours and locations—all convenient and cost-efficient to the *vendor*—made sense in a world where competition was limited and customers' alternatives were few. That world is fast fading. Brandeis University's Robert Reich notes that "worldwide competition continues to compress profits on anything that is uniform, routine, or standard." That means you can't win anymore with mass-market thinking, one-size-fits-all operations, and routinized processes. You can't win by grudgingly accommodating "exceptions to the rule." Nowadays, exceptions *are* the rule. In fact, exceptions rule. The organization that leapfrogs the competition is building its corporate system and culture to wrap itself lovingly around each and every customer.

To leapfrog the competition, we've got to break away from two beliefs that are bedrock in conventional management: (1) that our primary attention ought to be in making profit and (2) that mass markets exist and hence salvation lies in cost-efficiencies of standardization, routinization, and economies of scale. In contrast, the two commitments that will allow you to wrap your organization around the customer, and thus leapfrog the competition, are:

- Obsess about customers, not profits (Commitment 7), and
- Focus on market units of one (Commitment 8).

Commitment 7 is quickly stated; the chapter offers a short, empirically grounded statement of business philosophy: profits are a scorecard; they are not the game. Certainly, you've got to pay close attention to financials. You've always got to be concerned with them. The issue is what you choose to obsess on. Obsession on your customers will most likely yield higher financials. Paradoxically, obsessing on the financials will most likely yield the opposite result.

As this section will demonstrate, leapfrogging organizations begin with the philosophy that they are not in business to make a profit or to increase shareholder value but to create and maintain customers. If they do that well, their long-term profitability and stock growth will most likely shine. If they don't do that well, all the financial and restructuring wizardry in the world will only serve to keep the wolves at bay in the short run.

Commitment 8 takes this a step farther. First, it will challenge you to think "market unit of one" whenever you think *quality*. Quality is not merely meeting specs and delivering error-free product—quality encompasses the individual customer's entire experience with you and your organization. Using a seemingly ordinary story about the construction of a backyard fence, the chapter takes the moral further: if mass markets are indeed withering, if technology and competition force us to consider each customer's special needs, then we are compelled to take certain steps to start redefining our entire business in response to each individual customer.

As mentioned earlier, economies of scale should be capitalized on in both manufacturing and service delivery; but in the new economy, they will not be the precursors to competitive advantage. To leave the world of mass markets and economies of scale in favor of market units of one is a huge commitment to make, but it is the essence of leapfrogging far beyond competitors who are still trapped in the logic of uniformity and mass.

Obsess About Customers, Not Profits

> IT'S A paradox: The more you concentrate on profits, the less likely it is you'll achieve them. But focus your primary attention on your customers, and the profits and all the other good things will follow. This section tells you why.

Here's a little quiz. What do the following chairmen and CEOs have in common other than a successful track record: Paul Allaire (Xerox), Bernard Marcus (Home Depot), Edward McCabe (McCabe and Company), Robert McDermott (formerly with United Services Automobile Association), Howard Schultz (Starbucks), and Michael Eisner (Disney)? If you're stumped, here are some clues:

- Paul Allaire: "If we do what's right for the customer, our market share and our return on assets will take care of themselves."
- Bernard Marcus: "Take care of the customer, and the stock price will take care of itself."
- Edward McCabe: "You think I want my tombstone to say, 'He had twenty-seven offices'? What's important to me is that our company did outstanding advertising. ... The numbers are not achievements in themselves but the results of achievements."
- Robert McDermott: "As a company objective, service comes ahead of either profits or growth. Now profits and growth do matter ... but I submit that it's because service comes first at USAA that profits and growth have been so healthy."

121

- Howard Schultz: "I've tried to make decisions based on what's right for the company, not what's right for the stock price. That's one of the achievements I'm proudest of at Starbucks."
- Michael Eisner: "Our job is to make the best entertainment that we can. If you could have great entertainment and not as great profits, or great profits and not as great entertainment, I'll take the great entertainment every time. You keep making great entertainment, and the profits are sure to come."

These executives are offering us an important piece of wisdom. Profit and stock value are vital entries in the scorecard, the consequences of making the right moves in the game of business. Many managers still operate under the twin fictions that their primary business purpose is to increase profit and shareholder value. Whether this is legally true in publicly traded companies is open to debate, but from a strategic perspective it is dead counterproductive for any firm, public or private. Organizations that leapfrog the competition always pay close attention to profit and stock movement (as well as other key financials), but they understand that a business does not exist primarily for the benefit of controllers and analysts, nor should it be run under that premise.

In the words of Harvard's Ted Levitt: "The purpose of business is to get and keep customers." Similarly, Peter Drucker has argued for years that the only justification for an organization's existence is the extent to which it can service the needs of a particular constituency in society called "customers." In other words, though it sounds heretical, the primary allegiance of any organization ought to be to that constituency, not to its shareholders—a conclusion that, by the way, is formally institutionalized in the corporate credo of Solectron and Cemex. Those CEOs I quoted earlier know this lesson well, and it is precisely because they have learned this lesson that their organizations—and, therefore, their shareholders—have prospered.

Obviously, profit and stock value are vital indices. The interests of shareholders—particularly the large institutional investors that control more than 50 percent of U.S. companies' equity capital—should be a significant concern to any executive. Just as obviously, profit—and the need to reinvest it for the purpose of improving the company—must be a crucial goal for anyone in business; even nonprofit organizations have to declare a surplus over expenses to survive. And, by the way, as profit sharing and equity ownership become more widespread as compensation, you can bet that a lot more in-house people will pay a lot more attention to the gyrations of those numbers.

Moreover, any organization that hopes to be successful must be adept at managing cost, debt, cash flow, and assets. In fact, a publicly traded organization would also be wise to gain proficiency in managing earnings in such a way as to maintain consistencies and reduce unpleasant surprises to investors.

Clearly, therefore, attentive and astute financial management must be a given for any organization that wants to compete effectively. The issue becomes one of priority. Paying attention to the numbers is good, and effectively manipulating the numbers is good. But where do the numbers come from? What is the source of the big, steady boosts in revenue, margins, cash flow, and stock price? I have found that long-term financial success depends primarily on leaders' abilities to capitalize on globalization and technology and to launch dramatic breakthroughs in innovation, quality, service, and teamwork. That ought to be the top priority. Committing to wrapping one's organization around the customers (as well as committing to the other four Giant Steps) is the way to realize these goals.

The problem, then, is not management's concerns with financials. The problem occurs when financials such as profit and shareholder value are viewed not as the consequence of effective strategy but as the raison d'être of the business itself. At that point, an intriguing boomerang effect takes place: profit and shareholder value go down—if not quickly, then certainly over time.

Why should this be? Well, let's consider what happens in an organization or business unit when the top managers seriously adhere to—or manage as if they seriously adhere to—the premise that profit and stock value are the main business priorities. Certain trends inevitably emerge:

1. *Managers learn to become emotionally and analytically detached from their business.* When the company becomes simply an expedient tool toward the more "important" goals of profit and stock value, opportunism replaces a commitment to growing a business. When the primary commitment is to turn a profit, notions such as love of product, careful cultivation of customer relationships, and mind-blowing service delivery become quaint anomalies. One middle manager of a struggling firm once complained to me, "You know what the problem is around here? Nobody cares. Management speaks numbers, dollars, cents. Nobody speaks vision, passion, being the best."

Analytical detachment has a ripple effect throughout the organization. It is hard to sustain excitement and enthusiasm among employees if the only things that senior executives seem to care about are the returns—and inevitably, this focus means that the organization will be hard-pressed to retain top talent. As noted earlier, companies that leapfrog the competition share financial information and financial gain with employees, but even that's not enough. Increasingly, the high corporate performers today—such as Body Shop, Starbucks, ESPN, Gillette, Harley-Davidson, Swatch, and Enron—are noted for providing their employees not merely "jobs" but a "cause," a "calling" for the transformation of their industries, if not the world.

For example, Anita Roddick, founder of the hugely successful, environmentally focused cosmetics enterprise Body Shop, put it this way in a *Harvard Business* case: "Most businesses focus all the time on profits, profits, profits. I think that is deeply boring. I want to create an electricity and passion that bonds people to the company. Especially with young people, you have to find ways to grab their imagination. You want them to feel that they are doing something important. I'd never get that kind of motivation if we were just selling shampoo and body lotion."

Increasingly, leaders' *love and passion*—for the product and its customers—becomes the essential fuel for competitive vigor and customer response. An analytically detached obsession on the numbers dilutes that fuel markedly. One of the main reasons that the Big Three American auto manufacturers lost dramatic earnings, market share, and, more important, competitive positioning to foreign rivals in the 1980s is because their underlying assumption in the 1960s and 1970s was illustrated as follows: "GM is in the business of making money, not cars." This was why ex-Chrysler chairman Lynn Townsend, who presided over the unraveling of his company, could deride an investor's concerns about quality with "The only thing that people care about are the stock splits."

2. *Managers become obsessed with short-term financials, or "meeting their numbers."* This obsession takes on various forms. First, managers plunge into regular cost-cutting frenzies by spending more of their time looking inward than outward. Customers are put on back burners as managers spend their time and attention on variance adjusting, paper chasing, paper clip counting, and innumerable endless meetings to review progress on those fronts. Creative accounting becomes de rigueur, especially in the last few days of the quarter. These activities usually have an immediate, though marginal, impact on costs and cash flow. However, they also ensure that management remains buffered from customer and employee frustrations, daily shifts in markets, and the regular infusion of fresh competitors who you can bet are entering the playing field with interesting products and services.

Second, managers who focus on the short-term financials are more likely to employ sweeping meat-cleaver approaches to head-count reductions—approaches that often are not carefully thought out and integrated into operational efficiency and long-term competitive strategy but that serve well as quick fixes. It should not be surprising that, according to American Management Association research over the past decade, few downsizing efforts across American businesses have yielded lasting increases in productivity and profitability.

Third, the notion of "patient capital" becomes a self-canceling oxymoron, which leads us to the next point:

3. *Managers become overly cautious and conservative.* Managers become less apt to take risks and make necessary investments in new products and services, and in new quality and service initiatives. (Ironically, per item 2 above, it is solid quality enhancements that drive down costs.)

Instead, analysis paralysis and worship of algorithm become norms. Fast, guaranteed returns are implicitly expected from new ventures. Intuition becomes suspect; net present value proofs become a prerequisite to action, which means little action takes place. A barrage of stringent control mechanisms—both financial and hierarchical—are regularly imposed on managers in the name of fiscal responsibility, thus further eroding their creativity, initiative, and accountability. Products and customers suffer in the process.

4. *Buying success becomes preferable to earning it.* The implicit motto becomes "If you can't manage one company, buy another." When one's primary orientation is profit and stock value, management commitments requiring patience, risk, and unflashy fundamentals—all necessary to growing a business—become less attractive. It appears a lot easier to consolidate balance sheets with another firm than to go through the mundane grind of developing a product line and cultivating relationships with customers. The excitement of financial sleight of hand while "doing the deal" yields more gratification than visiting suppliers and sitting in on customer focus groups.

Certainly, some acquisition activity can make for prudent strategy, but managers who rely on portfolio strategies for market share and earnings growth are more likely to drive their company's profits and stock value down, as the research of Harvard's Michael Porter and New York University's Mark Sirower has shown (much more on merger and acquisition fads in Giant Step V). And as the raiders of the 1980s were delighted to discover, executives' obsession with wheeling and dealing for quick profits over the prior three decades led to the development of grossly undervalued empires ripe for the plucking. The final irony is that the purest examples of "buying success" strategies—the conglomerates—have consistently underperformed the Standard & Poor's 500 Index.

5. *To boost sales and revenues, the organization beats up on salespeople and tries to buy customers.* Because a commitment to quality, service, and innovation is basically lip service (after all, "profits are why we are in business"), then the ways to enhance sales are twofold:

- Use big carrots and big sticks to get salespeople to meet their numbers any way they can, no questions asked. Let those people in the field figure out how to sell square pegs to reluctant customers holding round holes. Apart from the fact that this strategy no longer works well, a couple of additional by-products emerge. One, the sales force is removed from operations and strategy, which lowers both operational efficiency and market-driven innovation. Two, after-sale service inevitably becomes de-emphasized, which, in turn, depresses customer loyalty and word-of-mouth marketing.

- Attract customers by buying their affections via regular price slashes and big-money promotions and advertising blitzes. This approach automatically shrinks margins and, as car manufacturers have learned, simply causes shrewd customers to postpone buying decisions until the next low-price promotion appears. Moreover, as Eastern Airlines found during the final stage of its corporate demise, cheap tickets cannot repair a reputation for shoddy service.

As numerous magazines have learned, glitzy promotions and incentive giveaways to new subscribers may boost circulation and cash flow in the short run, but in the long run they often lead to a spiral of cost increases necessary to maintain "soft" uncommitted subscribers and prospect for new ones to replace the dropouts. With tactics like these, it should not be surprising that the head of one major media organization—a gentleman who publicly declared his business strategy to be to "increase thy profit margin"—presided over an empire that lost $100 million in profits during his tenure.

6. *The "heroes" become the wrong people.* The heroes become those who count and analyze things rather than those who make and sell things. They become those who restructure and re-arrange boxes rather than those who operate and develop them. They become those who count beans rather than those who grow them. They become those who say no to risk rather than those who inspire others to try something new. Financial wizards and "paper entrepreneurs," along with their ever-increasing and

expensive staffs, attain the highest status and most power. Champions of quality, entrepreneurship, and customer care take a back seat when significant management decisions are made.

One additional clue: tell me who attends senior management meetings and I'll tell you the caliber of decisions that are being made. In many large American manufacturing firms during the 1970s and 1980s, for example, financial and legal folks significantly outnumbered manufacturing and engineering folks in top management meetings. With the wrong heroes, the priorities and activities of the firm become distorted, and the competitive vigor of the organization slides accordingly.

Back in 1988, I predicted Eastern Airlines' bankruptcy in a series of nationwide speeches. I am no soothsayer; I simply observed that Eastern management scored high on each of the six trends listed here. There was no one more financially adroit and profit-conscious than CEO Frank Lorenzo, but, to quote consultant J. Daniel Beckham, "Eastern is a tragic monument to what happens when an organization has a vision based on nothing more inspiring than a dealmaker's spreadsheet."

What is the bottom line of all this? Leapfrogging organizations operate by the principle that profits are the resultant scorecard of good management. They do not define good management. Companies that focus on creating value for their customers yield the highest total returns to investors. The story is the same when it comes to preparing for the future. David Aaker of the University of California at Berkeley studied 248 businesses and determined that the top-ranked assets and skills necessary to obtain a "sustainable competitive advantage" were, in order, reputation for quality, customer service and product support, name recognition, and the ability to retain good management and engineering staff. These factors were ranked higher than low-cost production, financial resources, and technical superiority, even though many of the firms in Aaker's sample were high-technology manufacturers.

Let's go back to the little quiz at the beginning of this discussion. The executives cited are all no-nonsense individuals who run tight, profitable ships. Had you invested in their companies at their inception, you would be a very happy camper today.

They are driven not by a spreadsheet but by an overarching vision of excellence on behalf of their customers, and their business decisions are consistent with that vision.

In contrast, those managers who live by the rule that their top priority is to make profits and enhance shareholder value will achieve precisely the opposite. Just give them time.

Commitment 8 —————————————————

Focus on Market
Units of One

COMMITTING TO the customer as the top business priority is
the first step. Thinking "one," or "market of one," means
viewing each customer as an individual market with individual
needs and individual idiosyncrasies. The capacity to think and
act "one" is an enormous advantage for leapfrogging the competition. In fact, vendors that believe they are engaged in simple product and service transactions will be a dying breed.
Here is a story of a fence that was not a fence but, rather, a solution to a deeply felt need. Unfortunately, the vendor didn't
see it that way.

My wife and I learned a sobering fact recently. The number one
cause of death for toddlers in California is drowning in a home
pool.

Because we live in California and happen to have two toddlers and a pool, my wife became, shall we say, concerned and
insisted that we supplement our existing pool cover with some
additional protective barrier that would prevent our sons from
even venturing near the pool. This wasn't simple paranoia on
her part. Our pediatrician told her that during the previous
month a child drowned after having somehow penetrated a
pool cover.

Anyway, we hired a reputable contractor to build a small
fence in the appropriate area. After hearing our concerns regarding safety and aesthetics, he proposed a reasonably attractive four-foot-high flexible green mesh fence, which we all
agreed would serve more as a temporary shield than as a per-

manent barrier. (We weren't prepared to build a ten-foot wall around the pool, but we figured that a discouraging fence coupled with an imposing pool cover would be the ticket.)

With all this in mind, my wife and I left our contractor alone for the day. When we returned, we were relieved that the new backyard addition wasn't an eyesore. And it appeared durable enough to withstand the pounding of even the most determined youngster.

So far, so good. But the next day I noticed that, since the fence was made of flexible mesh, there was a section near the gate where one could, with a bit of effort, bend and fold the bottom in such a way as to scoot underneath, if one had a very small frame.

Hmmm. Not good. We called the contractor, who explained that the mechanics of the swinging gate that he had installed prevented him from stretching the adjacent mesh to the same tension as the material comprising the rest of the fence. Hence, there was necessarily a slight bit of slack that could be exploited but, again, only with some effort.

The vendor-customer dynamics now shifted from logical to psychological. From our perspective, the fence was inadequate; it would have to be replaced or reengineered. The contractor's position was a bit different. He contended that he had spent an entire day building a fence reflecting the material, specifications, and price to which we had explicitly agreed. One small section of the fence had a bit of inevitable slack, but overall, it met our criteria for safety and aesthetics.

Besides, he reminded us, a four-foot-high mesh fence was never intended to be impervious. From his perspective, he had met the customer's requirements. If we wanted any changes, he'd be glad to oblige, as long as we told him precisely what we wanted and paid him for his labor.

So far, this sounds like a typical, mundane conflict—the kind that's boring if you're not one of the protagonists or that provides fodder for Judge Judy's TV courtroom. But I propose that this divergence of opinion illustrates a fundamental problem that exists in vendor-customer interactions today. More important, it illustrates the kinds of nitty-gritty issues that tomorrow's providers will have to confront with increasing regularity.

You see, the contractor's position was not unlike most vendors' positions these days: "Look, Mr. or Ms. Customer, we agreed on the specs and the services; I did them; here's the bill." Or, as in this case, "We agreed on the fence; I built it; here's the bill." A straightforward business transaction.

The contractor in this story represents every vendor we've all dealt with: the house painter, the dentist, the banker, the engineer, the insurance agent, the retailer, the publisher, the manufacturer, the distributor. Indeed, the contractor represents *us* if *we* are the vendor. And, in the old order of business—that is, the status quo we've accepted—the contractor's point is defensible. After all, who's to say the customer is right? Who's to say the vendor should suffer just because the customer doesn't like what was ordered? There was no malice here. On the contrary, the contractor listened to us the customers, and he responded in good faith. Further, the final product would surely pass the test of quality; it was a well-built fence. Besides, let's face it: there are no sure things in business transactions.

Times, however, are changing. Increasingly, the customer is less interested in the tangibles of the deal (the specs, the final product, the actual services rendered) than in the intangibles— the original motive and desire for purchasing the services in the first place and the extent to which those deep motives and desires are met.

This is a subtle but crucial point for any business to take seriously. The customer is illustrated by the position of my wife who, with some prodding, would admit:

> I didn't necessarily want a fence in the first place. I wanted peace of mind so I wouldn't have to worry about my kids. I thought I wanted a fence because that's all I could envision, but in reality, I wanted a solution to my problem. Now the problem still exists because I'm still worried that my children could find the soft spot and possibly scoot underneath the fence. So I'm stuck with having to watch them as if the fence didn't exist. Sure, I agreed to the fence; yes, I understand the mechanics of the gate; and, yes, things are better in terms of probabilities. But I still don't have the peace of mind I anticipated when I got into this deal in the first place.

In the old order, this line of customer reasoning is whiny and unreasonable. In the old order, the vendor defends his or her position contractually, and the customer either takes his or her lumps or takes it to court. But I propose that in the new order—the emerging world of business—this scenario will have a different ending. Customers—individual and corporate—will be less patient with legalism and contractualism. Vendors that rely on them, however sincerely, will fall behind in the race toward competitive advantage.

Here's what's happening: as we've already seen, customers are more demanding and fickle than ever before, with good reason. They're smarter and more aware. They have more and more choices, from a logarithmic increase among competing vendors all the way to the enormous self-help possibilities of the World Wide Web. *Hence, they will gravitate toward vendors who understand that business is no longer about buying and selling products and services. It is about addressing peoples' intangible motives and desires.* Read those last two sentences again, because 99 percent of businesses today are run with absolutely no understanding of this point.

In the new order of things (which is already starting to happen), what will count for customers is the *total experience they have with the vendor.* By "vendor," I mean both the organization and its representatives. The customer's appraisal of the total experience will be based on questions such as these:

- How easy is it to work with this vendor—before and after the sale?
- Does the vendor really, truly understand what I'm looking for?
- How responsive, caring, and concerned is the vendor toward me and my particular problems?
- How willing is the vendor to probe and listen, and then adjust and contort, to my idiosyncratic demands?
- Does the vendor know me so well that he/she can anticipate what I might want before I do?
- How effective is the vendor in devising a creative solution to my real problems and unique needs?
- To what extent does the vendor seek my input and solicit my involvement toward working together to meet my needs?

Reread these seven questions. They suggest a very subtle but crucial point: it's not marketing and sales wizardry that will create success with customers but your capacity to listen, understand, and respond in a way that the customer defines as value-adding. This point was driven home to me last year during a class session of my executive MBA course at the University of San Francisco. We were doing a case analysis of a major, faltering bank. One group took on the role of a new management team and made a presentation to the rest of the class about how they would turn around the bank's fortunes.

The group described the benefits of a whole new set of pro-posed technological investments that would boost the bank's data-mining capacity and allow the bank to target individual customers with numerous cross-selling opportunities, as in "We've pulled up your mortgage account and note that you've paid off 50 percent of your principle; did you know that this al-lows you to take an equity loan on . . . ?" or "We notice that you've got $50,000 spread across three accounts with us, and we'd like to recommend that you invest in one of our mutual funds."

I admit that I was impressed with the presentation. I thought the rest of the class would be too. After all, it was a "market unit of one" type of approach, and, besides, the students were all very technologically sophisticated, so they would no doubt appreciate the orientation of the group.

I was wrong. The students jumped on the group with com-ments such as "As a customer, I never gave you permission to look into my personal records!" and "You guys aren't helping the customer—you're just selling your own products!" and "If I was a customer, I'd tell you I'm quite capable of handling my own affairs, thank you!"

That's when I myself reread those previous seven questions. Good service? Value adding? The individual customer will de-cide! Not the techies, the marketers, the planners, or the sales-people. And to reinforce the students' reactions, here is an excerpt from a letter sent to the October 1998 issue of *Worth* magazine:

I recently received a stuffer with my monthly bank statement. Printed in very small type, it stated that information about me and my accounts would be shared with all of the bank's affiliated companies. These include brokerage, credit, mortgage, insurance, and marketing firms. If I did not want this to happen, my only choice was to write a detailed letter formally requesting exclusion from this galling practice. Now this bank is merging with another, much larger bank, meaning that most of its customers' personal information will be made available nationwide. Whatever happened to the sacred banker-client privilege?

Getting back to our contractor, the lesson is clear. "Market unit of one" means that my wife and only my wife will decide what's good for her unique needs. My wife and only my wife will evaluate her total experience of dealing with the contractor. In this scenario, the price and final tangible output are part of the experience, to be sure, but not the only parts, and not necessarily the most important ones. Right now, customers are beginning to take their total experience seriously, and they're starting to judge vendors on that admittedly nonrational basis. They're saying, Wait a minute. Officially speaking, I got my fence built or my house painted or my teeth adjusted or my bank loan granted or my insurance done or the product delivered. But, by George, I'm not happy with how things went or how things turned out. In the past, I, the customer, didn't take that experience seriously. After all, business is a contractual arrangement. But no more. I do take it seriously now.

Simply "listening to what the customer wants" and then responding will no longer be sufficient. In our discussion of Giant Step I, we saw that customers often don't know what they will want tomorrow. The fact is that they may not even be able to articulate what they want *today*. That was our problem with the fence. Writing in the *Wall Street Journal*, Brandeis professor Robert Reich argues that "ever greater value is being created by helping customers *discover* their unique needs and then tailoring products and designing services to satisfy them."

In the future, therefore, the successful businessperson/contractor will act as a consultant, helping my wife and me articulate our latent needs, and working with us to solve problems creatively. In doing so, he'll necessarily wind up doing things and partnering with other vendors in a manner he might personally find unorthodox (which, by the way, will expand his own skill base and networks).

Think about it. Suppose the contractor had approached the problem with the mind-set of a personal coach. He knows he brings to the party certain key skills and competencies in the building trade. Fine. But so do a jillion other contractors. His real value to us is his ability to use those skills in a manner that we the customers have never imagined and to form alliances with other vendors he may or may not have ever worked with before to help him achieve these goals.

Who knows? Maybe he would have created—on his own, with our help, or with the help of a new strategic partner—a creative type of childproof, adult-friendly barrier that not only would have been foolproof but that he could have parlayed into a new service niche or a new product line. Either way, a new business spin-off and revenue stream. (As a matter of fact, my wife and I have since learned that a local contractor and a nurse have joined forces in a very lucrative "childproofing" business.)

Or maybe, in alliance with a creative landscape architect, he could have used his ingenuity to create a beautiful new natural childproof barrier that we, the customers, didn't "ask" for initially, because we couldn't conceptualize it.

If this contractor applies imagination to solving our real problem, the consequences are powerful: he "wows" us with an innovative solution, he jacks up our loyalty (and resultant repeat business and word-of-mouth marketing), he differentiates himself from other contractors, he augments his fee, he broadens his skill base, he expands his network base, and he grows the scope of his business. In short, he perpetually redefines and reinvents his business because he's not limited by the products and services he thinks he sells. He's not limited by any mission statement that limits his business vision, either. His business is to apply his unique skills in an ingenious way to solve customer problems. Within those parameters, the nature of his business is perpetually changing, evolving, and growing.

What I'm saying may sound weird today, but I predict that it will soon be conventional wisdom. A whole new world is emerging, one where the products and the services in your current portfolio are going to be less and less relevant. The products and services that you're clinging to are becoming commodities fast.

Fences? They're commodities. Bank loans? Commodities, too. Personal computers? Long-distance telephone service? Custody of financial assets? Food-processing equipment? Gaming and gambling? Security systems for the home? Travel-booking services? All commodities. (If you don't believe me, talk to the people who must survive in these businesses.)

The value-add and the way to differentiate yourself and capitalize on new opportunities—thereby the route to competitive advantage—lie in focusing wisdom, attention, and resources toward addressing each customer's unique needs. Jim McGuirk, who runs the Unisys Federal Systems unit, tells me that in the notoriously fickle, price-sensitive government sector his people serve, they can no longer simply sell their traditional staple of mainframe computers. They've reconfigured their strategy and workforce to provide long-term customized information technology solutions (e.g., information systems engineering, data warehousing, Y2K solutions, telecommunications and network integration, intranet development, and facilities management) for each of their clients' specific needs. As part of this equation, they sell all sorts of mainframe as well as non-mainframe computer hardware—including competitors' products. Whatever it takes.

For example, in their recent work with the Internal Revenue Service, Unisys experts worked on integrating the IRS's existing IBM and Unisys machines because they determined that that was the most cost-effective path for the client. They did not try to sell the client replacement Unisys hardware. In fact, they suggested the purchase of more IBM machines. The initially skeptical IRS was won over and recently signed a rare twelve-year deal with Unisys as a result.

McGuirk had plenty of skeptics in his own company when he initiated his business approach three years ago. Government was considered a dead-end business. For that reason, one of the first things Lou Gerstner did when he took over IBM was dump IBM's own federal systems division. Meanwhile, from 1996 through

1998, McGuirk's division enjoyed a roaring 30 percent average annual growth rate compared with the 4 percent industry average. Moreover, as McGuirk told me, the same people who laughed at his 1995 goal of $1 billion in revenues by the year 2000 are stunned that he achieved it two years ahead of schedule.

At this point, some of you may be thinking, this is all well and good if you can somehow create services. But I'm dealing strictly in mass-market products. I can't afford to think about my business in terms of each individual customer.

My response? Good luck—you'll need it in the next millennium. The rules are changing. Mass markets are withering in the face of the onslaught by global competition and technological advance. "Mass customization" and individual tailoring are replacing undifferentiated, standardized, commodity-like products. At the 1996 Comdex convention in Las Vegas, Netscape CEO Jim Barksdale said, "We are entering the third wave of the Internet. . . . While the first waves of the Internet focused on users being able to easily find information, the mark of this third wave is that information finds the user. Our new products will have the intelligence to help you focus on the information you care about."

Netscape is not alone. Sun Microsystems and several small start-ups are now using Java programming to deliver individualized software programs, Web pages, news updates, and other specified data to each customer's personal computer. Search engines such as Yahoo!, Excite, and InfoSeek have moved in the same direction. Dow-Jones allows individual subscribers to create their own on-line *Wall Street Journal*, individually tailored to the reader's unique specifications. Time Inc. is talking about a goal of four million separate issues of *Time* magazine, potentially one per subscriber.

In the manufacturing arena, Levi Strauss & Co. is using a range of technologies, including EDI, CAD-CAM, and computerized fabric cutting to pilot the concept of custom-built jeans. The customer tries on a sample pair of prototype jeans in a selected location, and the data is beamed to a facility where a robot makes the jeans to order. There's a three-week turnaround with a $10 to $20 price increment over a mass-produced, off-the-rack pair of jeans.

At Westport, Connecticut-based start-up Custom Foot, the stores have no conventional inventory, just scanning-imaging devices that take twelve measurements of each foot and forward the data to the company's shoe contractors in Italy. Japanese-owned Paris Miki, the largest eyewear company in the world, now features a computer graphics system called Eye-tailor that designs custom rimless glasses, deliverable in less than a week. The system is already in use in more than 300 stores worldwide.

Meanwhile, twenty Matsushita employees in Japan can receive an individual customer's body specs from a prototype bicycle frame in a retail outlet and then draw from a technology allowing 11 million variations of road and mountain bikes in 200 colors, to produce the custom-built bicycle quickly.

There's no product or industry that is immune from this trend. Merck augments smoking cessation pills with tailored health management programs. Once a consumer fills out a questionnaire on habits, he or she receives a package with a workbook and a customized plan to quit smoking.

McGraw-Hill's Custom Publishing unit allows professors to create their own textbooks chapter by chapter by going on-line and choosing among hundreds of thousands of documents. They can add material not on the Web site that might ordinarily have been used as handouts. McGraw-Hill then puts together the final product and handles copyright issues.

At General Nutrition Centers (GNC), a pilot project in twelve of its Live Well stores allows customers to customize products from shampoo to vitamins by using machines similar to those used in hospitals to dispense medicines. After vitamin customers, for example, fill out a form about general health habits and their current vitamin use, the machine's computer program suggests an optimal vitamin package that it then dispenses in daily packets with the customer's name on it.

The Merck, McGraw-Hill, and GNC interventions illustrate yet another form of value-add. Companies that wrap themselves around customers are moving to provide them with tools and expertise so that they themselves can create their own individualized products and services. It's a very important trend. Pure on-line competitors such as Travelocity (travel itineraries),

E*Trade (investment), and Home Advisor (mortgage banking) are constantly raising the level of what consumers can do on their own, and they represent the zillion new Web offerings that are just beginning to scratch the surface of possibilities of self-help and solo production.

In response, cutting-edge "brick-and-mortar" competitors such as Rosenbluth Travel, Charles Schwab, and Countrywide Credit Industries are also providing Internet tools for individuals to create their own travel itineraries, investment portfolios, and mortgage loan packages, respectively, but—as a critical means of differentiation from purely on-line providers—they are offering individual customers an ever-widening menu of organizational support services around those tools.

It boils down to this: in every industry, the customer is telling vendors, "Either do things for *me*, or give me the tools and support so that I can easily do things for myself. But don't ever treat me like you would anyone else. Treat me as a unique entity."

Cisco Systems' CIO Peter Solvik envisions even more profound movement in the near future. In an interview with *Fast Company* magazine (February/March 1997), he said, "We're using the Web as a vehicle to move customer relationships to a new level. The only way to grow as fast as we're growing is to let customers do their own work—self-service. The Web makes that possible. That's today."

And in fact, Cisco currently logs over half million contacts from customers each month reporting technical problems and checking orders. More than two-thirds of those contacts now occur over the Internet. The company's Troubleshooting Engine, for example, allows customers to tap into an artificial intelligence system built from a cataloging of prior customer problems. The system poses a series of increasingly detailed questions to help customers diagnose and fix specific problems. Immediate feedback, immediate response. And if the problem remains unsolved, the systems immediately connects to real Cisco people who can help out, which, according to Slovik, is the next big wave:

> The next big opportunity is automatic service. We want our products to tell us when they have problems, and for us to be able to fix those problems without anyone logging onto our Web site. We'll

connect a customer's network to ours. A tool will monitor their network, check for bugs, figure out what new software the customer might want to buy, and make suggestions—without anyone initiating the transaction. This is still in the R & D stage. But it's where things are heading.

That is absolutely true regardless of your industry. Leapfrogging organizations in every industry are relentlessly cracking that once-inviolable, undifferentiated, opaque "mass" market, continually probing the possibilities of using new technologies and new organizational forms to establish one-on-one products and services with real people, no matter how big the market, no matter how distant the customer is from headquarters.

I hope it's obvious by this point, but I want to emphasize that Giant Step III is much, much more than a marketing issue. Certainly, it makes marketing sense to use data-mining technology to individually profile your customers, especially your more valuable customers. In fact, the Dayton, Ohio-based Dorothy Lane grocery chain has doubled its margins by doing precisely that and, just as significantly, has customized direct mail and special promotions based on profiled customers' individualized shopping history. This approach has allowed Dorothy Lane to boost its "favored customer" loyalty significantly while eliminating its dependence on inefficient mass-market promotion tactics such as newspaper ads and across-the-board price cuts.

That's commendable, up-to-date marketing. But in considering the implications of Giant Step III, a much bigger, richer picture is slowly coming into focus as we head to the next millennium: customized products, personalized service, one-to-one collaborative* communication (face-to-face or electronic), real-time response. In effect, market units of one.

The paradigm is shifting, and it's a lot more than good marketing. It's about defining the business. It's about engineers at the 3M computer components facility in Austin, Texas, asserting, "How do we even know what to make until we work it out with the customer first?" It's about the philosophy of celebrated

---

*Individual customers (units of one) are huge potential sources of collaboration not only for customer service but for product development and cost reduction efforts as well. More on this in Giant Step IV.

plastic injection molder Nypro to "organize around the customer's direction"—including building a microfactory near each one, because, as CEO Gordon Lankton says, "being next to the customer is so significant it outweighs almost everything else."

In the emerging marketplace of the year 2000 and beyond, the quality of your relationships will be even more important than the quality of your products. Moreover, relationships—not products or ads—will increasingly define your brand image. Robert Reich argues that in the future, the real value of great brands will be their "promise to deliver just the right package of specialized products, plus advice about the content of the right package, and continuing help thereafter." That promise is necessarily built on relationship.

Dayton Hudson chairman Bob Ulrich is fond of quoting Sears's vice president John Costello, who said "a brand signifies a relationship with customers. It's the best defense we have against price competition and it's the key to customer loyalty." To his own troops, Ulrich emphasizes that a brand relationship can only occur if the vendor cultivates it deliberately, consistently, and authentically.

That is the spirit behind Giant Step III. It's the spirit that underlies the strategic intent at Solectron, the first little case study in our discussion, and the other examples thereafter. Unfortunately, that's what our friend the fence builder (remember him?) didn't understand. When all is said and done, his job wasn't to meet specs, to meet a contractual obligation, or even to build a high-TQM fence with a friendly "customer service" smile. His job was to learn about us—my family, my home—to imaginatively create unique value for us, so that we would *want* to enter into a long-term relationship with him. And, by the way, if he continued to work *with* us that way, he himself would become a brand in our eyes.

Now comes the sobering news. It won't be easy to transform oneself from a transaction-driven, commodity-oriented business to one based on the selling of customized expertise and branded solutions. Joe Costello, the recently retired president of Cadence Design Systems, had to embark on a personal mission to transform his company from a vendor of electronic design products per se to one of customized services enveloping products. Even though he was able to document to everyone that the fastest growth in earnings and margins was coming from this new way of addressing the business, he still faced internal resistance.

Here's what he said: "Everyone is used to the traditional structure and roles—marketing, R & D, application engineers, and sales. All of a sudden, we say we aren't selling just tools. That raises an identity crisis for many people in the company." Costello found that the new organizational persona requires engineers to think like consultants and spend time on the front lines. It requires financial people to share data across the organization. In fact, it requires people in all functions and levels to share information openly, including with customers and suppliers. It requires people in sales to start thinking about after-sale relationships. It requires everyone to know the client's business, not merely Cadence's product line. This is a difficult transformation, to say the least, requiring constant pounding away at the old culture.

It's not just internal people who have to be convinced. Customers do, too. The folks at Unisys Federal Systems had a huge task educating government people about their new way of doing business. Only through the consistency, deliberateness, and authenticity that Bob Ulrich talks about were they able to build credibility and trust. Andersen Windows is having to educate the entire supply chain in its radical new concept of made-to-order windows. As an Andersen manager explained to me, "A lot of people in the industry do not understand the concept of product customization, or they are scared of any system that doesn't rely on mass inventory. We're even dealing with lumberyards that don't have computers. It's a tough sell."

Let's go back to our contractor. By insisting on implicit contracts and narrowing his view to agreements about fences, he's positioned himself as a commodity provider of commodity transactions. Whatever he gets paid today by us, he'll lose by a multiple tomorrow. No margins, no repeat business, no word-of-mouth marketing, no new alliances, no new business opportunities. He won't understand why; he'll blame politicians, immigrants, big government, or big corporations. Maybe he'll pour more of his limited resources into advertising, which will put some quick and dirty window-dressing salve on his undifferentiated service, and he'll be disappointed by the marginal impact that results. Maybe he'll merge with another contractor to compete by volume and price. Then he'll learn that volume—even if efficiently executed—makes little sense if mass markets are dying and customers reject standardized services. He'll learn that competing on price is ultimately devastating to both margins and customer loyalty—hence akin to slow self-strangulation.

If you're truly committed to leapfrogging your competition, here is my suggestion: plaster the message of Giant Step III on every business document, office wall, and meeting agenda from now on. Let it drive every capital budgeting, personnel, product development, and after-sale decision. It won't be easy, because you and I were incredibly intelligent in the old world but not particularly so in the new. But if we repeat this credo over and over again, we might finally start to believe it, and we just might start acting on it. We would then really wrap ourselves around each of our customers. They and our shareholders will thank us profusely.

GIANT STEP IV

TRANSFORM YOUR ORGANIZATION INTO A WEB OF RELATIONSHIPS

In 1996, 70 percent of Fujitsu's business was in Japan. However, profits over the prior few years had declined in that fiercely competitive, glutted domestic environment. In an attempt to jump-start the business, Fujitsu's PC division entered the lucrative U.S. laptop computer market. Sales inched up a bit in 1996, but as Fujitsu learned, the American PC market is as saturated as the one in Japan. In attempting to differentiate itself from its myriad competitors, the company realized that one of its main problems revolved around logistics.

Fujitsu's laptops were being fully manufactured in the Tokyo area. For the sake of scale and cost-efficiencies, the company would wait until a sufficient volume of orders justified the use of a cargo ship to transport the product from Japan to Fujitsu PC warehouses in Milpitas, California, and Hillsboro, Oregon. When all was said and done, it usually took a month to get an ordered product to retailers and end users. The delay was creating dissatisfaction among customers, and the yen's slide was exacerbating the financial impact.

Consequently, Fujitsu PC decided to outsource its warehousing and distribution functions to FedEx. Instead of shipping product by sea, Fujitsu could now fly small batches over to

145

the United States—which immediately meant significantly less transportation time and opportunity cost. Once product was in the United States, FedEx's core warehousing and distribution competencies, which exceeded the skills of Fujitsu, could now move the product to its final destinations on land much more quickly and efficiently.

Collaborative discussions between the two firms unearthed some additional opportunities. In October 1997, Fujitsu PC opened a customer support center in Memphis, Tennessee, not only to be close to the FedEx superhub but to offer customers faster service benefits. (A further cost-saving move, though an unfortunate downside for Oregon employees, was the closure of the Hillsboro facility.)

The close physical proximity allowed further discussions among members of the two companies, which led to the next leap in innovation. In March 1998, Fujitsu PC announced that it would be expanding the support center to included built-to-order configuration on its laptops. The configuration would be performed by the American firm CTI, a company with an established history of subassembly work with many of FedEx's customers.

The closed-loop alliance of Fujitsu PC/FedEx/CTI now allows Fujitsu PC a four-day distribution-to-market cycle with customized product as opposed to a four-week scenario with an undifferentiated product. The design, development, and basic manufacturing is still done by Fujitsu in Japan, but once the product reaches Osaka airport and FedEx takes over, the remaining functions are performed by FedEx and CTI. The result is that a customer who places an order on Monday at 4 P.M. can take possession of a Fujitsu "Built to Human" notebook computer by Thursday at 10:30 A.M.

The moral of the story is simple: to leapfrog the competition, you need allies: real allies with whom you can strategize and work to do extraordinary things that you could never do—or ever think of doing—on your own. Organizations like Fujitsu are capitalizing on a huge relentless trend that Peter Drucker aptly summarized in the premier issue of *Leader to Leader* in 1996.

I met with a very big company not long ago—around 80 or so on the Fortune 500 list. They expect to be number 5 on that list in 10 years, and I shocked them by saying that I don't think that list will exist, so that goal is meaningless. That list basically assumes that everything you do is under your roof and is owned by you and run by you. But already in many companies, most work is done through alliances, joint ventures, minority participation, and very informal agreements which no lawyer could possibly handle.

I don't agree with Drucker that the *Fortune* 500 list will be meaningless, but the trend he's citing is unequivocal. A recent American Management Association study, summarized in the April 1998 issue of *Management Review*, showed that 94 percent of surveyed firms currently outsource at least one *major* business activity. The fastest-growing candidates for outsourcing are traditional in-house functions such as accounting and finance (where outsourcing has doubled over the past three years), information systems (up 40 percent), and marketing (up 35 percent). As stated in the report: "If you can't recruit the necessary talent to do the work, consider handing the whole task over to an outside team of providers."

The conclusion: "If you can't recruit the necessary talent" suggests that you might be able to. That's a short-sighted presumption. In a knowledge-based free-market global economy, it is naive to assume that any one organization could ever lock up all the necessary resources and talent under one roof. Why would you want to, anyway? In a world where speed and agility are paramount virtues, and where the goal is to leap over—not waddle among—competitors, is it smart to weigh yourself down with a heavy, costly, often debt-laden, vertically integrated organization?

As Tom Peters has noted, the key nowadays is not to own the resources but to have access to them. So consider: why not have as small a workforce as possible, be able to turn on a dime, and *borrow* the best resources and talent from anywhere on earth? Why not determine what you're "world-class great" in and then link up with partners who are world-class great in those activities that are currently bleeding you costwise while under your roof? That's precisely what Fujitsu did.

There's a new, powerful business logic afoot:

- Premise 1: As noted earlier, we are all operating in a brain-based economy, where intangible assets such as intelligence, skills, and competencies are among the most crucial precursors of competitive advantage.
- Premise 2: In a brain-based economy, your company cannot possibly collect and hoard all the best talent and intellectual resources under your roof. No one organization, no matter how big, no matter how many acquisitions, can possibly corner this market—or even a fraction of it.

Therefore:

- Determine the competencies, technologies, and niches you're dominant in or what you aspire to be dominant in.
- Focus on that part of your business and invest heavily in it.
- Let go of everything else—automate it, divest it, or let another company do it for you.
- Look to grow partnerships with the best and the brightest, those who are either great in the functions you no longer want to keep in-house or great in the functions and activities that you want to further cultivate in the quest for extraordinary achievement.

In other words, start viewing your organization as a web of world-class relationships. Organizations that wish to leapfrog the competition continually cultivate trusted networks around the world; in fact, they begin to view their organizations as extensions of other organizations—their allies—all of whom contribute unique value.

While the well-known outsourcing phenomenon is germane to this discussion, what I'm talking about—and what Fujitsu and FedEx have demonstrated—is far more than the conventional arm's-length type of commodity exchanges that go under the name of outsourcing these days. I'm talking, instead, about genuine collaboration in developing and executing new strategic concepts. I'm talking about the fact that since technological advance has rendered time and place irrelevant (I can be anywhere and be connected with anyone and anything real-time), the smart organization is one that can quickly connect with talent from any source in any pocket of the world for any project and any goal—and thereby create a value-adding web of relationships globally.

This is why Fuji, an expert in photographic film and paper, joins forces with Xerox, an expert in photocopy equipment services, to create mutual value: each gains exposure in each other's national terrain, and just as important, Fuji learns American entrepreneurial skills and Xerox learns about being a "document" company.

This is why Gateway teams up with Yahoo! rather than building a search engine or spending megabucks to acquire one. While Gateway concentrates on its strength of custom-built computers, the Yahoo! search engine boosts Gateway's customer service by allowing Gateway's customers to both personalize their Internet experiences and directly access Gateway technical support and related services. Yahoo!, of course, gains access to Gateway's growing global, sophisticated consumer audience.

First Direct, the no-branch telephone bank owned by Midland Bank, can grow as fast as it has (650,000 customers in Great Britain since its launch in 1989; 12,000 new accounts monthly) and still stay lean, light, and creative for one simple reason: it focuses on leveraging its intangible assets—exceptional telephone service, database marketing, one-on-one consumer profiling, and rapid response to individual customers—while linking with a select set of outside partners who provide immediate ancillary services including car insurance and home security systems as part of the deal. (The effect of these efforts on customers is noteworthy: 90 percent of customers say they are "very" or "extremely" satisfied with the bank's service, while 80 percent say they have recommended the bank to a friend or colleague within the past year. Put those figures next to comparable data of conventional banks.)

Prior to its acquisition by WorldCom, MCI was basically (and still largely remains) an integrative software, systems, and marketing company that has outsourced services from paging to security systems, from manufacturing to technology R & D, to its more than 100 carefully chosen partners. (In fact, British Telecom, the pre-WorldCom suitor of MCI, was simply one of many companies—such as Microsoft and Westinghouse—networked together in MCI's constellation of partners). For years, it's been MCI's capacity to replenish its own in-house core strengths and orchestrate supportive talent from around the world that has allowed it to be much fleeter, much more cost-effective (and, many would argue, much more innovative) than the exponentially bulkier AT&T. That's what made the company so attractive to WorldCom to begin with.

Webs allow each participating organization to concentrate on developing its own special competencies and niches without being diverted by activities and functions in which it is not splendid—but which someone else in the web is. Hence, each webmate becomes an active vibrant part of a network tide that raises all boats.

Ideally, the strategic focus centers around a consolidation of brain and imagination toward goals that are potentially revolutionary. Consider these examples:

- Lego's Mindstorms Robotics Invention System for children, cited earlier in this book, the result of the collaboration between the Danish toymaker and the cutting-edge Media Lab of the Massachusetts Institute of Technology.
- Software database expert Oracle and credit card authorization king VeriFone bringing together their distinct pools of talent to create a powerful new Internet payment system.
- The alliance of Teledesic (a start-up of Craig McCaw and Bill Gates), Boeing, Matra Marconi, and, most recently, Motorola, which brings together four parties' unique, capabilities for the eye-popping goal of launching into space nearly 300 satellites by 2002, allowing anyone on earth to access the Internet without a computer or telephone link.

When a company starts thinking in terms of webs, all sorts of interesting new possibilities emerge. Merck partners with Walgreens and the Osteoporosis Centers of America to offer Walgreen's customers a low-cost test to measure bone density. The tests are developed by Merck in conjunction with the Osteoporosis Center and performed in Walgreens pharmacies. Merck gets the drug business. Just as important, Merck's goal of building its pharmaceutical information business is enhanced by the relationship.

Boeing, meanwhile, in developing its 777 aircraft, established 238 cross-functional teams whose participants included a wide range of employees from its customer and supplier list. United Airlines, All Nippon Airways, British Airways, Japan Airlines, Cathay Pacific, and others came from the customer side. The supplier network included Mitsubishi Heavy Industries, Fuji Heavy Industries, and Kawasaki Heavy Industries. Boeing borrowed the brains of exceptional players in creating a product they themselves would find exceptional and in doing so also established closer relations with them.

Little Irvine Sensors, the $14 million southern California manufacturer of sensors and high-density electronic products, uses worldwide networks to quickly become a global player in a capital-intensive business despite its small size and shallow pockets. Irvine Sensors has kept product development functions in-house, while farming out manufacturing, quality assurance, and worldwide distribution to sources as far away as Korea and Kuala Lampur. These global alliances have helped Irvine Sensors reap most of its 33 percent revenue growth abroad.

Savvy leaders are extending these arrangements to include competitors. Most conventional managers are surprised by this notion, for they are obsessed with destroying competitors. But this mind-set engenders two counterproductive forces. First, the driver of strategy becomes a narrow focus on beating someone else rather than creating new, exciting market opportunities that are much more lucrative. Second, managers become oblivious to the fact that some of these competitors can provide valuable sources of opportunity as allies on selected ventures. General Colin Powell has remarked that one of his most sobering realizations while chairman of the Joint Chiefs of Staff was that in the hardball world of geopolitics, it's no longer a simple case of white hats (us, the good guys) versus black hats (them, the Russians, the bad guys). The CIA and KGB now collaborate, as do NASA and the Russian Space Agency.

Competitors Rockwell, Northrop Grumman, and Honeywell worked together with customer Boeing to help develop the new 777. Sun Microsystems enthusiastically relies on rivals such as IBM and Oracle to help develop software and business applications for its burgeoning Java technology. Merck teams with competitors such as Astra, Johnson & Johnson, Biogen, and Rhone-Poulenc to produce a wide variety of pharmaceutical and genetics products.

When I worked with Visa International, I was intrigued to learn that the banks that issue Visa consider themselves fierce competitors, but they actively cooperate with each other in raising the ease of the card's usage among merchants and customers.

For me, a real eye-opener occurred when I addressed the annual meeting of the trust divisions of the New York Bankers Association. The speaker prior to me was a senior representative of high-profile competitor Fidelity Investments, who openly shared his insights with his competitors in the audience. Why? Because his competitors in the audience sold Fidelity products as part of their overall portfolio. That's the nature of the beast nowadays. Schizophrenia rules. In any given moment, depending on the context, AT&T and Motorola are each others' customers, suppliers, competitors, or joint venture partners. To expand on General Powell's sentiments, competition is no longer good guys versus bad guys. The relationships are far more incestuous than that.

Viewing the marketplace in terms of web relationships also leads to a new way of viewing customers: no longer as end points of a transaction but as ongoing, interacting partners with compatible goals, obligations, and commitments. Silicon Graphics teams worked closely with teams from customer Lucas Arts & Entertainment to generate new technological advances that allowed Lucas Arts to create special effects for *Terminator 2* and *Jurassic Park*, among others, while Silicon Graphics wound up with new products and skills to sell on the open market.

You may have already recognized that if you wrap yourself around each customer, à la Giant Step III, you've got a better chance of getting to the next level with your customer, which is Step IV. That is, once you do Giant Step III, there is a likelihood that the relationship can further develop into a mutually supporting web. A web with customers develops when the goals and payoff to both parties are beyond that anticipated in the "official" transaction, and the responsibility for the relationship is two-way, not simply the vendor's. Clinton, Massachusetts–based Nypro, recently named the *Plastics News* Processor of the Year, is a case in point. As noted in Giant Step III, the plastics supplier organizes its services around each customer, even to the point of building microfacilities near each one. However, it also invites—indeed, urges—each customer to be part of joint Continuous Improvement Teams with Nypro people. The teams are charged with finding innovative ways to reduce costs and improve manufacturing processes.

Hence, mixed teams of plastics maker Nypro and customer Vistakon, the Johnson & Johnson contact lens maker, work together not only to improve Nypro's product and delivery quality but also to improve each others' productivity on matters ranging from inventory to setup. They share databases, ideas, and resources. Whether with J & J, Gillette, Motorola, or GM's Saturn, these weblike teams have documented cost savings of hundreds of millions of dollars. In fact, a Vistakon manager states, "We are the biggest disposable contact lens producer in the world, and we couldn't have gotten there without Nypro." That's a manifestation of a Step IV web.

Smart companies move toward web relations with customers because they know webs mean profit, customer loyalty, and new core competencies. When EDS took over Rolls-Royce Aerospace Group's data management, it was initially on an "outsource" basis. However, per Giant Step III, EDS is now intimately involved in helping the Group substantially reduce its product development cycle time as well as improve the quality of product development. EDS calls it a "cosourcing" relationship. The two companies have gradually developed a Step IV collaborative web in which the parties physically intermingle with each other at work and hold ongoing, open discussions on planning, design, and execution. Rolls-Royce gains with the inflow of exceptional expertise that it doesn't have to "buy and own." EDS gains significantly greater "share of customer" business on a long-term basis and a wealth of new unanticipated expertise from its customer that it can market to other clients.

The intimacy of the web is such that EDS has built a research center near the Rolls-Royce facility, and several hundred Rolls-Royce people officially report to EDS folks. The web has grown to the point that EDS not only designs the engineering processes for engine development but will actually run the systems. In fact, the web is by now so tight that a chunk of EDS's fees are contingent on Rolls's performance improvement. Both parties feel a pressing responsibility and incentive to contribute to each other's benefit.

The relationship between Cincinnati–based Milacron's chemical management group and General Motors has a similar feel. The relationship began with Milacron totally customizing its operations for GM, and now Milacron manages cutting fluids, grinding wheels, and competitor products in several GM plants. In fact, it manages entire shop floors, and in a number of situations GM's United Auto Worker employees report directly to Milacron people. In addition to winning the Supplier of the Year award for the last two years, the business development payoff for Milacron is similar to that gained by EDS. In addition, there is a big payoff in entrées gained into the auto industry for a whole menu of products from other Milacron divisions. Yet another important entrée was summarized by senior vice president Alan Shaffer: "When GM goes to China, we go to China." GM, in effect, is helping Milacron further expand its business around the world.

Even in the so-called "mass-market," innovative organizations are moving toward establishing web relations with customers. Bill Gates is talking about not selling products but "membership" to Microsoft, where electronic media such as the Internet will allow Microsoft to dialogue frequently with each of its customers, solicit their ideas and interests, respond quickly, and thereby create a viable, ongoing Microsoft community. This is the model that companies such as Merck, Dell, Schwab, and Cisco Systems are embracing. Use technology to link with your customers individually, to know your customers individually, and to offer easy avenues for them to get immediate information from you (whether it's about health, technology, or personal finance) and to give immediate input to you (feedback, ideas on product improvement, trends). Parenthetically, on a less customized "low-tech" basis, Harley Davidson has used this model effectively for years. With newsletters, phone calls, face-to-face meetings, and mixer celebrations, Harley Davidson has learned from and bonded with its fanatical HOG (Harley Owners Group) membership.

Increasingly, cutting-edge vendors across industries are beginning to understand that relying on price-obsessed commodity transactions with customers is ultimately a dead end, whereas cultivating collaborative, two-way, mutual-responsibility webs with customers à la Nypro/Vistakon and Milacron/GM is the wave of the future. A 1997 Andersen Consulting report concluded that any strategy focusing solely on product and service enhancement will be "short-lived." Instead, "forging long-term relationships with customers is the key to stability in increasingly dynamic markets."

A growing minority of progressive vendors are taking the Step IV message so seriously that they are beginning to do the unthinkable: they are retaining only those customers who wish to enter a weblike relationship and letting go of those who don't.

Let's go back to Nypro. Over a decade ago, the company made a seemingly insane decision to slash its customer base from 800 to approximately thirty. Explained CEO Gordon Lankton, "This is a low-margin, highly competitive business. If you have 800 customers, how often can you call on them? How can you get to know them?" Nypro chose to stick with those customers (typically *Fortune* 1000 industrials) who they felt could grow into long-term profitable relationships à la Giant Steps III and IV. Within a few years, Nypro's business tripled. Today, with sixty close customers, the legacy of that decision is such that 1997 sales were $433 million with $20.9 million in profit, as compared with $72 million in sales and $1.2 million in profit ten years ago.

Ken Olevson, who directed a remarkable turnaround in the ailing turbine engine repairer Sermatech Klock (a division of publicly traded Teleflex) between 1995 and 1997, told me that one of the key steps in the process was letting go of established customers who were consuming more of the company's resources (floor space, budget) than the income they were generating. While Sermatech was shifting its management philosophy toward quality relationships, these customers remained interested only in price and continued to play off Sermatech against competitors. Amazingly, once the decision was made to divorce, the customers that Sermatech Klock let go represented more than half of their established clientele!

The point is simple: fire those customers who don't share your business philosophy. Fire those who don't want to grow with you. In fact, as Sermatech Klock did, be professional and pave the way for them to go to competitors. Then concentrate on building your "share of customer" with your remaining base and expand the base with philosophically compatible customers. The idea is this: you can make more money, and collaborate with the brains of more interesting people, if you concentrate your efforts on customers who see the value of webs.

I recently pointed out the implications to a major retailer. The company's own data indicated that 10 percent of its customer base was supplying over 50 percent of their sales. Obviously, you can't fire customers who wish to enter a department store, but at least why not bring in those 10 percent loyal, knowledgeable customers as valued members of a web? Sure, for starters treat them better, the way we've seen Canadian Pacific Hotels do with its top clients. But now take it a step further: solicit their input, bring them into meetings, ask them to work with in-house people on key decisions regarding merchandise and marketing, and make it worthwhile for them to do so with appealing incentives. In other words, invite these customers into the web. Tap into their brains and obvious commitment to you. These long-term, knowledgeable customers can be far more valuable than consultants—and a helluva lot cheaper.

All in all, this discussion has significant implications for any organization. Let's review the facts. First, networks are rapidly growing in fits and starts whether you do anything about them or not. The enormous growth in outsourcing is one telltale sign. Another is the explosion of networked technology. Netscape cofounder Marc Andreessen notes that the 1990s has seen "the networking of the world, or the interconnecting of all businesses and a growing number of individuals in a seamless electronic web." Yet another clue is the boundary collapse across traditionally distinct businesses; for example, telecommunications is now an amalgam of voice, video, and data enterprises, while insurance, banking, and brokerage businesses are melding into an intertwined "financial services" industry.

The network trend is so pervasive that in a 1995 summit at MIT, one participant described the year 2020 as follows: "We imagined a world in which there are many, many firms with only one person, and many others with fewer than fifteen people. These firms would come together in temporary combinations for various projects. Work is already organized like this for producing movies, organizing conventions, and constructing large buildings."

Leapfrogging organizations don't wait for this trend to overwhelm them; they're at the forefront in capitalizing on it. They initiate the webs, they guide them, they orchestrate them. By embracing cooperative relationships with the cream of the crop (not necessarily the cheapest of the crop), organizations can sharply accelerate product development and market penetration, as well as significantly reduce operational and distribution costs—all vital tactics to nimbly vault over conventional wisdom and existing competition.

Thus, the picture of the leapfrogging organization will not be the solid, massed pyramid bolted to one locale and one way of doing things but, instead, an ever-multiplying, often temporary set of overlapping weblike circles—spread everywhere, permeable and ephemeral. Savvy leaders will transform their organizations into value-adding networks, combinations, clusters, and alliances, where each party brings to the table unique talent and expertise. Cultivating constructive relationships for the purpose of achieving extraordinary goals will be so important that it is safe to say that the value of your organization's relationships will be as important—if not more important—than the value of your organization's products.

One last point. The fuel of this Giant Step is *trust*. Not blind trust, but the kind of prudent trust that allows partners to be open, inclusive, and collaborative with one another rather than operating within the typical arm's-length, legalistic, often adversarial context that describes so many "partnerships" today.

Recently retired AT&T vice president William Moody, in a December 1996 talk at the University of San Francisco, said that the whole issue of trust is receiving rapidly increasing attention at his company—for reasons similar to the ones outlined here. Moody is no fool, and he readily admits that not everyone is trustworthy. Yet he also observes that real trust is an all-or-nothing affair. The organization, argues Moody, has one of two choices: "Either you build systems that unleash trust, or you build systems that diminish trust."

In most cases, it's the latter that predominate, and leaders in industry after industry are realizing that this must change. I gave a series of lectures at the Steel Service Center Institute in 1997. In the audiences were executives from every segment of the rough-and-tumble steel distribution system—from raw materials to finished product. Repeatedly, the topic that galvanized the most interest was this issue of trust. As one steel man told me, "in our business, trust is a joke. It's something you look up on page 45, paragraph 2, subsection 3 in a 50-page contract. We've got to learn how to trust other players in this business, or else we're all going to get killed. But people are afraid to take the first step."

Leaders must take that step, because the notion of distrustful webs is an oxymoron, a self-canceling phrase. Whether we're talking about joint ventures, activity-based accounting, or virtual alliances, trust is the glue that binds. The days of dealing with partners in an arm's-length, closed-door, hyperlegalistic manner or, even worse, rewarding purchasing managers for jerking around and lying to suppliers to save two bucks—those days are dying fast. Repeatedly, leaders in companies who are pursuing a Giant Step IV strategy have told me that they look for great and compatible webmates, not necessarily the cheapest, most expedient, or biggest ones. They look for webmates who share similar cultures, a similar vision about what the future can be, and similar values about how to get there. In short, they look for mates they can trust in sharing ideas, work groups, planning sessions, and databases. And they act with the assumption that any chosen ally is indeed trustworthy until that party violates that trust—and then they're out, regardless of tenure or price.

For fifteen years, Bank of America has used Milwaukee-based M & I Data Systems to develop and manage its ATM systems. Was M & I the lowest bidder? Not at all. It offered a competitive price, to be sure, but according to a senior B of A manager, it's kept the job because of "shared corporate values" and because M & I can best "help the bank decrease time to market for new product introduction and anticipate the dynamic changes in the financial industry without jeopardizing quality." Quite a different charge than simply running ATMs on a commodity "outsource" basis.

Meanwhile, a senior M & I official noted, "Our relationship with the Bank of America has evolved to a mutually beneficial partnership which is based on a high level of trust. This trust has been earned over the past 15 years. . . . Our relationship is characterized by an open and continuous exchange of ideas. This environment of mutual respect allows us to conditionally learn from one another." That's the spirit that M & I feels will propel it to even greater opportunity now that Bank of America has been absorbed into NationsBank.

If you're sincere about transforming your organization from an "I am an island" pile of bricks and mortar into a web of value-adding relationships, Commitments 9, 10, and 11 provide a number of practical paths toward this goal:

- Get real about what it takes to build a web team (Commitment 9).
- Invite your competitors in; don't fence them out (Commitment 10).
- Bless thy complaining customer (Commitment 11).

Commitment 9 puts the spotlight on relationship building. If you're really serious about creating value-enhancing web partnerships with customers, suppliers, and so on, challenge yourself to apply the Commitment 9 criteria for cultivating real dream teams, not pseudo-teams. The words here are *cultivate*, which means "grow, nourish, replenish," and *real*, which means "genuinely bonded with common goals, philosophies, values, and a sense of trust."

If you can meet the standards of this Commitment, you're already well on the road to transforming your organization into a web of relationships. The subsequent two Commitments, however, will really add fuel to the fire.

Commitment 10 calls for developing a new perspective about your competitors. Commit to transcending the simplistic us-versus-them mentality of the past. Respect your competitors, yes; monitor them, of course; but stop draining your creative energy by trying to come up with ways to "beat" them. Instead, use them as a spur to develop creative impulses that will grow your own business. And if competitors have special expertise or connections that can help, broaden your vision to include them in your strategic web rather than seal them out.

Commitment 11 challenges you with a particularly difficult challenge: deliberately create inviting, two-way webs with *complaining* customers. Yes, view all your customers as potential partners. But assuming you want to keep their business, pay careful attention to the complainers. Why? Because the complainers often hold the keys to greatest change, by surfacing important weaknesses and by prodding you to challenge the very way you run your business. Organizations that consciously create enticing webs to draw in valued but dissatisfied customers will not only keep those customers (and other dissatisfied customers who don't complain) but will also propel themselves forward in ways that they may never have anticipated.

Get Real About What It Takes to Build a Web Team

WEBS REQUIRE intimate teamwork. Lots of it. If you're sincere about cultivating genuine teamwork with your webmates (including partners, suppliers, and customers), ask yourself how your current alliances stack up on the eight points described in this section.

The December 22, 1997, issue of *Business Week* featured an article entitled "A Marriage Made in Hell," describing the failed alliance between American advertiser Foote, Cone & Belding and its French counterpart Publicis. Words such as "undercutting," "betrayal," "cheated," and "lied to" were sprinkled in the story.

Unfortunately, this is not an unusual tale. All too often, alliances such as strategic partnerships, joint ventures, product swaps, and equity investments are determined on the basis of a compelling logic about supposed synergies. But just as often, the people who make and applaud these deals fail to consider whether the relationships among the people who will live and breathe the alliances are in any way value enhancing.

Accordingly, it is not surprising how T. K. Das and Bing-Sheng Teng of the City University of New York recently summarize their research in *The Journal of General Management*:

> The number of newly forged alliances has been growing at more than 25 percent annually in recent years. Nevertheless, while many firms are rushing into such alliances as a quick-fix solution to their problems, the failure rate of strategic alliances has been consistently high. . . . Many partners terminated their alliances before achieving intended objectives. It has been a busy two-way street: companies

keep pulling themselves out of alliances even as more companies continue to forge new alliances.

This is all particularly ominous in view of the fact that the requirements for intimate, collaborative webs go well beyond what's usually acceptable in conventional partnershipping and outsourcing. Transforming your organization into a web of relationships means that the kinds of problems cited earlier could be devastating to your competitive position. With webs, the stakes are higher, and your exposure to the nuance of relationship is greater. Why? Well, let's review the basic premises of Giant Step IV. I have argued the following:

1. If any part of your organization is not a strategic point of differentiation, let it go. Cultivate relationships with exceptional players who are strong in what you're not. Release your cost centers and value-detracting overhead, and start pouring your capital and attention into what will make you a truly great company, à la Rolls-Royce Aerospace's perspective on EDS.

2. Even as you invest in your strategic point of differentiation, look among the best and brightest on the planet to join forces with, to chart new paths, and create extraordinary ideas, concepts, and products that you couldn't do alone, à la Fujitsu/FedEx/CTI, Lego/MIT, Teledesic/Boeing/Matra, Marconi/Motorola, and, again, Rolls-Royce Aerospace/EDS.

Points 1 and 2 are about organizational and personal relationships that take potential webmates to a new level of reality. Deal makers often patronizingly dismiss this relationship factor as "soft" stuff. But as Tom Peters has aptly noted, the "hard" stuff is soft and the "soft" stuff is hard. Doing the spreadsheets and the financials is less difficult than putting together people and systems to create something wonderful.

The examples cited in the prior section illustrate web relationships that are moving in the right direction. Although there is no one simple formula for creating successful webs, here are eight factors to consider if and your partners are serious about traveling this road. Rate yourself and your partners (current or potential) on this scale, and then ponder the brief postscript that follows.

1. CONSENSUS

Do members of your team share the same overarching goals and the same sense of commitment to the group? Consider these questions:

- Do you all agree on the team's vision and purpose: why it exists, where it's going, what it's trying to do, what its core priorities are? Or do these issues generate confusion and uncertainty—maybe even conflict—among members?
- Are you all committed to the same values, such as these: what do we stand for, how do we define success, what is ethical and fair behavior, and how should we behave toward each other? Or do the values that are ostensibly followed amount to so much lip service?
- Do people feel a sense of ownership in the team? Do they feel like they're a genuine, involved, participating, egalitarian part of it, and do they feel that this ownership is an important part of their work life? Or are they noncommittal, grudging participants, perhaps because they feel that membership in the group has little compelling purpose or payoff?

2. TRUST

Do members of your team really trust each other? Ask yourself these questions:

- Do people believe each other when communicating? Or are they a bit anxious that they are hearing partial truths and that hidden agendas exist?
- Do they believe that they can depend on and count on each other? Or do they feel that relying on others' goodwill and expertise is either naive or dangerous?
- When people interact and communicate with one another, is *honesty* the operative descriptor, or are *manipulation* and *deceit* more appropriate?
- Do team members feel safe with each other, or are they wary of each other's motives?

- Do people feel confident about each other's professional capacities and efforts? Or do they feel uncomfortable, perhaps suspicious, so that they've got to scrutinize others' actions to get the "right" results?

3. CANDOR

How open are your team members with each other? Ask yourself these questions:

- Can they be open and straight with each other about concerns, anxieties, hopes, fears, joys, or angers? Or do they wind up holding things in, muttering under their breath and throwing verbal darts at people behind their backs?
- Can they be forthright with each other about problems the team faces? Can they openly exchange criticisms of each other, the team as a whole, and the status quo in general while simultaneously generating alternatives and reviewing ideas for the future? Or do they tend to pull their punches with each other, carefully sniffing the wind before communicating at all?
- Do they share their "wins" and "losses" (goal attainment, setbacks, personal learning, personal reactions to events) with each other? Or do they camouflage these experiences for political reasons, while rationalizing negative outcomes with excuses and finger pointing?
- Are the communications and information-exchange among people marked by words such as *direct, frank, straightforward, undisguised,* and *plainspoken*? Or just the opposite?

4. RESPECT

To what extent do members of your "team" feel—and demonstrate—that they hold each other in esteem? Consider these questions:

- Are people aware of the full set of each other's skills, experiences, and expertise? Or is there a myopic ignorance of people's full array of talents?

- Do people genuinely—even naively—listen to each other's ideas and concerns? Or do they simply defend and promote their own preconceptions, with only a pretense of paying attention to what others believe?
- Do people publicly honor and recognize each other's efforts and contributions? Or are accomplishments taken for granted?
- Do people value each other's time? Or do they act in a way that suggests that others' time doesn't have much importance?
- Do people hold agreements and promises among themselves as sacred? For example, if someone says he will publicly support someone at a meeting, he does; if someone says she will show up for a meeting, she will—on time and prepared. Or are agreements and promises viewed expediently as "maybe—if it's convenient?"

5. CARING

Do people seem genuinely concerned about each other's personal welfare, as human beings? (Yes, this is a particularly squishy-soft concept, but it's quite important for intimate teamwork.) Again, some questions:

- Do people show sympathy for each other when personal and professional problems arise or empathy when occasions for joy arise? That is, are they sincere in showing concern to someone who is in distress, writing little notes and cards, giving gifts on birthdays and anniversaries?
- Do people help each other succeed and grow, and then share in the excitement of each other's accomplishments? Or are such concerns deemed unnecessary or childish?
- Do people transcend codependency—that is, do they hold each other to high standards of performance and provide each other with a fourfold combination of straight feedback, no-nonsense expectations, coaching, and compassion? Or do they confuse caring for people with indulging them, thereby—in the name of "caring"—failing to insist on high standards or to coach poor performance and

inappropriate behavior? Or even worse, do they justify a mistaken view of caring by inappropriately "rescuing" people whose behavior and performance consistently falls short of the mark?

6. COLLABORATION

Do people (both as individuals and as representatives of their organizations) emphasize working together, behaving as if their own goals and those of others in the team were in harmony?

- Do people act as if their own success will be enhanced by the success of the team, or do people act as if their own needs and those of the team are contradictory concepts?
- Does individuality emerge as unique contributions to the team or as egocentric self-aggrandizement?
- Do the individuals in the team share information, tools, and other resources with each other? Or do they tend to hoard and protect turf?
- When the team is working together, is the dominant mode a search for "win-win" solutions, or is the dominant mode a "win-lose" perspective in which team members are in subtle battle with each other for ostensibly scarce resources and rewards?
- When difficulties or crises occur, is the dominant response cooperative problem analysis? Or is it cover-my-rear blame analysis?
- Do team members make sure that every team member is included, is "in the know" and "in the loop"? Or does a laissez-faire, "I'm not my brother's keeper" mentality prevail?

7. MEANINGFUL RECOGNITION AND REWARDS

Do recognition and reward, formal and informal, reinforce team activities?

- Are team members recognized and rewarded for contributing to the team purpose and charter, or do team members feel that they're better off pursuing their own individual and organizational agendas, even while outwardly appearing to participate?
- Are recognition and rewards directly and significantly linked to team performance (achieving team goals)? Or are compensation and other goodies determined strictly by individual performance?
- Are team members recognized and rewarded for helping and coaching other team members? Or are such behaviors considered inconsequential when rewards are handed out?
- Are team members recognized and rewarded for a willingness and ability to learn and practice new, important skills and knowledge? Or is training and development considered an occasional "soft" perk (or obligation), not carefully aligned with team priorities?

8. TEAM INFLUENCE, AUTHORITY, AND BUSINESS CONNECTEDNESS

One can't separate the effectiveness of a partnership team from the total corporate environment within which it operates; hence, to what extent is the "team" integrated as an influential part of the partners' businesses?

- Are team purpose and goals clearly aligned with larger corporate strategies? Or are the purpose and goals seemingly unconnected to the bigger picture?
- Are "star" players represented on the team? Is membership on the team considered a plum assignment? Or is membership on the team considered a backwater assignment, maybe even counterproductive for career advancement?
- Does the team have the authority to do what it was organized to do? Or is a lot of time wasted playing political games and trying to overcome corporate resistance and bureaucracy?

- Is the organization investing financial, managerial, and time resources in the team, or does it let the team "sink or swim" with little support, hoping it somehow will survive?
- Does top management trust and respect decisions made by the team? Or does top management frequently second-guess, interfere in, or simply fail to act on the recommendations made by the team?

POSTSCRIPT

OK, I'm the first to admit that these eight dimensions represent ideals and that the questions themselves are stereotypical extremes. I know of no web whose partners would score perfectly on these dimensions. I suspect that only at the Pearly Gates would we find people who work in flawless harmony.

Nevertheless, the points are useful benchmarks of genuineness. I am confident that the Publicis/Foote, Cone & Belding alliance would have failed miserably on many of these dimensions. Using these criteria, I would also argue that many publicly trumpeted alliances are on shaky grounds. Furthermore, I predict that the seemingly successful webs cited in the prior section will remain successes only if the parties involved continue to score well on these eight dimensions. Hence, if you're serious about creating value-adding webs, and if you know that teamwork is key to leapfrogging the competition, you won't shirk from using the eight dimensions as a means to monitor your progress. It's a never-ending job, but the results are worth it.

Invite Your Competition In—
Don't Fence Them Out

VALENTINE'S DAY cards are probably seldom exchanged between executives of Sony and Philips, or Mercedes and Toyota,
or Microsoft and Sun. And you can be darned sure that FedEx
and United Airlines took full advantage of the 1997 UPS strike
and the 1998 Northwest Airlines strike, respectively. In short,
you don't have to love your competitors, but you'd be doing
yourself a great service if you judiciously included some of the
better ones in your web. The flip side is that obsessing on
"beating" your competitors will hurt you even more than it
will them. Read on.

Healthy competition is natural and inevitable in thriving economies; it's what makes capitalism such a powerful economic
force. It is so important that the exhaustive research of Harvard's Michael Porter allowed him to conclude that "vigorous
domestic rivalry" is the primary determinant of any nation's
economic strength within the international community.

In real life, however, many executives spend big bucks
and time obsessing about beating, pulverizing, or eliminating
their competition. But this path leads to neither progress nor
prosperity.

I have in front of me a *Wall Street Journal* article that describes how a senior executive of a large corporation "barks"
(very appropriate word) the following: "I want my people to
destroy our competitors, I want them to kill and crush them."
In my own consulting practice, I've frequently heard these
words used as strategic objectives. It all sounds tough and virile,

but let me briefly propose two major reasons that this sort of macho posturing is both counterproductive and outdated.

1. *When managers focus on squashing competitors, they are operating from neither a position of power nor a position of innovation.* The key to competitive advantage is to create new opportunities and lead the market rather than pay undue attention to what today's established competitors are doing. A strategy that is preoccupied with "beating" competitors is reactive, fear based, and myopic. It is reactive because management decisions by definition revolve around what others are currently doing; in effect, management that obsesses about beating competitors necessarily allows others to define the game and make the first moves.

Besides, because unexpected sources of competition are incessantly cropping up, an organization with a "kill the competitor" mind-set is forever frenetically doomed to run around and around, spending its creative energy trying to stamp out new fires.

A "crush the competitor" priority is also fear-based because the driving force for organizational motivation and teamwork is negative: to somehow liquidate a so-called dangerous alien (the competitor) before "it" destroys us. On both an organizational and a personal level, this approach is anxiety laden and exhausting.

Finally, a preoccupation with "beating" the competitor is myopic because the organization inevitably operates under the delusion that there are limited possibilities (death to the competitor) rather than a full range of exciting uncharted ones. Put it all together and it's easy to see what happened to Novell.

Between 1990 and 1993, when its stock price peaked, Provo, Utah–based Novell dominated the fast-growing corporate network software market. But Microsoft was growling and positioning its own Windows NT products as viable alternatives. So former chairman Ray Noorda, rather than concentrating on building Novell's momentum and brand name in this niche, instead became obsessed with "beating" Microsoft—even on the latter's turf of consumer products.

Novell's in-your-face assault of Microsoft's market involved a variety of costly acquisitions (such as Borland's WordPerfect word-processing suite and QuattroPro spreadsheet software). These acquisitions initially created an image of Novell as the new mano-a-mano competitor of Microsoft. But appearances deceived. The company's strategic focus became blurred and confused. Moreover, the acquisitions drained the company of the resources necessary to develop new product quickly and expand its presence in its hitherto profitable network business. Most important, says current CEO Eric Schmidt, "Novell was so distracted by all of its acquisitions, it missed sight of the importance of the Internet." This was an important oversight, because the common language of Internet threatened the proprietary nature of Novell's products.

Within four years, Novell's market share in its traditional stronghold had plummeted, whereas Microsoft's NT had climbed from practically 0 to 36 percent share. Further, Novell's forays into Microsoft's arena (word processing, spreadsheets) were a disaster.

Under new CEO Eric Schmidt, the company is seeing a tentative turnaround: fourth-quarter 1998 revenues of $298 million, an 11 percent increase over fourth-quarter 1997 revenues. Market share has stabilized at 50 percent. And in September 1998, Novell scored a first-to-market coup over Microsoft with its delivery of its latest product, NetWare 5. The reason for this turnaround is that Novell has let go of its "crush the competition" obsession and gone back to focusing on networked products (like NetWare), as well as a variety of Intranet and Internet services.

As mentioned throughout this book, cutting-edge companies are primarily interested in changing the rules of the entire game with fresh, unique market offerings. Review business history of the past twenty years and consider the breakthrough impact of Schwab's discount brokerage services, Dell Computer's no-intermediary distribution system, Amazon.com's cybermarket, Hewlett-Packard's LaserJet printers, and Merrill Lynch's early asset management account offerings. You'll probably conclude, as I did, that successful companies such as these were less obsessed with "killing" established players than in carving out new niches and creating hitherto nonexistent possibilities for their own businesses. Bottom line: the focus on beating competitors reflects narrow thinking—and narrow thinking will inevitably yield narrow results.

2. *When managers overemphasize the idea of beating competitors, they become oblivious to something more important: that some of these competitors can provide valuable sources of strategic opportunity as allies.*

Starbucks CEO Howard Schultz has correctly noted that "adversarial or distant relationships are not inevitable—nor are they the best way of doing business. Much can be gained by enlisting partners and colleagues who are committed to the same goals." Though it may stretch credibility, this statement applies to competitors. In fact, in today's helter-skelter economy, a failure to seek webs that pool expertise and resources even with traditional rivals can be damaging.

Here's why. When it comes to competition, I've already noted that the world is no longer a simple good guy versus bad guy affair. It's a much more tangled and ambiguous theater, as I found out when I downloaded my latest version of Microsoft's Explorer using my Netscape Navigator. Or when I learned that Novell CEO Schmidt met with Microsoft chairman Bill Gates several times in 1998 to discuss potential collaboration between the two companies (already, Schmidt is stating that Novell is repositioning NetWare to coexist with Microsoft's NT).

The reality, although it may violate conventional wisdom, is that competitors can be potentially valuable partners. Kirin, the largest brewery in Japan and third largest in the world, has for years had a licensing contract with its competitor Heineken, the number two in the world, to produce each other's beer in its manufacturing process—which means the parties must exchange information about technology and brewing formulas. The rationale is the same one underlying Seven-Up/RC Bottling Company's practice of brewing the product of competitors' Lipton and Arizona in the same tanks: lower production costs, lower shipping costs in targeted areas, better utilization of excess capacity.

Or consider this example: a number of local daily newspapers—from the Waco, Texas, *Herald Tribune* to the *Chicago Tribune*—are currently delivering the national edition of the *New York Times* to their interested subscribers. The *Times* typically pays the local paper about $0.25 for each home delivery ($0.50 on Sunday). This allows the local dailies to spread their fixed costs and raise their gross margins, while the *Times* capitalizes on established distribution systems to build its own revenue stream. *Times* executives now view these other dailies as complementary, not as competition.

A similar sentiment exists between CBS and NBC: CBS "shock jock" Don Imus is carried by MSNBC, augmenting the revenues of both companies. When CBS's 1996 show *Ink* bombed, ABC was not particularly overjoyed. Why? ABC has a stake in DreamWorks, which produces *Ink*. As an ABC executive commented: "It's planned schizophrenia. The rules are different."

Yes, indeed, they are, which means you can't automatically exclude competitors from your web. When Netscape and America Online agreed to produce compatible products a couple years ago, strategic alliance consultant David Raphael of Belmont, California–based Marcar Consulting told me, "They've figured out that they stand to make a lot more profit from standardization than from killing each other." Undoubtedly this relationship also helped pave the way for AOL's recent acquisition of Netscape, a move that may have enormous significance for E-commerce. Just as important, the fact that a collaborative history between the parties existed prior to the merger dramatically improves the odds that the deal will succeed.

You'll always be facing competition from somewhere, but you're more likely to leapfrog over it if you can selectively and collaboratively draw resources from any and all world-class players, including carefully selected competitors. Remember Sun's relationship with IBM in the development of Java language? The fact that IBM is so much larger than Sun means that more IBM people are currently working on Java than are Sun people.

In the brutal terrain of jet engine manufacturing, General Electric has joined forces with Pratt & Whitney to develop an engine for the Boeing 777-600 series aircraft that will be launched in the year 2000. Raphael notes that if both companies pursued the traditional course of "crushing" each other in pursuit of 777-600 contracts, each company could anticipate $200 to $300 million in operating profits over the next ten years. But Raphael's calculations indicate that this alliance will generate $900 million in operating profits over the same time period. Split two ways, that means a winning $450 million for each partner.

Furthermore, the alliance will allow GE to attain the standard chairman Jack Welch imposes on all GE businesses, which is to be number one or two in the sectors in which it plays. Without this alliance—especially given Rolls-Royce's presence—it is less likely that GE would attain this standard.

Finally, the alliance allows both parties to consolidate their experience and expertise toward creating a radically new type of engine. GE and Pratt & Whitney thus leapfrog over today's competitive feuding by collaboratively developing new technologies and infrastructures that will no doubt serve both of them well in the years to come in other markets.

If the action of take-no-prisoners GE is a surprise, how about the action of hypercompetitive Proctor & Gamble? On August 20, 1998, Proctor & Gamble hosted a two-day Internet summit in its Cincinnati headquarters. The summit was revolutionary for two reasons. First, P & G is revving up the stakes on Internet marketing and is, if appropriate, prepared to move 80 percent of its enormous advertising budget to that medium within five years (just as it moved 80 percent of its advertising budget from radio to TV within the five year span of 1950–1955). Second, P & G recognized that big steps in these unchartered waters require brainpower that exists beyond P & G walls and hence invited a wide array of outside guests to discuss new possibilities—including rivals such as Unilever and Clorox. In the consumer products world, reported one publication, that last step was "unthinkable." In the new world, I predict this step will be very thinkable. (By the way, to complete the web, the summit was broadcast live on the Internet, allowing anyone with a PC—competitor or otherwise—to "attend.")

Two notable quotes provide a useful final perspective on this issue. One, from Harvard's Paul Lawrence, writing for a 1997 American Management Association circular: "It is imperative for future managers to understand cooperative business alliances because, in the decades to come, managers will either be part of an alliance or be competing with one."

Combine that thought with this one, from Stewart Alsop, writing in the September 30, 1996, issue of *Fortune* magazine: "[In] today's computer business [who nowadays isn't in the computer business?], alliances with other companies—including competitors—are often more important than good relationships with customers."

In short, adopting a new inclusive mind-set allows you to see the world of "competitors" anew. Raphael's advice in this matter is straightforward. If you want to collaborate with competitors, first, be open to possibilities and simultaneously be careful. Second, start with a highly focused scope, a project, like both GE and P & G have done. Third, build trust and success and grow the partnership incrementally. Finally, never forget that partnerships—like marriages—require patience and persistence.

I think Raphael is right on target, and I would add to his list. I have found that differences in corporate cultures, systems, technologies, geographic distance, and, increasingly, disparate language, religion, and social mores must be ironed out. Permeating the entire partnership, and muddying the waters further, an air of distrust and sometimes mutual fear frequently exists and must be overcome, regardless of whether the partners previously were competitors or not. To do all of this, persistence is clearly a must.

The bottom line: choose the competitors that are world-class players in areas in which you're not, focus on establishing mutually enhancing goals, follow the eight "dream team" rules cited in Commitment 9, and something magical and paradoxical occurs: competitors wind up helping you leapfrog the competition.

These, then, are the reasons that the whole "crushing" mentality is a dead-end, which itself is a testament to a couple of larger trends in business today. Crushing becomes particularly self-defeating in a world that is becoming more and more interdependent. In an interdependent economy, our self-interests and destinies are dependent on others. Accordingly, the quality of relationships that one establishes with customers, vendors, suppliers, and partners becomes a key strategic success factor.

Collaboration, candor, and trust within these relationships become strategic imperatives. In this kind of world, organizations that insist on playing the role of squinty-eyed, fast-shooting cowboy or goon-like Mafioso will not fare well.

Once we eliminate crushing from our planning repertoire and focus instead on leapfrogging, we are free to consider more sensible advice about dealing with competitors:

1. *Accept them.* They or others will always be there; that's the nature of free markets.
2. *Be aware of them.* Keep a general lookout, but don't get bogged down in the paralysis of incessant competitive analysis.
3. *Respect them.* Welcome them as spurs to your own motivation and efforts; remember that pride, arrogance, and a "not invented here" corporate culture are always precursors to a fall.
4. *Whenever possible, join them in a web.* They may have valuable skills and networks you don't and vice versa; so dialogue with them, learn from them, and probe joint opportunities with them.

Bless Thy
Complaining Customer

ARE YOU including customers in key meetings, as FedEx and Fujitsu do? Are you sharing databases with your customers, as Cisco Systems and Nypro do? Are you living with your customers on their premises, as EDS and Milacron do? Good, that means you're starting to think in terms of webs. Then let me now test your courage and humility to the nth degree: are you willing to include your vociferous, irritating, *complaining* customers in your web? If you don't want to keep their business (remember our discussion of "firing" customers), the answer to that question is an obvious no. But otherwise, bringing complaining customers into your web can be a stroke of genius.

First, let's agree that there are customers from hell out there. Kris Anderson of Minneapolis-based Performance Research Associates hit the bull's-eye when she said, "If you don't believe there is such a thing as a customer from hell, you must be a consultant or a CEO. No one who works with the public on a regular basis can doubt their existence." Starry-eyed souls who spout the line that "the customer is always right" are usually well buffered from the bizarros of the world whom the poor frontline folks periodically have to deal with.

There is no excuse for tolerating individuals who are ugly, abusive, destructive, or potentially violent with your staff. Customers from hell exist, and they must be dealt with firmly, fairly, quickly, and unapologetically. Any other response is an insult to your employees and a double-insult to the vast majority of customers who are decent human beings.

177

On the other hand, my colleagues Ron Zemke and Chip Bell, also of Performance Research Associates, point out that there's a critical difference between *a customer from hell* and *a customer who's been through hell*. But they often look alike. Bell contends that because the number of customers who are truly malicious or evil is extremely rare, it's far better to first assume that they've been through hell. And if they really have been through hell, then you had better believe that other customers are going through hell, and you're going to wind up losing everyone's business. I would take it a step further: each time you respond inappropriately to customers who have gone through hell, you push them closer to the door marked "customer from hell."

On the other hand, you can view a customer who has gone through hell as potentially one of your most value-adding partners—if you (and your company) really and truly listen to his or her concerns and then respond appropriately, sincerely, and dramatically. Here's why: every customer complaint is a golden nugget of information for any company, which is why leaders should gratefully pounce on them. They can use complaints as fuel to improve current operations. They can use them as leverage to enhance product and service quality and to educate personnel as to what's really important. They can analyze them to glean subtle clues for breakthroughs in the products and services themselves. That's because savvy leaders know that customers who actually take the time to complain are as valuable to bottom-line financials as any MBA analyst or high-priced consultant.

To be sure, complainers are bothersome. But remember that each complaining customer is telling the vendor three things:

1. *My business and I are still wooable* if you personally show me you care about me and fix your mess (even though I say you've lost me, if I didn't care, I'd just walk).
2. *I represent others* (you ought to thank me; quieter customers who are just as disgruntled have silently moved on or are looking to do so at the first opportunity).
3. *I am telling you the end result of glitches* in your systems and business philosophy (consider me a fire alarm that's

warning you that whatever it is you're doing, you had better change, and fast!).

So, to reiterate: yes, indeed, there are customers from hell, and they'll come at you without provocation. Dump them politely but fast. Prosecute them if they go over the edge. Don't ever expect your frontline people to tolerate their abuses.

But, remember, customers from hell are the rare exception to the rule. Before you label every angry complaining customer a villain, think about your dependence on these people, think about how valuable it would be to respond to them in empathetic, constructive, inclusionary, weblike ways, and think about what a pain in the neck we all are when we act the role of customers in our personal lives and are turned away, disappointed.

Customers' perceptions are usually well founded. You know this from your own experiences as a dissatisfied customer. Therefore, if you want to differentiate yourself in the marketplace and use complaining customers as allies in leapfrogging the competition, consider the following steps:

1. MAKE IT VERY EASY FOR CUSTOMERS TO COMPLAIN.

I mean really easy. Have a well-publicized twenty-four-hour, toll-free phone line with many extensions staffed by competent, well-trained, carefully selected individuals who are especially good at tracking and handling complaints. Create easy-to-fill-out survey cards with return postage on products, and mail them with invoices or other correspondence. Position suggestion boxes in as many sites as possible. Consider adding home phone numbers to all business cards. And don't forget to establish easy electronic accessibility to your central terminals.

If you're not sure whether you're hearing enough, periodically interview a sample of customers to find out specifically how to make it easier for them to convey any problems or frustrations.

Proactively solicit complaints. Customer service departments and toll-free customer assistance centers are not enough. You—yes, you—should call customers and ex-customers directly with a list of specific questions, and you should do so regularly. (More on this later.) Carefully probe what didn't work, what didn't go well, or what could have been done better. Hold regular focus groups with customers; solicit specific, even "minor," sources of hassle and irritation. Don't hire consultants to do it for you. Every manager should be a part of at least one focus group a month.

Learn from Milliken's (textiles) and Northwest Mutual Life's practice of flying in customers and putting them up on-site to air their views, or Stew Leonard's (grocery) bimonthly customer focus groups, attended by top management. Take the attitude of one California hospital CEO who makes it a point of visiting discharged patients at their homes, where they're secure and comfortable, to really get good feedback.

2. WORK LIKE MAD TO RESPOND TO EACH AND EVERY COMPLAINT.

Begin by logging every customer complaint from all sources and insisting that everyone in management access that information in any decision making. Follow the lead of an L. L. Bean executive who said, "Track, by computer, every customer complaint. Update and follow up daily." Or Staples (office supplies), which tracks every complaint and uses those data to drive the adjustment of products, policies, and guidelines.

Then take it a step further with the responsibility for follow-through. Once the information is available, somebody has to contact each complainer and see that the problem is fixed, customer satisfaction is assured, and appropriate changes are championed throughout the organization. Every manager's job description should include being that "somebody" regularly, every month.

Two key points here: first, complaints must be handled "fast and friendly." By *fast* I mean from the customer's time perspective, not from the legal department's. By *friendly* I mean that customers are delighted by the empathy that somebody in your organization shows for the hassles they have had to undergo. Ron Zemke's research indicates that nearly 40 percent of a customer's perception of service is influenced by how well the vendor responds to unforeseen problems. Employees at Ritz-Carlton hotels, Disney theme parks, and Dell Computer phone lines seem to "get" this, and it pays off at those organizations.

Second, the system (structure, policies, habits) must be fixed so that the glitch that caused the problem will not occur with a future customer. Fixing the system also will allow you to take advantage of the complaint to innovate in your product and service offerings. One 3M executive mentioned that more than 50 percent of the new product innovations in his division came from the ideas of complainers. Unsurprisingly, he geared a lot of his time to listening.

Remember, if you don't do number 2, number 1 is a waste of time. Stew Leonard, Jr., once told me an interesting story. His grocery store has a large suggestion box that is usually filled to capacity by the end of the day. Every morning the information of the prior day is logged, and by late morning the list is on every manager's desk. Action is expected immediately; problems are to be solved that day, if possible. "A couple years ago we became complacent," Leonard remarked. "We began to make up the list every three or four days instead of every day. The volume of suggestions gradually went down. But our focus groups told us that dissatisfaction was going up. This was weird: we never told customers that we were not responding to the suggestion box every day, but somehow they figured it out. As soon as we went back to our once-a-day commitment, the suggestion box started to fill up again."

3. EDUCATE, EDUCATE, EDUCATE.

In orientation. In management development sessions. In memos and briefings. In meetings and stump speeches. Use case studies of complaints in training classes. Include a "customer panel" in every management retreat. Teach people about the strategic and financial value of complaints, about the need for urgency in responding, and, perhaps most important, that everyone owns the problem—not just the "customer service" people. Teach people why it's counterproductive to label complainers as "difficult customers" or "customers from hell" who "gripe" and "bellyache." Instead, teach people that complainers are better viewed as allies, consultants, guests of honor—anything as long as it reflects their contribution to the success of our organizations and our careers.

4. APPROACH COMPLAINTS AS OPERATIONAL PROBLEMS AND STRATEGIC OPPORTUNITIES.

This means putting complaints in the category of research and information, not personal attacks. It means replacing blame analysis with problem analysis. It means using complaints to help develop better operations and "planned recovery systems" for when things do break down. It means viewing complaints in the Renaissance tradition, in which the critic was your ally, helping you better focus on reality. A few years ago a health-care executive told me that once his hospital system literally relabeled "patient complaint" forms as "consultant reports," managers began to pay close attention to the information.

5. MAKE COMPLAINTS VISIBLE.

Post quantitative complaint data publicly on walls and Web sites. Post raw unedited letters and phone call transcripts on bulletin boards. Reprint them in newsletters. Read and discuss them in meetings. Publicize responses to the complaints. Identify and laud the folks who did the responding.

6. ADJUST QUALITY MEASURES, PERFORMANCE REVIEW, AND COMPENSATION ACCORDINGLY.

What gets measured and rewarded gets done. Quality measures should always incorporate pervasive customer complaints. One manufacturer found its customers rated the product lower because the user manual was so poor. Federal Express's Service Quality Index yields a score based on the highest-to-lowest hassle factors as experienced and defined by the customer.

Key questions for managers' performance evaluation and pay might include the following: how many complaints have you solicited? How many firefighting teams have you been on? How have you used the input of complainers to improve this organization? Rewarding managers for simply "reducing" complaints will only encourage cheating. What's desired is their discovering and acting on complaints.

7. REWARD COMPLAINERS.

These people can help your business prosper, and their advice is often priceless. Visible displays of your gratitude not only make good common sense but also send a signal to them and to your organization. Consider thank-you notes and phone calls, small cash rewards, plaques and certificates, gifts, "consultant of the month" awards, feature stories in company newsletters, and periodic celebrations with complainers as guests of honor. Even better, reward them by officially inviting them to join your problem-solving teams, which is the next point.

8. MAKE THEM PART OF THE TEAM.

Here's the climax: bring in disgruntled customers as a part of your extended web. They've got plenty to say, plenty to advise, and, on top of that, they're the ones who are paying the bills. Consider the value of having an unhappy customer share his experiences and opinions with your staff or be part of a training session (from personal experience, I can assure you that nothing grabs managers' attention like eyeballing a customer who lays it on the line). Consider the value of inviting an unhappy customer (with pay) to join a project team aimed at radical improvement of operations or a team aimed at revamping the procedures followed by frontline people who regularly deal with customers. In short, instead of viewing complainers as "difficult" customers or as nut cases, why not assume that they're mad as hell about something and that by complaining they're doing what a lot of other silent, unhappy customers only fantasize about doing? By including, involving, and inviting the complaining customers as part of your team, you can take their pent-up energy and funnel it into a constructive consultative role to help figure out ways to solve these problems so that nobody else experiences them. And when you do that, a few nice things occur. One, their dissatisfaction with us disintegrates. Two, they can help unearth current problems and develop solutions that make a real difference to customers. Three, they and their stories galvanize you with a sense of urgency—and enthusiasm—as dramatic changes are executed in the organization. All rather vital spurs to leapfrogging the competition, don't you agree?

In fact, as we end this Giant Step, let's note that if we can stretch ourselves to include so-called "complainers" in our web, there's no reason that we can't commit to getting *anyone*, anywhere who is world-class into our web as quickly as possible.

GIANT STEP V

EAT CHANGE FOR BREAKFAST— SERVE IT UP FOR EVERY MEAL

Bernard Rapoport is the chairman and CEO of the billion-dollar American Income Life Insurance company, a Waco, Texas-based company that concentrates on providing insurance to members of labor unions. As an active, vigorous eighty-two-year-old, he has a rather unique historical perspective on things, and he tells an instructive story about his childhood in Texas.

"Whenever we climbed into our Model T Ford for the trip from San Antonio to Austin, we could expect to have four or five flats along the way. They were bothersome, but fortunately all it took to fix a flat back then was to take the tire off, put a cold patch on the inner tube, and get back on the road. It took maybe a couple of minutes.

"But there was one day I've never forgotten. Just as we were coming into Austin, we felt yet another flat. We stopped, climbed out of the car, and when Papa looked at the tube, what he said was, 'Oh, my God, there's no more space to patch. We're going to have to buy a new one.'

"I suspect that's the state of the world today. We've run out of patch room. For so many of the problems we face in this world, it's time to buy new tires."

That is the essence of Giant Step V—your role as a leader is to help people in your organization cease patching problems with old solutions and help them instead put on new tires, new solutions, to navigate the highways of the emerging millennium successfully. It's the most important and the most difficult task any leader will face.

I thought about Bernie Rapoport's story during a recent conversation with a CEO of a struggling $100 million company. He complained that every year he would wind up spending literally two months immersed in an abhorrent, wasteful, budgeting process. I pointed out that companies such as Quad/Graphics place minimal emphasis on annual capital budgets and instead use computer technology to crank out a daily income statement that goes immediately to decentralized business units (all with P & L accountability), which in turn use it as a daily guide for financing. I told the CEO that his own company was set up to do the same; his newly decentralized structure was in place, as was the information technology.

The logic was compelling: Quad/Graphics chairman Harry Quadracchi asks, "Why is it that so many companies insist on having a twelve-month budget, drawn up in November of one year, based on still-incomplete numbers, that will be the Bible for running the company as far away as December of the following year?" The CEO I conversed with ruefully admitted that he was spending nearly 20 percent of his fiscal year on this minutia rather than using the time to concentrate on growing his business.

"So," I said, "what are you going to do? Are you going to at least investigate the possibilities?" Embarrassed, he muttered something and quickly changed the subject. His response basically meant only one answer: negative. His complaints notwithstanding, he was apparently resigned to the known routine of patching old tires.

"Change" and the need for it is the hot issue nowadays. We talk about it a lot in management retreats, but back home, the audio of talk and the video of action are often at odds. Big batches of sound and fury are followed by tepid, tentative action, or quick, short-lived fads. Fundamental overhaul is rare; a culture of constant renewal is even rarer. As author and consultant Jim O'Toole has noted, we often fall back on the "ideology of comfort and the tyranny of custom."

Why is this? Why is change such a challenge for us? Why do we have such a difficult time dealing with it? Dan Sweeney, a vice president in IBM's consultancy practice, recently E-mailed me some thoughtful perspectives on this question.

"I think we all have an inherent belief or assumption that our lives, and especially our business lives ought to be stable—they ought to be predictable. We think, at least implicitly, that stability, constancy, and predictability are the natural ways of things.

"In fact, we as managers work very hard to bring our business operations and organizations to a point of stability, constancy, and predictability—to an equilibrium position. We strive for a smooth-running, fine-tuned, variance-free operation. This, after all, we have been taught, is a mark of a good manager. This is the way, we believe, things ought to be. Certainly, to the degree that knowledge is power, and change invalidates that knowledge, then change robs us of power. Change robs us of our ability to know and therefore to manage our future. It robs us of our sense of control over our affairs. The prospect of such a loss will indeed raise fear and anxiety in the hearts and souls of executives used to dealing from reliable knowledge and exercising its consequent power."

Well put. So what's the solution? Sweeney has a couple ideas:

"Purge the assumption of stability from your view of the world. Recognize that stability, constancy, and predictability are unnatural circumstances. Stability itself is an aberration. Recognize that life, even our business and economic life, is inherently dynamic, largely unpredictable, somewhat random, and happily full of surprises.

"Don't concentrate on the past except as a source of lessons. Don't expect things to return to a 'normal.' Don't try to alter the present; it's simply too late—you can't do anything about it. Keep your management attention clearly focused on the only thing you can influence—but that you know the least about—the future."

Sweeney is definitely onto something. During a panel discussion with attendees of the American Management Association's M2 conference in San Francisco in November 1998, participants regularly brought up the need to "manage change." Peter Drucker, who happened to be moderating the panel, finally had enough. "All this talk about managing change is nonsense," he admonished the panel. "One can't manage change. One can only be ahead of it."

A participant later told me, "I guess Drucker was saying that you have to be proactive in making change." I agreed but suggested that her perspective was only a small part of the message.

I myself am speculating on Drucker's motive, but I think he hit on a much larger truth. "Managing change" sounds nifty, because it suggests that there is some sort of nice, neat, orderly, linear, predictable, routine path to change. Perfect fodder for bureaucrats and for consultants peddling this year's fad. Wrap change around a technique and an orderly structure—in other words, "manage" it—and you'll be successful.

And it's all nonsense. Change is messy, unruly, chaotic, and unpredictable. It wreaks havoc on plans and egos. It rips an organization inside out. It's not an analytically detached process; it's an emotional process—both painful and joyful.

Yes, of course you should have goals and a broad plan of action. But realize you can't control the process. You can't predict either the unfolding events or the outcomes. In other words, don't worry about the inevitable chaos; expect it, deal with it, revel in it. You lead change, you cause change, you prepare people for it and pull them along, and then, like heading into Class V white water rapids, you get swept into it and confront the realities as they come at you fast and furious. And then you celebrate like crazy when you come through it. Frankly, that's why change is so attractive to so many entrepreneurial businesspeople—because it requires constant innovation and because "managers" haven't figured out a way to fence it in and anesthetize it.

Back to Dan Sweeney, who was astute enough to offer one last piece of advice: mainly, to stay alert to the dangers of incrementalism. He quotes an executive in the 1940s:

"The businessman who concentrates on incremental (present) decisions makes no major gamble and takes no major risk save the risk that his business may fail (or succeed) incrementally. The businessman who probes the future with strategic decisions plays for much larger stakes."

That statement was made over fifty years ago. Today, the stakes are higher. So much so that if you're not playing for large stakes, you're simply not playing. Leapfrogging the competition is about going for the largest stakes of all, and by definition, you can't leapfrog across a chasm in little steps.

This message was brought home to me vividly during a meeting at the national headquarters of Toyota Motor Sales, U.S.A. During our meeting, one Toyota vice president, Bryan Bergsteinsson, summarized the reality set at Toyota with one simple, powerful declaration: "*Kai-zen* is not enough." *Kai-zen*, of course, is the Japanese term referring to continuous improvement of current processes. It is the foundation for modern TQM efforts. It is the core of incremental efforts in strategy and operations. In most organizations, *kai-zen*—whether referred to by that name or not—is at the heart of management philosophy and change interventions. Saying that *kai-zen* is no longer enough borders on radicalism. At Toyota, saying that *kai-zen* is not enough stops just short of heresy.

But "nonrevolutionary change makes no sense in the face of the emerging consumer revolution," as senior vice president Douglas West explained to me. With consumers able to choose from a myriad of cars from a variety of powerful global competitors, and with their ability to use new retailers (e.g., Car Max and AutoNation) and new distribution sources (car brokers, the Internet) to vastly enhance their options, Toyota is learning what every business in every industry is learning: incremental change via "continuous improvement" of products and processes is absolutely necessary for surviving, but it is no longer enough for thriving. To leapfrog the competition, and to make sure nobody is going to leapfrog over you, much more is required.

How much more?

Well, CEO Jim Thompson of the Vallen Corporation, who is transitioning his company from a seller of low-margin industrial

safety products to a purveyor of high-value industrial safety expertise, tells me that "we have to change faster than the outside
environment does." That's a tall order, and he's absolutely
right. And this is where leadership comes into play. As futurist
Alvin Toffler has observed, "the manager who can't conceive of
a radical alternative to the way things are being done . . . isn't
going to survive very long." Neither will his or her organization. Leaders develop radical alternatives, and, just as important, they mobilize others to do the same. Nypro executive
Brian Jones summarized it nicely in Tom Peters's newsletter *On
Achieving Excellence* a few years ago:

> "I went to business school, and they teach you fundamentals of
> management—direct, control, plan, cut costs. It's the wrong thing
> to teach. They should be teaching people what their job is, which is
> to reinvent the system within which people work."

Over the past few years, my research has led me to conclude
that the most effective leaders are those who view their role as
provocateurs of change. It's those managers who combine expertise, initiative, and the personal responsibility to provoke
change—regardless of whether or not their people are theoreti-
cally "ready" for it—who will most likely guide their organizations to leapfrog their competition.

I find it intriguing that three exceptional leaders—Lars
Kolind (Oticon), Harry Quadracchi (Quad/Graphics), and the
late Bill McGowan (MCI)—independently voiced the same
opinion: that the leader's job is to be not the chief "organizer"
but the chief "disorganizer."

Most of us have sufficient skills and motivation to succeed as
leaders. What we most often lack is the will, the perseverance,
the obstinate pigheadedness to be disorganizers—that is, to
ruffle routines, disrupt complacency, challenge processes, and
cause constructive disequilibrium—and to do so every day because we believe that it's our job to do so. It's our leadership responsibility, even our fiduciary obligation. When we take all
that on, we begin to understand the magnitude of Giant Step V.
This section provides a few clues about what leaders can do to
create an organization that does indeed serve up change for
every meal.

First, managers who live Giant Step V are bone-honest: when they talk about making change, about mobilizing to leapfrog the competition, they walk the talk. They engender a sense of understanding (why the need to leapfrog), they impart a sense of urgency (why we need to change *now*), and they lead a daily discipline that is visibly consistent with the new priorities and values they are espousing.

Furthermore, they not only delineate a stretch-the-envelope visionary direction for the organization, but they also ensure that it inspires everyone emotionally to make the leap of faith. They ensure that it becomes shared and "owned" by everyone. As part of this process, they carefully avoid the pitfalls of fads; they reject the idea of pat solutions and magic bullets. They are skeptical of any quick-fix programs and painless promises of salvation. They know that leapfrogging the competition requires all-hands courage, commitment, perseverance— and shared sacrifice.

Next, leaders who live Giant Step V have the self-insight and self-confidence to change themselves, not just their organization. While they are uncompromising in viewing their role as provocateurs of change, they seek constant feedback from employees and customers alike, and they are not afraid to adjust their personal styles or short-term decisions when it helps the organization make big transitions toward big goals.

Finally, they are eternally vigilant against the danger of complacency and arrogance; in fact, they feel and induce a sense of urgency *especially* when the numbers look good. They know that after they do leapfrog the competition, a kiss of death is just staying put, as in, "Why fix it if it ain't broke?" Leapfrogging the competition requires eternal vigilance, which no doubt is why Intel chairman Andy Grove so aptly entitled his most recent book *Only the Paranoid Survive*.

It should be no surprise that dominant players such as Microsoft, Intel, and Gillette manage to avoid the dread disease of complacency, because the spirit of Grove's message is maniacally endorsed by chairmen Bill Gates, Andy Grove, and Alfred Zeien, respectively. So if your company's numbers look good today, beware! There's always tomorrow. If you successfully leapfrog the competition tomorrow, beware again! There's always the day after tomorrow. Accepting and confronting that reality is at the core of Giant Step V.

This section discusses all these attributes and behaviors in some detail and provides a fitting finale to the challenge facing any organization that wants to thrive in the emerging millennium. When all is said and done, carrying out these five Giant Steps requires leaders who themselves are not afraid of change; in fact, they relish it both personally and professionally. With leaders like this, transformation occurs, and our organizations are imbued with life, direction, and hope.

Giant Step V is a call to arms to all would-be leaders. It is particularly important because without a leader's unyielding commitment to carrying out Step V, Steps I, II, III, and IV will simply not occur.

To serve up change as the exciting strategic opportunity that it is, this section will show that one needs to embrace four personal Commitments:

1. Get honest—walk the talk (Commitment 12).
2. Don't get snookered by fads du jour (Commitment 13).
3. Sponge up daily doses of reality (Commitment 14).
4. Beware the danger of success (Commitment 15).

The message of Commitment 12 is simple: if you want to make change in your organization, you've got to emulate the behavior you want to see. No more lip service. No more programs of the month. No more audio-video mismatches. Commitment 12 notes that the essence of leadership is visibly challenging the process in moving toward your goals—daily. To help you do that, the section provides a powerful prescription I call "U2D2."

The underlying theme of Commitment 13 is that if you are committed to leapfrogging the competition, you have to avoid management fads du jour. Like the Sirens beckoning Ulysses, management fads entice all of us. And like those ancient ladies, they will destroy. To drive the point home, Commitment 13 presents the fallout from three management approaches that have genuine merit as concepts but that in practice have too often become destructive fads. I'm speaking about TQM, reengineering, and the mania of deal making for deal making's sake.

Commitment 14 warns us that even as we are making change, we must stay in touch. This Commitment challenges us to enthusiastically seek a *daily* dose of reality from all key stakeholders—customers in particular, employees, and partners—and to insist that all our colleagues do the same. No more substituting laundered reports for face-to-face interactions with critical constituencies. No more surrounding ourselves with gilded trappings and yes-man gatekeepers for the purpose of seeking shelter from people with whom we ought to be rubbing our bellies.

We must continually soak up direct, unfiltered feedback from key constituencies, especially customers, to get a reality check on how we're doing vis-à-vis our strategic priorities. It is that unfiltered feedback that will fuel us to change far quicker than simply attending an off-site or reading yet another article entitled "Change or Die."

Commitment 15 is the wrap-up that reminds us that one of the best predictors of business failure is business success, because success in so many companies is followed by that intervening variable called complacency—or even worse, arrogance. As we saw in the earlier discussion of the Thomas Lawson Syndrome, business history has too often been littered with the carcasses of companies that believed their own press clippings. This chapter relates a more subtle fable, about one company that seemed to follow the right path toward listening but in reality was too comfortable with itself to follow up on the information that emerged—until too late.

The message is clear: beware the danger of success, even after you initially leapfrog the competition. There's always tomorrow's race, and then another the following day. Leapfrogging the competition is not a one-shot affair. That's what makes the business of business so fascinating and so compelling.

More than fifty years ago, the prominent educator and philosopher John Dewey noted that the great discoveries in science and medicine "always entail the destruction of or disintegration of old knowledge before the new can be created." He concluded, therefore, that what our society needs are many iconoclastic individuals, each of whom is a "minister of disturbance, a source of annoyance, a destroyer of routine, an underminer of complacence."

Our organizations need leaders with those attributes to confront the chaos of today's marketplace. That's the message of Giant Step V. After reading the remainder of this book, you might just be ready to label your job title as Minister of Disturbance or Destroyer of Routine on your business cards. Will you at least consider it? Because that's who you'll need to be. The following sections will show you how.

Get Honest—
Walk the Talk

Too often, executives and managers believe they can achieve meaningful change in their organizations while, on a personal level, maintaining their current behaviors, current schedules, and current calendars. It doesn't work. Leapfrogging the competition is a process that requires leaders who personally eat change for breakfast, every day, to demonstrate publicly commitment to a cause. If you're ready to walk the talk, the following section will provide both an antidote to the "how to get started" blues and a path toward sustaining the momentum.

The late Bill Graham built an exceptional organization in the late 1960s, Bill Graham Presents, to promote, produce, and manage rock concerts. In the hitherto chaotic, sleazy, and sometimes violent world of rock concerts, Bill Graham Presents redefined the terrain with a mix of precision, control, creativity, and love, which is precisely why most major rock bands insisted on using Bill Graham Presents. They knew that a Bill Graham Presents concert would be tight, professional, and enjoyable. They could count on the fact that every detail—such as staging, sound system, lighting, seating, ticketing, security, ancillary product sales, personal attention, and final payment—would be taken care of by people who knew and loved the business intimately. Customers, in turn, knew that a Bill Graham Presents concert would be honest, clockwork-efficient, safe, and fun. This was a radical change.

Graham was not universally liked, but he inspired the utmost respect in the industry and a fierce loyalty among his employees and clients. He articulated an uncompromising image of the perfect rock concert, and he demonstrated what music people called "the mania"—an absolute passion, even fanaticism—for his craft and for the myriad details necessary to bring the image of the perfect concert to fruition. More important, he was able to convey that image to others and inspire them to share his crusade. By role-modeling his own passion, by holding himself and others to higher-than-high professional standards, by fomenting creativity and pure fun as crucial strategic priorities, and by being willing to hire passionate people and turn them loose to make it happen, he inspired a legacy that has endured at Bill Graham Presents even after his death.

Bill Graham walked the talk. He challenged the conventional way of doing business, called for a dramatically different business model, and spent his daily actions building support, cooperation, and momentum for his quest. Bill Graham illustrated a set of change—tools that I've come to call "U2D2." Consider U2D2 a prescription that, if taken daily for the rest of your professional life, will allow you too to become a credible, transformational leader, one who will be able to create a corporate culture where change is devoured at every meal on behalf of exceptional causes.

Before ingesting any prescription, a smart consumer like you demands to know its ingredients. Fair enough. The basic elements of U2D2 are *understanding, urgency, direction,* and *discipline.* Let's review each in turn.

U1—Understanding

Leaders are often ineffective at creating change because their people are in the dark. I cannot tell you how often I have spoken to employees and managers who are ignorant of the organization's market pressures, financial burdens, and strategic dilemmas. That's a major reason that they're suspicious of change or resistant to it.

Effective leaders work daily to ensure that everyone in the organization understands why perpetual change is necessary. They share the dangers and opportunities that confront the company, the steps that might be taken and why, and the sorts of contributions and behaviors that are required from everyone. They use all communication channels—newsletters, E-mail, intranets, public forums, small-group discussions, one-on-ones— to disseminate news and information about new competitors, new technologies, and new partnership opportunities. They discuss the numbers: sales, margins, cycle times, investor reactions, customer service issues, customer defections, and quality data. They talk about trends in costs, earnings, returns, and market share. They explore options and responses, both strategic and tactical. They invite response and feedback. They demand that written and electronic sources of direct communication be accessible to everyone. They insist that everyone be "in the know." They are rabid partisans of Giant Step II.

Even beyond this: by their own behavior, effective leaders personally demonstrate in every little way their personal commitment to keeping people "in the know." It might be Microsoft's Bill Gates, diligently responding to scores of E-mail messages from employees daily or Atlantic City Medical Center's George Lynn holding freewheeling public "speakeasies" with employees in all shifts. It might be Springfield Remanufacturing's Jack Stack regularly debating the implications of a multipage financial statement with groups of blue-collar employees. It might be Nellcor Puritan Bennett's Ray Larkin or Southwest Airlines' Herb Kelleher roaming their company sites to be personally accessible to anyone.

The idea behind U1 is simple. You won't generate ownership or commitment to any intervention if people don't "get" what you're trying to do, and why.

That's why understanding is the first component of U2D2. When executives tell me that their most pressing frustration is getting people to "buy in" to the need for change, I suspect that the executives are the only ones who have intimate access and exposure to the reasons that the interventions are critical.

U2—Urgency

Effective leaders are repulsed by complacency. When they hear sentiments such as "If it ain't broke, don't fix it," they become alarmed. Effective leaders realize that today's numbers (earnings, market share, etc.) are simply a reflection of what the organization did yesterday. If the numbers are good today, the organization made the right moves yesterday. But because only the naive believe that tomorrow will look like today, only the doubly naive believe that perpetuating yesterday's moves will lead to tomorrow's successes.

Accordingly, injecting a sense of urgency into the organization becomes a top priority for real leaders. Their ongoing preoccupation is shaking people out of their comfort zones. I read an article recently that said that if you live in an urban "war zone" and you don't feel paranoid, you're crazy. Effective leaders demonstrate a healthy sense of paranoia for similar reasons. They couple it with liberal doses of excitement in the face of new business possibilities, based on the "data" of the understanding phase.

They cap it all off with an unbridled passion for excellence in quality, service, innovation, and teamwork. They realize that management is an emotional process and that the information gained in the understanding phase must be augmented with an enthusiasm to improve continuously and a passion to lead the market in some arena. This is why Bob Ulrich, when he headed retailer Target and more recently while at the helm of parent Dayton Hudson, has continued to hammer home his message "Speed is life." Ulrich is alluding not only to the reduction of cycle times, although that clearly is critical; he's also referring to the importance of an all-hands urgency to try things, to get on with things, to complete things, and to do so in a timely way.

One would think that if the organization's numbers are bad, the leader's task vis-à-vis urgency will be easier. Sometimes that's the case, but often, when companies finally do take action in the face of bad numbers, it's a panic reaction, not urgency. Panic is characterized by knee-jerk, cover-thy-rear behavior that temporarily douses immediate fires without moving the organization toward genuine transformation. It usually follows a long period of complacency. It's based primarily on raw fear, not a healthy excitement. It's mostly flame-broiled sizzle, not steak.

Astonishingly, bad numbers often fail to ignite people to action. People's capacity to cling to behaviors that no longer work is extraordinary. Denial ("the numbers will be better next quarter"), sham action ("let's get another consultant's report"), and just plain fear of moving beyond a comfort zone all collude to preclude genuine change.

Several years ago, Nellcor CEO Ray Larkin shared an insight with me while in the midst of a frustrating period in which he was attempting to stimulate change in the face of rising costs and product development problems: "One of the hardest things I learned was that the facts don't speak for themselves. People are capable of rationalizing the most damning facts. Data can't replace leadership." That's why urgency must go hand in hand with understanding.

Whether today's numbers are good or bad, effective managers fuel the fire. They continually challenge the process—in meetings, in budgeting decisions, in performance reviews, in policy debates. As USC's Warren Bennis notes, they create outright disequilibrium. And in moving the team, these leaders are patient with those who struggle to change, while they are unapologetically impatient with career skeptics.

A few years ago, AlliedSignal CEO Lawrence Bossidy put it well in a *Harvard Business Review* interview: "The leader's job is to help everyone see that the platform is burning, whether the flames are apparent or not."

D1—Direction

Direction tells us who we are and where we're going. In ambiguous, unstable times, people need a sense of coherence in their work lives. Effective leaders place great emphasis on ensuring that people in their organizations feel, own, and live an overarching vision, a common philosophy, an inspiring purpose, and a collective set of values and ideals.

Understanding and urgency rev up people with reasons and fuel for change, respectively. Direction gives them the positive path and the vehicle to channel their creative energies. Direction is not simply a mission statement or a sound-bite "vision." Per our discussion in Giant Step I, it is a perpetually evolving set of answers to questions such as, What is our business? Where do we want it to go? What do we stand for? Who do we serve? But just as important: what makes us unique? Interesting? Controversial? Special? What are we world-class-great in doing? What markets and products will we be unequivocally preeminent in? How will we *amaze* customers? What are we going to do that will blow people's minds?

A good direction is exciting. Effective directions stir people's emotions; they kindle excitement; they arouse and animate. They provoke an image of grand possibilities and engender pride in standing head and shoulders above the rest of the mob in a crowded marketplace. To notify employees and customers that "the Ritz-Carlton experience enlivens the senses, instills well-being, and fulfills even the unexpected wishes and needs of our guests" is a lot more inspirational than a goal of simply running a good hotel. To offer Starbucks customers "a sanctuary from their hectic lives . . . an escape, a state of mind, and a rich comforting place that provides a sense of community" means a lot more than a goal of selling good, cost-efficient coffee. To challenge employees with the image of creating a new world in which every adult and child uses a computer in every home, in every office, and in every schoolroom—as Apple and Microsoft have done in different contexts—is something that transcends the notion of manufacturing hardware and software.

A good direction is controversial. As Sun Microsystems CEO Scott McNealy put it, "I want Sun to be controversial; if everybody believes in your strategy, you have zero chance of profit." Per Giant Step I, if everyone thinks your direction is reasonable, then you're probably mired in conventional wisdom. Jack Welch was even blunter. In an interview with the *Wall Street Journal*, he asserted that "you've got to be out there on the lunatic fringe." Lunacy is definitely controversial, but as we've seen throughout this book, today's lunacy is tomorrow's conventional wisdom; today's conventional wisdom is tomorrow's historical footnote.

A good direction is shared. In 1987, when then-CEO George Lynn launched PACE (Patients Are the Center of Everything) at the two hospitals that comprise the Atlantic City Medical Center, he made sure to embed it into everyone. Daily problem-solving dialogues became de rigueur among managers and employees: who exactly are our patients? What does it mean for us to say that patients are the center of everything? How do we ensure that patients are the center of everything? To realize our ideal, what changes do we need to make in our organization structure to achieve our priority? Our budgeting? Our leadership styles? Our physical architecture? Our relationships with physicians and each other? Gradually, a shared picture of a hospital driven by patients emerged.

Direction provides people with an alternative to dissatisfaction with the present, as well as an alternative to passivity and despair. Just as important, it unifies and bonds people, providing them with the "big tent" of community heading down the same road. When direction is shared, conflict yields healthy problem analysis, and diversity of opinion leads to innovative decision making. The reason is that everyone knows that disagreements are fueled by a common purpose. That is why the spirited debates within Atlantic City Medical Center were a sign of a healthy organization.

But when direction is not shared, when overarching priorities, values, and commitments are at loggerheads, then conflict breeds turfism and blame analysis, and diversity leads to divisiveness. Organizations become fragmented. Confusion reigns: What are our priorities anyway? What are acceptable behaviors? What's OK to do? What are we really emphasizing around here? People become cynical, passive, and unfocused. Self-protective power plays and fiefdoms emerge.

Leapfrogging the competition won't work unless direction is a collaborative, all-hands affair. What this means is very simple: suppose I go into your organization and pick ten people at random—any department, any level, any job title, any site, any length of tenure. Further, suppose that I individually ask each of them questions such as "What are the ideals of this organization, what does it stand for, what's special and unique about this company to your customers, what does this organization do better than anyone else, what is the core set of principles that define your organization?" and so on. Suppose I simply ask, "What is your company vision, what is its business philosophy, and where is your company heading?"

Now, here's the climactic question. Will I get the same response from everyone? For that matter, will I get any response other than "I don't know" or "I'm not sure"? And suppose I follow up with yet another question, such as "To what extent do you embrace (live, own) this vision? To what extent do you talk about it and live by it in your day-to-day problem analysis and decision making?" What responses would I get from those ten randomly chosen individuals?

In a speech in Gothenburg, Sweden, a couple years ago, I posed the "shared" direction challenge to a large audience that included about thirty managers from Markpoint, a printer manufacturer. Markpoint is one of the best-managed, quality-oriented, employee-involved firms I have seen for a long time. In private discussions afterward, I was intrigued that managing director Torkild Jensen and his team were concerned by my comments. They were refreshingly candid in confessing that even in their team-based company, they could not be at all certain that all hands even understood the company vision, much less agreed or felt ownership with it. I bring this up precisely because I consider Markpoint to be a role model in many ways, and hence it makes me wonder even more how most organizations would stack up on this "sharing" dimension.

I would argue that an imperfect "vision and business plan," if universally shared and endorsed, is a much more powerful predictor of business success than a so-called perfect vision and plan that is neither understood nor universally endorsed.

Finally, direction must rest on the foundation of understanding. A direction that does not reflect an accurate read of market realities may lead everyone on the same path, but the path leads over a cliff. For years, IBM's direction—built on premises of mainframes, centralized corporate information systems, employment guarantees, and starched white shirts—carried the day. But as market realities shifted, the direction became a liability. It needed to be renewed, which has been CEO Lou Gerstner's major accomplishment over the last three years. The direction pioneered by George Lynn for Atlantic City Medical Center rested on an understanding of the changing world of hospital administration and on the urgency that transformations in health care delivery were necessary right away.

D2—Discipline

This is not about punishment or kinky sex. It's about consistency and persistence in execution. It's about the leader's daily behavior and decisions being aligned with the direction. It's about rejecting lip service, pseudo-support, and expediency. In short, it's about honor and integrity.

Discipline is the daily grind that makes things happen and lets people know you're worthy of your word. For three years after the launch of PACE, I watched George Lynn look and sound like a broken record. He talked about PACE every day, in every meeting. He roamed both hospitals in the system, visiting housekeeping and nursing groups at 2 A.M. to talk about PACE and the importance of linking everyday behaviors to it. I once watched him politely turn down a request by the chairman of the hospital board to meet on a particular date because of a prior commitment with a group of front-line employees set to discuss the implications of PACE.

Lynn was relentless. He spurred his people to develop measures against which progress toward PACE could be monitored, and he held them accountable for their performance thereafter. Charts, graphs, and key indices were omnipresent—tacked on walls, discussed in meetings, digested by all as the organization moved toward its big goals. Lynn himself reviewed business decisions in reports and meetings in terms of their "fit" with PACE.

As we first noted in *Jumping the Curve*, Lynn insisted that his managers analyze operational problems, personnel decisions, and vendor relationships in terms of PACE. He told them that he wanted them to have the same emotional reaction to PACE that they have toward budget variances. He "stacked the deck" and helped "create small wins" (new project successes) by picking people who were visibly committed to PACE. He invested heavily in service quality training, and he enlisted the help of 3M as a partner and mentor. He blessed self-managed teams that were willing to try new initiatives consistent with PACE, and he promised that he would personally protect anyone from retaliation by any manager who was threatened by the process.

And he delivered. For Lynn, the fact that patient satisfaction scores, physician referrals, and operating margins improved steadily over the next two years reinforced the validity of the PACE direction and added fuel for yet more urgency and more discipline.

Lynn has since moved along from Atlantic City Medical Center to be CEO of AtlantiCare, a health care holding company of which the Medical Center is a subsidiary. Last year, Lynn and I reminisced together about PACE. He noted with pride that the eleventh annual PACE retreat was coming up and that PACE is still thoroughly ingrained in hospital strategy and operations. He also noted that the administrators of the two hospitals of the system—both of whom had grown up with PACE—are still fully committed to the process, even though the specifics of PACE have necessarily changed in response to the enormous changes in health care over the past decade.

Of the entire U2D2 process, Lynn told me that he found the discipline phase the most personally taxing. "Continuing the grind is the hardest part of it," he said. But that's the essence of good discipline and, all too often, it's where many of us fall short.

What gets leaders through that daily grind? I am convinced that it must be an unbridled passion and commitment to a cause. Analytically detached, unemotional "professional management" will no longer cut it. You have to really *believe and love* the path you're taking. You've got to see what you're doing not as a job or "career-enhancing option" but as a *crusade*. Like Bill Graham did, like George Lynn did, like many of the leaders cited throughout this book have done. Without that emotional foundation, the grind grinds you down. With it, you gain strength and ingenuity you never thought you'd have.

One last point: in his discipline while at the helm of the Medical Center, Lynn was persistent but prudent; he was not a dogmatic bull in a china shop, running roughshod over people. There were times when he tactically stepped back, gave some leeway, held off. But as a result of everything else he did every day, it was clear to everyone that he never lost sight of his primary direction or of its urgency.

Study the personal history of inspiring leaders such as Mohandas Gandhi and Nelson Mandela, and you will note occasions where they seemed to back off or compromise on specific decisions, thus incurring the wrath of their more extreme colleagues. But for Gandhi and Mandela, such actions were temporary and necessary blips on a long road; there was never the slightest doubt of their commitment to their ultimate cause.

Great business leaders are the same. When leaders with direction and discipline compromise, they are rightly seen as prudent and tactical. In contrast, when managers without direction and discipline compromise, they are rightly seen as opportunistic and weak. Of the two Ds, direction points out the path, but it only comprises 20 percent of the battle. Daily discipline is the 80 percent sweat equity, the day-in-day-out stuff that demonstrates authenticity and separates real leaders from the shams.

Well, there you have it: a prescription to help you walk the talk. Listen to the good doctor: take U2D2 several times a day, every day, until you retire—and you will retire a successful change agent with a legacy of having helped your organization repeatedly leapfrog its competition.

Commitment 13

Don't Get Snookered
by Fads du Jour

WARNING: THIS is a politically incorrect section. I have already mentioned that real change too often grinds to a halt because of the "don'ts" that we do. This next section describes some particularly glaring don'ts and contrasts them with healthy alternatives. The section title should be a clue to what's coming: in the Age of Consultants, we're constantly being enticed by quick-fix, high-priced, one-size-fits-all elixirs that offer, at best, a pseudo-guarantee of business success. They can be costly distractions from the hard work that really needs to be done. Let's dive into three of the most sacred fads: Total Quality Management (TQM), reengineering, and deal-making mania. The point is not to vilify but to demonstrate that the process of creating real value-adding change leaps over reliance on silver-bullet techniques. As you read the next section on TQM, for example, feel free to interchange TQM with the name of any program of the year (or of the month) that you've lived through, and you'll know why that program most likely failed to achieve the changes it was designed to bring about.

I don't know exactly when it happened, but somewhere, somehow, total quality management (tqm) segued into TQM. The former—think about the three words individually—pertains to what I consider to be just plain effective management: creatively and eclectically doing whatever it takes and using any tools and methodologies (statistical, technological, financial, marketing, strategic, leadership) to create a quality organization, a quality product, a quality culture, and quality people—all for the purpose of attaining organizational success.

The latter, TQM, is a product in and of itself. There are literally hundreds of versions of this product in the marketplace, each designed, sold, delivered, and defended by different batches of consultants, staff professionals, and academics. And therein lies the problem. Like so many other change interventions, TQM became a fad, and fads don't fare well in the long haul.

Put together all the independent research conducted by consulting firms Arthur D. Little, Ernst & Young, A.T. Kearney, and McKinsey & Co., and you come up with the conclusion that only about one-fifth—at best one-third—of TQM programs in the United States and Europe have achieved noteworthy improvements in quality, productivity, competitiveness, or financial returns. This is a frightening conclusion given the hype that has accompanied TQM for years. It's even more serious given the fact that three-quarters of reasonably sized American firms claim to have invested in some form of TQM.

The findings themselves no longer surprise me, and that doesn't make me special. Managers are beginning to realize that quality is sacred; TQM is not. There's another difference: quality is about unbending focus, passion, iron discipline, and a way of life for all hands. TQM is about statistics, jargon, committees, and quality departments.

Yes, of course, the two concepts sometimes converge, but there are at least seven fad-filled reasons that they are likely not to—not even in organizational environments that desperately cry out for quality improvements.

1. *TQM focuses people's attention on internal processes rather than on external results.* Despite all the lip service to the contrary, the actual day-to-day mechanics of most TQM programs hypnotize—if not require—people to become internally focused, even as all the action is happening externally. People become preoccupied with internal performance measurements, conformance indices, and technical specifications. Paying attention to these data can be a useful part of discipline, as noted earlier. But a *preoccupation* with them inevitably diminishes managers' attention to external factors such as constantly

shifting customer preferences, technological breakthroughs, and new competitors capitalizing on them.

Thus, what an internally focused company actually does may result in a product or service that, in the eyes of the customer, is outdated, blandly conventional, insufficient, or just plain irrelevant. As one manager said, "Before we invested in TQM, the rap on our company was that we churned out poorly made products that customers didn't want. Now, after TQM, things have changed. We now churn out well-made products that customers don't want."

2. *TQM focuses on minimum standards.* Zero-defects products and no-rework efficiency are laudable goals, and they must be pursued. If TQM can help, well and good. But today those are minimal standards. Attaining them means you get to play in the arena; they're not guarantees of success. Unfortunately, TQM seduces many people into believing that minimum standards define quality. They do not. In today's frenzied global economy, quality also includes the capacity to offer customers things that add excitement, ease, and value to their lives. Quality means offering your customers products and services that are "wow—look at this!" Quality means offering customers personal experiences with your company that they will find easy, useful, "cool," and fun. In customers' definitions of quality, zero defects is merely one small part of that package.

3. *TQM develops its own cumbersome bureaucracy.* Of course, we don't call it a bureaucracy; we merely create reams of paper and sign-offs, a formal hierarchy of councils and committees, a plethora of meetings and techniques that must be adhered to, and a steadily growing staff that does little but monitor—some would say police—it all.

This has little to do with energetic, lithe, market-driven quality. Quite the opposite. Moreover, many people start viewing the whole concept of quality as a number-crunching paper chase or as a "whip." In one company, an hourly worker told me he was so fed up with the paperwork that "I sign off on the crap because I don't want to hassle with it anymore." In another company, a line manager of a successful operation begged me to tell corporate to "stop force-feeding their formula on us; they don't know what we do and they don't listen!"

4. *TQM does not demand radical organizational reform.* If your organization is weighted down with excess management layers, bloat in corporate staff, a proliferation of functional fiefdoms, and a compensation structure removed from quality, all the TQM training in the world won't jack up your quality. The plain fact of life is that authentic quality improvements demand the flattening of structures, the liberation of line management from corporate control, the freeing of front-line people from upper management, the meltdown of functional foxholes, and a compensation system for both managers and executives that is closely tied to quality indices (e.g., like that at Ford Motor and FedEx).

The problem is that while TQM gives these issues lip service, it rarely confronts them head-on. Too often in TQM, tough, painful, structural changes play second fiddle to the more visible carnival of motivational balloons and wall posters, innumerable classes with big binders, and slick presentations with fancy graphics.

5. *TQM appeals to egotism and quick-fixism.* In their efforts to sell TQM seminars and programs, too many vendors have subtly pandered, perhaps inadvertently, to these myopic traits. I've seen representatives of well-known consulting and seminar outfits promote their own companies and wares by presenting a fantasy picture of a clean, orderly, straightforward, eminently logical, user-easy path to success, with some ego-gratifying quickie results promised for good measure. Good marketing it may be, but good quality it ain't.

6. *TQM drains entrepreneurship and innovation from corporate culture.* The foundation of TQM is "continuous improvement." Continuous improvements on current operations and products are necessary, to be sure. But obsessing internally until one achieves a zero-defects "do it right the first time" routine is a dangerous luxury that often slows down new breakthrough streams in products and services. It is the latter that is the cornerstone of business success.

We are faced with a paradox that I described earlier in this book. On one hand, a company that aims at leapfrogging the competition must pursue constant improvement toward perfection in what it is doing now. On the other hand, that same company must encourage risk and tolerate errors in pursuit of the destruction of the status quo (products, systems, technologies, business models) and the creation of the new. Typical TQM, at best, only addresses the first part of the equation, often myopically, as noted in points 1 and 2. It does not address the second part of the equation at all, which means that the organization's capacity for entrepreneurship and innovation become seriously impaired.

7. *TQM has no place for love.* By this outrageous statement, I mean that when all is said and done, TQM attempts to make quality happen via an analytically detached, sterile, mechanical path. What's often missing, frankly, is emotion and soul. Go out and look at all the earnest individuals diligently following the step-by-step processes they've learned in TQM (and, for that matter, customer service) training classes, and ask yourself, Where's the love of our product and our customer? Where's the joy of the pursuit of excellence? Where's the passion in the doing and the creating? Where's the fun in being here? Where's the rage and agony in the slightest snag in product or service quality? If you can't find evidence of these, you probably won't find real quality, either.

A few years ago, in Tom Peters's newsletter *On Achieving Excellence,* business writer Paul Cohen wrote extensively about Maine-based Thos. Moser Cabinetmakers. This ninety-person company is winning the loyalty of a growing army of highly demanding consumers around the country with its array of exceptional products and services. Moser quality is superb, even though statistical process control charts and quality committees are conspicuously absent. Thomas Moser explains his company's approach to quality by noting that, first, most products on the market today "lack soul" and, second, "There's a set of values resident in our furniture that attracts customers. They're not just buying something to sit in, something well-made and well-designed, or something the neighbors will envy. Those are all motivations, but there is a strong emotional component to the objects themselves that motivates people to buy."

Moser goes on to say that what his company brings to the picture is *soul,* including creative craftsmanship of "absolute integrity" and an in-house delivery service (itself a profit center) that guarantees gentle, caring, precise, on-time delivery across the country. Small wonder that Moser can say with all sincerity, "We don't sell furniture." Not your usual TQM lingo.

Max DePree, chairman of another acclaimed furniture manufacturer—Herman Miller—would agree. His words may be a bit hyperbolic, but even I—an ex-professor of statistics and psychometrics—can buy the spirit that led him to say, "Managers who only understand methodologies and quantification are modern-day eunuchs."

These seven points go beyond TQM; they are a reflection of fad thinking rather than genuine change in any intervention. To be sure, even conventional TQM can provide a genuine service when it gets people sensitized to the concept of quality and helps them get disciplined in their efforts to attain quality. But as some of the Baldrige winners who have gone bankrupt or gone hurting can testify, TQM is, first, not automatically synonymous with either quality or "tqm." Second, it is not automatically synonymous with the only success that ultimately matters: whether the organization thrives. Writing in *Management Review* back in June, 1992, Tamara Erickson of Arthur D. Little conceded that TQM might lead to improvement in narrowly defined processes where customers are known and efforts easily measured. However, as she cogently observes, "Automobile manufacturers strive to improve fuel efficiency. Detergent makers become intent on improving the whitening power of their products. While these certainly are not unwise targets for improvement, they are unlikely to move a second-tier firm into a leadership position."

And, of course, market leadership, as described in this book, is what leapfrogging the competition is all about.

THE CRITIQUE of the TQM fad can be applied directly to the reengineering fad, especially reasons 1 (internal obsession), 4 (same old structure and pay), 5 (egotism, faddism), 6 (drain on entrepreneurship), and 7 (no love).

So does that mean that we can place a "Reengineering, R.I.P." tombstone in the business-fad graveyard? Not yet. Besides, reengineering as originally envisioned, had real merit. It promoted the idea of using information technology to link processes—such as product development and customer service—that sliced across functional groupings, so that work flow was organized around those integrated processes, not around typically discrete functional fiefdoms. Very wise. But it was when the apostles (a.k.a. faddists) took over that reengineering began to be viewed as a magic cure-all elixir for organizational woes. If you want to leapfrog the competition, keep the following caveats in mind with regard to any change process.

Thomas Davenport, who preceded Michael Hammer and James Champy in developing the concepts of reengineering, asked a simple question a couple years ago in *Fast Company* magazine: "How did a modest insight become the world's leading management fad? How did reengineering go from a decent idea to a $51 *billion* industry?"

The answer is simple. As long as people are willing to pay for quick fixes and snake oil, someone will be out there selling them. Eventually, reality sinks in. Today, the $51 billion industry (what Davenport derisively calls the "Reengineering Industrial Complex") is itself downsizing dramatically, a delicious irony.

Managers are gradually realizing that the underlying premises of reengineering (e.g., eliminating counterproductive organizational barriers and process steps) are eminently sensible, but they've always been around. Further, the premises of reengineering are easy to understand in principle but damnably difficult to execute in practice. That's why the research findings on the actual efficacy of reengineering interventions are sobering, to say the least. Studies indicate that 85 percent of interventions just plain and outright "fail." Even the follow-up research of CSC Index (the original James Champy purveyor of consulting services) concludes that about two-thirds of interventions have yielded "mediocre, marginal, or failed results."

Here's the reality flash: reengineering "died" not because there's anything "wrong" with it. Quite the contrary; reengineering is one (though not the only) sensible way for leaders to rethink their business and overhaul their organization. The reason reengineering has so often failed is that managers buy it as a magic elixir and implement it as a silver bullet. If they were serious about reengineering as a genuine, radical change process, not a fad, they might approach it the way a volunteer work group did as described in a wonderful little story in the March 18, 1996, issue of *Fortune* magazine.

It was a story about a volunteer work group in Hewlett-Packard's North American distribution organization. In a short time-frame of nine months, this work group managed to completely reengineer the creaky, slow process by which product reached the customer. Among other things, the group reshaped a process that involved seventy separate computer systems and indeterminable byzantine steps into a single, unified database covering everything from customer order through credit check, manufacturing, warehousing, shipping, and invoicing.

But what was unique about this group is that reengineering wasn't "done" to them. In fact, nothing was done to them. The team leaders went out of their way to step aside, not provide pat answers, and—amazingly enough—not have any sort of "organization" at all. That is, team members did not have any formally defined responsibilities; it was up to them to figure out, individually and as a team, what to investigate, what to ask, what to work on, and what to strive for. People were given free reign to form any project, to access any data, to challenge any process. To quote Julie Anderson, one of the team leaders: "We took things away: no supervisors, no hierarchy, no titles on our business cards, no job descriptions, no plans, no step-by-step milestones of progress."

The team leaders provided some broad directional parameters, but primarily training, tools, support, and encouragement.

They created an environment marked by openness, inclusion, and accountability. The idea was to reduce the myopia and defensiveness that comes from formally assigned responsibilities and to create a sense of personal ownership. People used their own wit and wisdom to challenge the process and come up with a radically different alternative.

The leaders seemed to have instinctively understood something else: that although reengineering involves automation and technology, it is not equivalent to them. Reengineering may even require some staff cuts, but, argues Davenport, that was never meant to be a primary goal. A couple years ago the *Economist* noted that "the 'soft' side of reengineering (winning over the workers) is even more important than the 'hard' side (such as installing new computers)."

Davenport is even more adamant. Again, in *Fast Company*, he asserts that reengineering is only valuable to the extent that "it helps people do their work better and differently. Companies are still throwing money at technology—instead of working with the people in the organization to infuse technology."

That certainly wasn't the case at HP. The leaders there approached their task with a Giant Step II perspective. They showed courage and foresight in flooding the work environment with knowledge.

As you consider this little story, don't you get the sense that in that pocket of HP, successful reengineering actually happened, and it wasn't a one-shot fix? Don't you get the sense that the leaders inspired a U2D2 process? Finally, don't you get the sense that not many organizations have tried to implement reengineering this way? No wonder the track record has been dismal.

Remember, on the surface, reengineering as the top-down imposed magic potion (a.k.a. fad) looks appealing. Reengineering as the hard, collective, committed work is much more challenging. But unlike the fad, it's the real work that generates genuine change.

"In these days when there seems to be a compulsive urge to acquire other companies. . . ."

AN EVEN more controversial fad is the art of deal making. First, a caveat: I am not against mergers and acquisitions (M & A). I love it when two top performers meld to reinvent the marketplace in a way neither could have done either alone or in a joint venture. But often, deal making becomes a compulsive eating disorder rationalized by fancy labels such as "synergy." Meanwhile, "vision," in the words of strategy gurus Gary Hamel and C. K. Prahahlad, becomes "window dressing for a CEO's ego-driven acquisition binge." When that happens, you can kiss off any hope of leapfrogging the competition. The following section explains why.

These are the first words of a business text published in . . . *1968*! Today, that compulsive urge has reached epidemic proportions: $1.7 *trillion* in deals in 1998 alone. Huge companies are gobbling up each other as if there's no tomorrow. Westinghouse and CBS, Seagrams and Universal, Morgan Stanley and Dean Witter, Boeing and McDonnell Douglas, Compaq and DEC, SBC and Ameritech, NationsBank and Bank of America, Citicorp and Traveller's, AT&T and TCI, Daimler and Chrysler, and Exxon and Mobil. The list goes on and on.

The press, excited by the carnage, splashes the news of the next deal every day. Self-anointed pundits dutifully bless the feeding frenzy as a sound, even necessary, corporate strategy and predict that in a few years only two or three players will be left in every industry.

Excuse me, but could I please inject a little reality flash here?

Forget for a moment the aforementioned specific examples. Let's simply concentrate on what it takes to leapfrog the competition.

Where exactly is the logic that says that two ineptly run, bumbling corporations that join forces will somehow give birth to a sparkling, inspiring hybrid? Where is the logic that says two turgid, bureaucratic companies that consolidate their balance sheets will magically transform themselves into a fleet, flexible, entrepreneurial entity? Or that two companies that

have individually managed to generate flat earnings and declin-
ing share in their current markets will somehow be able to right
all wrongs by jumping into bed together?

Oh, I've heard the buzzword answers: synergy, cost savings,
economies of scale, cross-business opportunities, distribution
channels for products, products for distribution channels, et
cetera, et cetera.

But if things are so rosy, then how do we explain the
following?

- The cover story of the April 28, 1998, issue of *Barron's*,
  the investor's Bible, was entitled, "Why Mergers Don't
  Work." One summary statement from the *Barron's* report
  declared, "Most of the research indicates that between 60
  percent and 80 percent of mergers are financial failures."
- The cover story of the October 20, 1995, issue of *Business Week* (titled "The Case against Mergers"; subtitled
  "Even in the '90s, Most Still Fail to Deliver") concluded,
  "The surge of consolidations and combinations is occurring in the face of strong evidence that mergers and acquisitions, at least over the past 35 years or so, have hurt
  more than helped companies and shareholders."
- New York University professor Mark Sirower, author of
  The Synergy Trap (Free Press, 1997) concluded his research with the indictment that "acquiring firms destroy
  shareholder value. This is a plain fact."
- Renowned financier Warren Buffet, chairman of Berkshire Hathaway, wrote in the 1995 annual report, "We
  believe most deals do damage to the shareholders of the
  acquiring companies."

I'm looking for answers. Why did the much-ballyhooed "synergy" used to justify Viacom's purchase of Blockbuster turn
out, to use the February 21, 1997, *Wall Street Journal's* language, to be "illusory" and "sour"? Why did the acquisition
mania of advertiser Saatchi & Saatchi wind up emasculating it?

Why is the once vaunted "synergy" among Pepsi Cola, Pizza
Hut, KFC, and Taco Bell now considered a "liability" by the very
people who until recently strongly supported their consolidation

under one PepsiCo umbrella? Why did former AT&T CEO Bob Allen remark that his managers were spending way too much time and resources tracking, controlling, and integrating the vast cacophony of businesses that AT&T was involved in?

Lest anyone misunderstand, I state unequivocally that I'm not against mergers and acquisitions. Under the right circumstances, they can be a powerful strategic weapon. Companies such as Microsoft, Hewlett Packard, 3M, Milacron, and Johnson & Johnson have grown shareholder value with the help of infrequent, small, prudent acquisitions that fit nicely into a larger, well-defined strategic direction—a direction, by the way, based primarily on internal growth.

Companies like USA Networks, Lucent Technologies, Cisco Systems, and WorldCom have made more frequent, sometimes large, acquisitions, but they too have fared well because they haven't used acquisitions primarily to build scale so as to produce and market today's buggy whip more efficiently. Instead, their acquisitions focus on absorbing cutting-edge talent and next-generation technologies aimed at tomorrow's marketplace. USA Networks, for example, with its acquisitions of Lycos, Home Shopping Network, Ticketmaster Online, Citysearch, and First Auction is, according to CEO Barry Diller, positioning itself for a leadership role in creating an interactive, customer-individualized cyberspace and video shopping experience.

Finally, all the aforementioned companies have fared well because they have a proven track record of fast, successful integration of acquired assets.

Notice the key words in the above paragraphs: "infrequent," "small," "prudent," "strategy based primarily on internal growth," "cutting-edge talent," "next-generation technologies," "aimed at tomorrow's marketplace," "not primarily to build scale," and "fast, successful integration." These criteria immediately eliminate 90 percent of the high-profile M & A deals going on today.

Let's take it a step further.

For the past few years, I've argued that consolidating the balance sheets of two corporations with the typical justifications of cost savings, synergy, global reach, and the like will pay off only if one can make two critical assumptions. These are such critical, obvious, yet so often overlooked assumptions that I'm calling them Harari's Rules for Healthy ROM (Return on Merger).

Assumption 1 is that it will be possible to integrate two complex, disparate organizations into a seamless whole within a cost-effective, timely manner.

This is a big assumption, for the research indicates that, at best, integration is often an uphill, long, bloody, earnings-draining battle. At worst, it's a slow strangulation. Witness the AT&T-NCR fiasco over the past few years. AT&T was simply never able to absorb NCR into its business design and processes, which resulted in a $10 billion loss, a horrendous diversion of management attention, and ultimately a costly divestiture. More recently, Boeing's acquisition of McDonnell Douglas has sucked the company of valuable resources, fouled up its production capacity in its core business, and distracted its top managers from the kinds of strategic thinking necessary in a hypercompetitive world market. Small wonder that over the past few years AT&T under Bob Allen was a loser of a stock, while Boeing's recent woes are causing similar shareholder angst.

The actual work of integrating two companies is damnably difficult. And messy. And grindy. Many CEOs don't want to be bothered with such "details." It's a lot easier to do the deal than to implement it.

Assumption 2 is that there are no fleet, irreverent competitors out there who are capitalizing on new technologies and business designs that will literally obsolete the new hybrid's products and services.

The $55 billion SBC/Ameritech deal has a semblance of logic as long as we assume that wired voice transmission remains the defining force in the telecom business. But the assumption doesn't stand. Wired voice transmission has become a low-margin, no-growth commodity, with nearly 900 providers in the United States alone. As noted earlier, the future of telecom belongs to companies who are racing ahead in bundling voice, video, and data in a high-speed, high-bandwidth digital wireless format—companies such as WinStar, Qwest, Level 3, Lucent Technologies, and WorldCom. Further, as a recent *Business Week* report notes, "The Internet is also giving rise to new products that could undermine traditional phone services. The one that sends shivers down the spines of telecom execs: software that lets you place phone calls over the Net."

Rich Karlgaard, editor of *Forbes ASAP*, would agree. He says that these M & A feasts are simply an attempt by "telecom dinosaurs" to "try to stave off extinction." Sarcastically, he notes that "the only hope for America's aging circuit-switched, copper-based telephone companies is to raise enough capital through mergers to fund a massive overhaul into high-capacity lines and Internet protocol switches." Highly unlikely. Even if the new megacompany could transcend the Thomas Lawson Syndrome, the effort would be monumentally costly and lengthy.

The face of business is changing so rapidly that consolidating the weight of two big companies today often dooms them toward slowness, yesterday's product line, and mass-market approaches to customers. You don't need a crystal ball to predict that executives will tenaciously justify prior big-bucks investments, even if those decisions make little sense in emerging markets. You don't need to be an econometrics genius to figure out that rosy projections of postmerger share and earnings are built on today's realities, ignoring the entrance of new technologies and vendors that render those realities obsolete.

The feeding frenzy in banking circles is a case in point. A senior executive of a major East Coast bank privately conceded to me that, by and large, the M & A track record in the banking industry was miserable. He went further. Describing his own bank's acquisition activity, he said, "Even under the best of circumstances, what's the point of investing all this money in obtaining a new chain of branches when all the trends suggest that branches themselves will become less and less valuable as assets? We don't need to use our resources to buy our competitors' assets. We've got to put our attention and capital into preparing for the future, not get ourselves locked into old ways of doing things." He was referring to the fact that the future of banking isn't in branch activity; it's in digital commerce, remote and home banking, debit and smart cards, database management, personal portfolio management, customized trust services, and applications tailored to each individual's unique financial planning needs. It's not only that you don't need bricks-and-mortar branches for these services, but in the age of deregulation and disintermediation, you don't even have to be a bank to provide those services.

And what about cross-selling as a rationale? Recently, one executive answered that question when he told me, "Why in the world would any bank believe that just because I keep a couple accounts with them for sheer convenience, that I'll also buy my home insurance and mutual funds from them?" Pointing to his laptop, he said, "Here's my bank. I've got choices around the world right in this little box."

I've said it throughout this book: in the emerging brain-based economy, it's not the biggest organizations that will thrive but the most agile, innovative, and future oriented. It's intangibles such as speed and imagination that will grow your business and allow you to leapfrog the competition. If an acquisition makes you faster, more agile, more customer responsive, more technologically cutting-edge, and more innovative in preparing for tomorrow's business models, then that acquisition might help you leapfrog the competition—and I as an observer and investor applaud it.

But the fact is, many of the postmerger megahybrids that dominate the headlines wind up as slow, clumsy, hyperbureaucratic, debt-burdened beasts who are bolted to the ground with excessive sunk costs, fragile patchwork infrastructure, passé products, incompatible systems, conflicting cultures, and outdated business models. As WinStar CEO Bill Rouhana told USA Today technology writer Kevin Maney regarding the SBC/Ameritech deal, "Merging gives them more of the same. It doesn't make their networks more modern or change the way employees act or are trained. In many ways, maybe getting bigger makes them more clumsy. They'll get even more bureaucratic. More layers of management."

As WorldCom, Milacron, and others have demonstrated, there are valid reasons to embark on carefully considered M & A ventures. But given the clear and present danger in so many deals, why do so many executives swarm to them like bees to honey? The answer: faddism. Yes, for all of the snazzy financial sleight of hand involved, many of the M & A activities are initiated as fads. Regardless of the weighty rationales that are pontificated as to why the deals get done, here are eight of the *real* reasons that leaders fall prey to deal-making faddism:

1. *Easy pickin's.* It's easier to finance a deal nowadays, so why not? In contrast to the prototype debt-financed takeovers in the 1980s, many of the deals today are equity driven. The late 1998 market correction slowed things down for a bit, but the revived bull market continues to give companies artificially greater purchasing power by allowing them to use their inflated stock as a currency for acquisition. So on the surface, it appears like a no-lose proposition: you can quickly double the size of the company without going into massive debt—at least in the very beginning. But, of course, the real costs and opportunity costs soon grow exponentially. And what's going to happen when the next inevitable market corrections occur?

2. *No vision, no alternative.* In the absence of any coherent, exciting, imaginative strategy for internally generated growth, a CEO may feel pressure by analysts to "do something," which usually translates into making a splashy acquisition. It takes vision, confidence, and integrity to say no and to say you've got a viable alternative, like Michael Dell of Dell Computer does. Dell is constantly inundated with investment bankers and other self-serving sharks who urge him to do deals. His position is that Dell Computer's breakthrough business models generate growth rates that dwarf anything proposed by the deal makers; he's got much better, more innovative plans for his capital, thank you very much. But many CEOs succumb to Wall Street pressure because they have no imaginative alternatives, and hence strategy is defined as the next acquisition.

3. *Opportunism and expediency.* Quick fixes tantalize many CEOs. Why work hard to build a company with breakthrough product and service when you can double your size and press exposure by—poof!—putting your signature on a contract and then "delegating" the postdeal implementation trauma to others? But soon reality strikes: you can cut costs by slashing budgets and people, you can use scale to muscle vendors and spread costs, but then exactly what do you do to *grow* this company in big enough boosts to justify the megainvestment? (Some of

these deals will require a doubling and tripling of earnings just to achieve a 10 percent return.) Don't look to cross-selling as a panacea, and don't assume you can simply buy market share. Industry after industry is becoming "unbundled," with consumers exercising freedom of choice, unwilling to be herded like sheep. If you can't provide consumers with something new and cool, your financials go sour, no matter how big and efficient you are.

4. *"Me too" myopia.* Everyone else is doing it, and their photo is on the front page. Knee-jerk response: panic or envy. I better do it too. (Besides, I wanna have my picture on the front page, too; see point 5.)

5. *Megalomania.* When British pharmaceutical Glaxo Wellcome initiated the megamerger with Smith/Kline, chairman Sir Richard Sykes said he wanted to be head of the biggest drug company in the world. The deal collapsed because the two chairmen couldn't agree on who would be the big honcho. Back in the United States, NationsBank CEO Hugh McColl says he wants to be head of the biggest bank in the United States. *Voilà!* NationsBank/Bank of America. Note: not the "best" drug company, not the "best" bank. But the *biggest.* Ergo, ego.

6. *Top management payoff.* The company may falter, but as the top dog, my net worth will soar whatever happens. May 13 headline in *USA Today*: "Mergers May Not Be Companies' Best Investment." May 14 headline in *USA Today*: "Ameritech Chief Stands to Make a Fortune From Its Sale to SBC."

7. *Fear, fear, fear.* What do I do? I haven't a clue. New, fast, innovative companies are entering the marketplace in droves. Solution: find another scared, unimaginative company to ingest. (There's got to be a logic there somehow.) *Wall Street Journal* analyst Holman Jenkins describes these deals as "about protecting the existing assets from obsolescence." A purely defensive maneuver born of fear, and a very expensive way to buy just a little bit of time.

8. *Obsolete premises.* As we've discussed earlier in this book, things we can see and touch, such as buildings and equipment, are much less valuable than things we can't, such as reputation and customer service. Jim Billington, writing in *Harvard Management Update*, reminds managers that "products and

services have no intrinsic value outside of customer demand."
In the twenty-first century (a.k.a. now), tangibles such as size,
mass, physical assets, "products," and so forth, will be much
less valuable than intangibles such as speed, ingenuity, radical
foresight, and customer delight. A lot of the deals today are put
together by folks who just don't "get" it. As the next millennium roars toward us, they're preparing their companies for
success in the twentieth century.

Faddism no longer offers safe harbor, even if it's disguised as a
megamerger. You can't hide from the vagaries of the market by
simply getting bigger. You can't buy success. You can't eliminate
competitors. New ones, hardy ones, pesky ones come out of the
woodwork daily with offerings we never even conceived of.
Neither can you win by playing with the old rules of volume
and cost.

   Nevertheless, the search for the quick, predictable fix continues, even if successive results contradict each other. Today's acquisition for "synergy" is followed by tomorrow's divestiture in
order to "get back to core businesses," which is then followed
by tomorrow's merger for "operational efficiency," which in
turn is followed by tomorrow's breakup to "get back to ba-
sics," and, well, you get the idea.

   As usual, the best word on all this comes from Peter Drucker.
In the September 22, 1990, issue of *Time* magazine he spoke
of why M & A seems to be the corporate strategy of choice.
"I will tell you a secret," confided Drucker. "Dealmaking beats
working. Dealmaking is exciting and fun, and working is
grubby. Running anything is primarily an enormous amount of
grubby detail work and very little excitement, so dealmaking
is kind of romantic, sexy. That's why you have deals that make
no sense."

   There's a fundamental axiom in biology that also applies to
organizations: two dinosaurs mating will have a tough time giving birth to a gazelle. Nevertheless, they keep on trying. The
deals keep on hatching as some magic cure-all. Are you a company like Daiwa Bank, faced with minor inconveniences such
as financial catastrophe, scandal, and criminal indictments?
Have no fear: "Merger may be the answer" (from Reuters). Are

you a big airline with hostile labor-management relations, inefficient hub-spoke systems, and disgruntled business travelers? No problem. The solution involves "considering mergers" (from the *Wall Street Journal*). There's no end in sight to the delusions.

So I ask: is there anyone out there who'll raise a voice to declare that the emperor has no clothes? That's a rhetorical question, of course, but it brings us right back to the precepts of Giant Step V. Yes, there are times when it is prudent for a leapfrogging organization to do a merger or acquisition; in fact, there are times when it would be foolish not to. But when dealmaking takes on a life of its own, when it becomes the primary hope for organizational renewal, or when it gets to the point that it "beats working," then you can be sure that the changes it begets will be value detracting in the long haul.

Let's keep that in mind the next time a whiz kid dangles the magic elixir of consolidation as our salvation. And as we end this politically incorrect section, let's remember something even more important: transcending all fads du jour—no matter how well packaged or well hyped—is an absolute necessity for leapfrogging the competition.

Sponge Up Daily Doses of Reality

ALTHOUGH IT may linguistically be a paradox, you need to be grounded to best leapfrog the competition. That is, you've got to be intimate with all aspects of the marketplace if your leap is going to take place in precisely the right direction and at precisely the right time. To be intimate, you've got to really know your stakeholders—from customers to employees to suppliers to partners. And to know them, you've got to get reality checks from all these sources every day.

Norman Brinker, chairman of the $2 billion Brinker International restaurant chain, likes to hang out anonymously in the parking lots of his properties and ask customers what their experience has been. Paul Orfalea, chairman of Kinko's, likes to take regular shifts working as a front-liner in copy centers in the United States and abroad. Jack Welch and Michael Dell spend 40 to 50 percent of their time interacting with customers.

Why do they do it? I'm sure their response would corroborate the comment made by Honeywell CEO Michael Bonsignore. In the middle of a hectic global travel schedule meeting customers around the world in autumn 1998, Bonsignore told the *Wall Street Journal*, "I learn a hell of a lot more doing this than sitting in my office reading historical information. Today, we can't be making decisions based on historical information because things are changing so fast."

That's why sponging up daily doses of reality—in this case from customers—is so important. It lets you know what's on their minds now. It gives you clues as to what might be on their minds tomorrow. It provides you with their reactions and feed-back to what you're doing. It fosters urgency, action, and ac-countability. It generates a lot of interesting new "what if?" ideas. It helps guide your leaps.

Sponging up daily doses of reality requires—minimally—what Tom Peters has called "naive listening." By listening, I do not mean the slow, expensive, detached, overgeneralized sur-veys that are read only by a special few in the company and acted on by even fewer. True listening involves humble, open "taking things in" from the perspective of a learner. True listen-ing entails focused, two-way collaborative interactions, face-to-face whenever possible. Remember, as noted in Giant Step III, "listening" is more than a formal, passive "focus group" activ-ity. Listening involves spending time with customers, getting to know their business needs, paying attention to their subtle con-cerns, probing issues and generating ideas together, and, of course, your taking notes throughout so that you can share data and insights with colleagues thereafter.

In the March 10, 1997, issue of *Forbes*, Peter Drucker argues that managers spend so much time perusing computer-generated output that they actually become less well informed about the outside world, "if only because they believe that the data on the computer printouts are *ipso facto* information."

Drucker's solution? "I tell my clients that it is absolutely im-perative that they spend a few weeks each year outside their own business and actively working in the marketplace. . . . The best way is for the chief executive officer to take the place of a salesman twice a year for two weeks."

I'd go a step further. Naive listening to "plain, old," ordinary customers ought to be part of everybody's job, every day. It doesn't matter whether you're an engineer, a purchasing man-ager, a secretary, an analyst, an IS specialist, or a controller; you ought to be spending time on customer sites, in customer focus groups, at trade shows, on sales calls, and on the toll-free line, listening, absorbing, probing, questioning, dialoguing, and jot-ting down ideas.

A few years ago, Cadillac's turnaround from a defect-ridden hog to a high-performance work of elegance was attributed in no small part to two steps taken by the GM division. First, dealerships became "listening posts" with immediate access to the company headquarters whenever vital customer feedback needed to be communicated. Second, executives began to call five randomly chosen buyers each week.

Good things happen when everyone takes on the responsibility of sponging up daily doses of reality. Imagine this possibility: every manager in your company receives the name of at least one randomly chosen customer every day to call or visit and ask a few simple questions about his or her experiences with your product and company. For good measure, the manager is then responsible for seeing to it that any problems or suggestions that emerge during these discussions are followed up with action right away *and* that the organizational systems that caused the problem or inhibit implementation of good ideas are attacked ruthlessly. Imagine the impact of everyone doing this every day. The task need not require a big chunk of time, but it will force everyone to make some important changes to their current calendars, with good reason. People will quickly get very clear about how they're spending that daily calendar time, and they'll get doubly clear on what's really value-adding behavior in their work life and what isn't.

The idea is for everyone to make time to interact with and absorb knowledge from customers directly, unfiltered, every day. And because customers change every day, listening to them—really listening to them—will force you to eat change with every meal. The plat du jour may vary, but the meal will prove tremendously satisfying as what you learn helps position you to leapfrog the competition.

Sponging up daily doses of reality becomes a vibrant part of the corporate culture, a way of staying in touch with today's customers and getting important clues about tomorrow's. Sponging up daily doses of reality not only helps guide our trajectory as we leapfrog the competition, but it helps ensure that we don't jump too far beyond our customers. This is an issue that's germane in any industry, but high-technology firms face it constantly as they pump out new generations of awe-inspiring products with extraordinary rapidity (one manager of a Silicon Valley firm described his company's products as "out of date before they're out of the carton"). Regardless of our industry, we want to "pull" and "stretch" our customers along with us per Giant Steps I through IV, but getting daily personal contacts with customers helps ensure that we don't make the alternate error of leaping way ahead of their ability or desire to stay with us.

All of this is why sponging up daily doses of reality should be a necessary part of everyone's daily job requirement. No more "I'm too busy (or important) for that." No more "That's the job of the customer service department." The message must be clearly sent: it's everyone's job to soak up daily doses of reality with real, paying customers.

A few suggestions on how to accomplish this:

1. Every organization can identify multiple categories of customers. You need to sponge up reality from each, but keep your priorities in mind. I throw my hat in with colleague Bob Le Duc, who tells his clients, "Ignore the end user at your own peril."

2. A big addendum to point 1: the only customers that count are external customers. Internal customers, *sayonara*. Companies can no longer afford to carry the overhead of jobs, functions, and activities that are buffered from external (read: real) customers who pay the bills. As the manager of a corporate group in one airline carrier told me, "The 'internal customer' schtick is a cop-out because as long as you or I satisfy the next internal person in the chain, we don't have to worry whether what we have done has any positive impact on the paying customer. In fact, we can easily say, 'I am not responsible for what happens in the marketplace; my job is to serve my internal customer.'"

The solution for anyone not immediately linked to customers? Figure out ways to join forces with colleagues who are directly serving external customers. Start by joining project teams and cross-disciplinary efforts that direct their attention to real customers. Let me repeat the message: if you're not currently sponging up a daily dose of reality from external customers, get started right away.

3. If everyone's sponging up reality in different ways and times, the information you gain should be consolidated and

made available to everyone. Otherwise, the learning and follow-up actions of one individual or group will be unknown to others. What a waste of valuable knowledge! What a depressing cap on collective brainpower!

Hence, develop a variety of media by which people can share the knowledge they've picked up. Throw the daily doses you've sponged up into a centralized database or expert system accessible by all. At Buckman Labs, the K'Netix system fits this bill seven days a week, twenty-four hours a day. You can be at home with your PC, or you can be at one of the many Buckman sites around the world. It doesn't matter. You can be connected right away to a massive database that is user-friendly and provides the information you need and that is automatically updated whenever you or anyone else adds information to the file.

Let's not overlook low-tech methods. Newsletters, educational forums, small meetings, one-on-ones, and public celebrations all play a role here. The important thing is to share the daily dose of reality as widely as possible.

4. Sponging up daily doses of reality means more than merely absorbing and accessing information; it means acting on it. If it's a customer complaint, do something about it and do something about the system that caused it and will, presumably, cause it again. If it's insights, observations, or suggestions that could impact tomorrow's customer, get a pilot rolling.

Ideally, if people follow these steps, what emerges is not merely a passive "listen to the customer" scenario, but per Giant Steps I, III, and IV, an active *collaboration* with customers focused on a common cause, such as "trend sniffing," cost reductions, expanded service delivery, and new product development. That's when daily doses of reality regularly permeate the organization. That's when fresh, new ideas percolate naturally. That's when you and your customers help each other leapfrog the competition.

5. Customers are your most crucial constituency, but try to include all important stakeholders in your daily dosages. Like suppliers. Like employees. Like strategic partners.

Underlying points 1 to 5 is a basic philosophy of seeking feedback about ourselves. Among the interesting things ex-New

York City mayor Ed Koch used to do was to ask citizens a simple question: "How'm I doin'?" The fact that Mayor Koch would continue to ask that question is one reason he remained popular with many New Yorkers despite the emergence of some embarrassing scandals during the final years of his tenure.

What is the significance of that simple little question? Certainly, voters like to have their opinions solicited in a direct, personal manner. So do employees and customers, for that matter. But I think there is something else going on. Most of us run our careers assuming—or hoping—that we're doing just fine with our employees, bosses, colleagues, customers, regulators, and any other relevant constituency. Sometimes we're right, sometimes we're wrong. But is it wise to run our careers like a crap shoot? More often than we'd like, we wind up facing distressing situations that could have been avoided, such as a customer or valued employee leaving us "without warning," or a cash-flow crisis that erupts "out of the blue," or an "unheard of" competitor who enters our industry with a new technology, or a "surprising" performance review from our boss or from the investment community. Common sense suggests that if we can gather valid feedback about ourselves, we are more likely to adjust our behavior so as to be more effective in influencing people and achieving our goals. Certainly, multirater or 360-degree feedback is helpful in this regard; so are consumer surveys. However, asking six colleagues or 600 customers to fill out a static questionnaire once a year or so is hardly sufficient. If we're serious about getting constant reality checks that allow us to adjust and weave and bob as we relentlessly pursue our leapfrogging goals, then a lot more probing of the environment is needed, and it needs to take place much more frequently.

The bottom line is, you've got to initiate the inquiry. If you wait for employees or customers or anyone else to tell you how you're doing or to provide you clues as to where you need to be heading, you'll be waiting a long time. If you want to avoid land mines and seize opportunities, patience is not necessarily a virtue. I am reminded of a favorite cartoon of mine. Two big, mangy vultures are sitting on a branch overlooking a deserted landscape. One vulture says to the other, "Patience, my ass. I'm gonna go kill something." Instead of assuming timely feedback will come to you, go out and get it.

The late Sam Walton defined good management in terms of *listening*. It's an art that reflects integrity and requires practice. Do yourself a favor and don't wait for feedback to come to you. Develop your own personal listening strategy and persevere in implementing it—every day. Make sure everyone else on your team does the same. The payoff will be unimaginable.

Commitment 15

Beware the Danger
of Success

YOU'VE FAITHFULLY executed the first fourteen Commitments. You're leapfrogging your competition. All is well—or is
it? There's one final hurdle you must consciously and continually confront. . . .

In business today, daily surprises mock careful planning and
can sabotage your company's hard-earned reputation. The only
guarantee is that there are no more guarantees. Many of the
most exciting brand names in business today didn't even exist
twenty years ago—or five years ago. Meanwhile, companies
that were heroes yesterday are not necessarily heroes today
(witness the difficulty faced by brand-name institutions such
as Westinghouse, GM, Eastman Kodak, and TWA). But at least
those companies are still around. As noted earlier, nearly 50
percent of the 1980 *Fortune* 500 no longer even exist, having been consolidated, or deconsolidated, or masticated into
unrecognizable bits, or just plain Chapter 11—liquidated into
oblivion.

Evolution is natural and relentless. As we know from biology,
many species that once dominated were in no way immune to
extinction. Back in 1992, the *Economist* noted that "big companies assume the trappings of solidity and permanence, [but]
the most remarkable thing about big companies is not their
longevity but their transience. . . . Companies are not enduring
institutions. Nor should they be."

In fact, a 1983 study conducted by Shell found that on the
average, corporations live half as long as individual human be-

232

ings. For every centenarian (GE or Proctor & Gamble), there are countless companies that are stillborn or don't survive adolescence. Either companies keep up with the market or they're relegated to has-been status, regardless of their glowing history, puffy public relations press, or awesome balance sheet size.

So-called "excellent" companies are not immune from these cold realities, either. Remember back in 1985 when a cover story of *Business Week* blared out, "Who's Excellent Now?" The article updated some of the "excellent" companies described in Tom Peters and Bob Waterman's 1982 *In Search of Excellence* and found that thirteen of them were having serious problems in the merely three years following publication of the best-seller.

The story was sensational, suggesting that Peters and Waterman were all wet with their eight principles of excellence. But a careful look at the data, including the trends and charts provided in the cover story itself, made it clear that those companies stumbled because they *deviated* from the eight principles that had made them excellent in the first place. In short, they got fat, dumb, and happy. They believed their own hype, and, worse, they believed the hype made them impervious to market realities.

In a similar vein, of the organizations cited in the first edition of *The 100 Best Companies to Work for in America*, written by Robert Levering and Milton Moskowitz in 1984, only about 50 percent made it to the second edition published in the early 1990s. Some companies didn't make it for obvious reasons, such as they no longer exist (e.g., People Express). But others failed to make the grade because either their standards have slipped or employees' standards for healthy work environments have risen. I suspect both trends are occurring simultaneously. Again the marketplace—in this case the marketplace for labor talent—is the great equalizer.

The bottom line is that no company is so big or so "excellent" that its finances and reputation can't be toppled. Excellence—or success—is not a static concept. Business is a long-running motion picture with perpetual ups and downs, not a still-life snapshot reflecting a fantasy of permanence. No company is "entitled" to success tomorrow just because it is hailed by investors and management gurus today.

Here's where it gets interesting. Companies that fail as a result of blatantly poor management are a dime a dozen, but what is more intriguing is when failure occurs on the other side of the coin—that is, when failure follows success and ostensibly good management. This occurs more often than we care to admit. Look at the history of individual companies and you'll find that a good predictor of today's business *failure* is yesterday's business *success,* because almost inevitably there are some little intervening variables in between—such as complacency, arrogance, and smugness.

Let me illustrate with a story about a certain company that understandably requests anonymity. A few years ago, this company was a $30 million organization doing exceptional things in the areas of customer responsiveness, new service innovations, and successful niche targeting, which no doubt helped explain its 25 percent annual growth rate over the prior five-year period. A few years ago, management sincerely believed it had licked the complacency/arrogance problem. Senior managers understood that their customers were very demanding and that the firm's ambitious business goals could not be attained unless all hands—including nonmanagement employees—were committed to those goals and empowered to do whatever it took to achieve them.

Accordingly, management spent a lot of time and money creating a good work environment for employees, an environment that not only satisfied their financial needs (the company paid darn well) but also allowed them the opportunity to take on many exciting responsibilities and new customer-driven projects hitherto reserved for management.

Sounds great so far, right? It certainly appeared that way a few years ago. The company was written up very positively in newspapers and received cover stories in trade publications. Its financials were solid. Employee and customer turnover was low. Everything appeared to be hunky-dory.

Until I sat in on an extraordinary series of in-house sessions, that is. Each session involved a cross-departmental, diagonal slice of employees and managers from corporate and field divisions. The purpose of the sessions was for employees to tell senior managers face-to-face how well or poorly the latter were doing in creating the "right" environment—that is, an environment that enhanced both employee morale and productivity, and one that contributed to the goal of total customer responsiveness. These goals were part of the organization's mission statement and values. Hence, the sessions were geared to letting employees tell management how well the company was living the mission and values, how honestly management was "walking the talk," and what needed to be done to rectify gaps.

I commended the senior managers for their "how'm I doin'?" courage. How many companies do you know in which top managers even attend forums such as this, much less initiate them?

On the other hand, I thought that the members of the top management team initially felt pretty confident, even a bit cocky. They assumed they wouldn't learn too much from these meetings. After all, this was a company noted for doing all of these wonderful, progressive, "excellent" things, such as focusing on the customer, flattening the organization, sharing financials with employees, and so on. Besides, by most formal measurements of organizational success and the low employee turnover rate, things seemed to be moving forward swimmingly.

The managers were wrong. Did they get an earful! Here they thought they were doing everything right, but somewhere, somehow, they had taken their eyes off the ball. After the sessions, I summarized the employees' comments into five categories, and here they are:

1. *Management doesn't listen.* Employees argued that they frequently proposed improvements in operations, service features and company marketing efforts. They argued that they also frequently voiced concern about company policies that inhibited their ability to innovate and serve the customer.

They pointed out that managers frequently heard but did not listen. The evidence of this assertion? "Nothing is ever done. There's no follow through. Managers say, 'Yeah, good idea,' but they often say they have to take it under advisement and then they just drop the ball."

Employees felt increasingly frustrated and noted that the organization's effectiveness and integrity suffered as a result. Even worse, they argued that senior management knew very well which middle managers were especially culpable in this regard, yet senior management did nothing about it. This meant that all the good intentions were perceived as just that: good intentions, not to be confused with hard business decision making.

2. *Budgets are used as excuses.* Employees argued that, on one hand, management encouraged them to be innovative and come up with new ideas for cost-efficiency and customer responsiveness. On the other hand, middle and senior managers often told employees that new ideas—even little ones—would have to be shelved; "the budget" wouldn't allow a test or implementation of the ideas. Employees argued this all-too-frequent response signified that the top organizational priority was apparently "Keep your nose clean; don't make waves."

They suggested that managers themselves should be willing to take some risks in reinforcing innovation and investing for the future rather than holding up "the budget" as something so sacred. Or, minimally, they suggested that managers take on the responsibility of coaching employees who have creative ideas on how to modify or sell the idea so that it would be approved.

3. *Data and numbers replace real information.* True, management shared budget and sales data, as well as income statements, with employees. Employees thought that was dandy, but they argued that being inundated with sheets of financials missed the point. Rather, they needed to understand the significance of those numbers. They wanted to know what management thought about the numbers and why. They wanted to know how management used those numbers in formulating policy and capital budgeting decisions. They wanted to know how the numbers impacted management's strategic goals and priorities.

Just as important, they wanted to be included in discussions on these topics. In short, they wanted impersonal data transformed into real knowledge. They said that if this were done, they would be better equipped to accept and execute company strategy and policies, and, more important, they themselves would be better equipped to make fast, "right" decisions consistent with company values and priorities.

4. *Delegation is spurious.* Employees applauded management's goal of turning more and more operational responsibili-

ties to them. But they noted that, often, delegation was a sham for one of two reasons. First, delegation was sometimes just another word for *dumping*. In their quest for total customer service, managers and salespeople made big commitments to customers, and then "dumped" all the work on employees who sometimes had to work all night to meet the deadlines and specifications negotiated by managers. Or, in their efforts to keep the organization lean and trim, management often would not hire additional people, and frequently they did not replace those who left the firm.

Rather than overhauling the work processes to eliminate as many unnecessary old activities as possible, management would simply dump the old workload requirement of two or three people on some poor survivor in the name of "empowerment." This, said employees, was a prescription for burnout and cynicism.

Second, employees felt that too often managers' implicit unspoken message was "I'm empowering you, but you had better run it by me anyway," or "I'm delegating this to you, but do it the way I would have, or just do it the way it's always been done." Or, as per criticism 1, "I'm empowering you but have to take your idea under advisement." Employees argued that these messages made "empowerment" something to be avoided.

5. *No recognition or appreciation exists.* Employees acknowledged the fairness—even generosity—of their paychecks. They appreciated the friendly, informal corporate culture. They endorsed the company's emphasis on customer service. But they felt that it wouldn't hurt managers to show some form of sincere personal gratitude when employees knocked themselves out in meeting deadlines or made creative contributions that translated into the company's bottom line. Employees said that frequently their heroic efforts on behalf of the company and its customers were not even acknowledged by managers. Employees often felt used and taken for granted.

Managers were surprised—indeed, stunned—by this feedback. Some were more than a little dismayed. I pointed out that they were fortunate to have learned important lessons. They learned that just because there's no crisis doesn't mean that

things are OK; critical problems are invariably brewing and fes-
tering. They learned that despite their progressive management,
there is always room for improvement. They learned that their
people were not complaining or whining for selfish reasons;
rather, they were turned on and demanding more opportunities
and (nonfinancial) rewards for contributing to the company's
well-being. How exciting! I saw the situation as a terrific opportunity for quantum improvement.

I also warned of potential dangers. It was clear that the senior
managers' progressive styles of management raised employees'
expectations not only for the company but for their own work
lives as well. I warned management that if, after conducting
these dramatic forums, they reverted back to employee criticism
1—that is, "management doesn't listen"—employees' insecuri-
ties, disillusionment, cynicism, and anger could potentially sky-
rocket, more so than if management had done nothing.

I urged management to react quickly and visibly to the important feedback they received. I urged management to hold
more forums and to work in partnership with their employees
to collaboratively alleviate the problems they raised. Finally, I
wondered aloud whether similar surprises would occur if management held the same forums with customers; I urged management to consider doing so.

Those on the senior management team assured me they would.

They didn't. Things stayed the same. Despite the small size of
the company, management remained blissfully ignorant of realities in the trenches. They looked at the numbers and concluded
that the gravy train would run forever. They were wrong.

And so management got another surprise. A year later the
company saw a rash of good people beginning to leave the company. These were some of the best and brightest, the ones who
became the most easily disillusioned. Some of them joined competitors; a couple became competitors themselves by starting
their own businesses and offering new and better services. Management saw a deterioration in the capacity of the company to
deliver fast, efficient, customized services. Among those who remained, morale dropped and fresh ideas withered, all of which
began to adversely impact the monthlies.

The board grew restive and began to rein in some of the more progressive management interventions in favor of more conventional controls and bureaucratic processes. This, in turn, exacerbated employee disillusionment and turnover; in fact, it generated some management disillusionment and turnover—all of which, in turn, further depressed customer responsiveness, and so on, and so on. Within just a one-year span, the lovely numbers had dropped precipitously, and the company had turned from star to goat. No more cover stories in magazines.

Once again, management learned some painful lessons. First, the success-to-failure life cycle for organizations used to be decades; in today's madcap world it can be just a few years, months, or weeks. (Think about Compaq, which went from champ to chump to champ within an eighteen-month cycle around 1990.)

Second, the numbers that a company achieves today—say, market share or earnings—are a consequence of what management did *yesterday*. But tomorrow's numbers are a reflection of what management does *today*. There's always a delayed reaction in the marketplace. And what may have been good management yesterday—hence, good numbers today—is often *not* what is good management today—hence, bad numbers tomorrow. In short, no guarantees, no entitlements.

The update: a now smaller, humbler company has painfully pulled itself out of the morass by focusing management attention on some of the things it should have done two years previously.

Will the company be a success story again? I can't predict. No person or algorithm can. New surprises are undoubtedly just around the corner. But from talking to the new CEO, I can assure you that management has learned the most important lesson of all: *beware the danger of success*. It now truly appreciates the old Chinese curse "May you get what you wish for."

Business success is what every manager wishes for, of course. But managers must never forget that eternal vigilance and immediate aggressive response are necessary to combat the complacency, arrogance, smugness, and protectionism of old practices that seem to be inevitable by-products of that success.

How do you think you and your company stack up on this issue? Always keep this issue close at hand, in your hip pocket, as you navigate Giant Steps I through V.

Why end this book with a reminder to beware the dangers of success? Because if you embark on these five Giant Steps and the Commitments needed to fulfill them, I believe you will leapfrog your competition and do so quite effectively. You'll be very successful. So much so that you might be tempted to catch your breath and relax. Don't. People catch up to those who are sitting back. And nowadays, life cycle times are shrinking exponentially, be they cycle times of products, technologies, or organizations themselves. One leap is no longer sufficient. Recently, Lars Nyberg, CEO of NCR, astutely commented on his company's rather dramatic transition from a "dog" label while in the AT&T fold to a revival entity boasting both independence and profitability: "This is no time to declare victory. The challenges only increase as we look to grow the business."

So beware the danger of success. Keep on leapfrogging. It'll certainly propel your organization's fortunes. And on a personal level, I guarantee that it'll spice up your work life, your intellect, your reputation, and your pocketbook. I wish you the best of luck.

A SHORT EPILOGUE:
PUTTING IT INTO PERSPECTIVE

In 1455, the Gutenberg Bible came off a crude printing press, signaling a momentous shift in society and in history. The invention of movable type gradually precipitated a widespread availability of books to the masses and, ultimately, the democratization of information.

Yet as James O'Donnell, professor of classic studies at the University of Pennsylvania, points out in his Web site, not everyone was initially thrilled with this new technology. Many took the position expressed by Vespasiano de Bisticci, who wrote in 1490 that in his library, "All books were superlatively good and written with the pen; had there been one printed book, it would have been ashamed in such company."

Perhaps the most vociferous criticisms came from Benedictine monks, many of whom were scribes who wrote out the books by hand. The patron saint of critics, O'Donnell notes, was the Benedictine abbot Johannes Tithemius, who argued the following:

- Printed books (which use paper) would not last nearly as long as manuscripts prepared on skin.
- Print is uglier than the beauty and art gracing the pages of illuminated manuscripts.
- Print is more defective because printers make more errors than do scribes.

Tithemius was right on all three counts. His criticisms were articulate, reasonable, and valid. They were also irrelevant. The new technology had unleashed a momentous force with its own life, a force that others capitalized on and took to new heights. The world would never be the same again.

My colleague Stanley Nel, dean of arts and sciences at the University of San Francisco, believes that Tithemius was not simply standing up as a union shop steward or a corporate protectionist against the impact of the new technology on the livelihood of the Benedictines. "At a much deeper level," Nel says, "he was mourning the passing of an age and a way of life."

I believe that Nel is correct and that the same issue is germane today. In response to the convulsive changes in today's marketplace, all of us can and perhaps should mourn the passing of an age in which we are knowledgeable and comfortable, an age in which we can point to wonderful memories. But as Nel points out, we are then left with one of two choices. "We can fight to protect our privilege and keep our comforts. Or we can give thanks that we will be able to participate in the coming revolution."

This latter sentiment underlies the spirit in which I wrote this book. The five Giant Steps tell us how to leapfrog the competition, of course. But their real value is that they do so by providing us tools to capitalize on forces as momentous as the ones faced by the Benedictines and, using Nel's sentiment, by empowering us to do so with gratitude and grace.

The revolution that Nel correctly alludes to is already here. Retiring EDS chairman Les Alberthal notes that "the rate of change is occurring faster than we can comprehend." We can't delay the changes; we can't hold back the tide; we can't build a fortress against inevitabilities.

When I watch old western movies, I am intrigued by the scenes in which a clerk taps out an urgent Morse code message on the telegraph. It's not uncommon to have onlookers watch (in awe?) as this clerk (a nerd/geek?) fiddles proficiently with this strange futuristic technology. I am amazed at how far we've come in only 100 years and how much further we're going to go. Just as we chuckle at all the excitement generated by "primitive" technologies such as telegraph and movable type, managers fifty years from now will chuckle at our own primitive technologies that we think are so cool today. Because hindsight is 20-20, they'll also smile in sympathy at our current attempts to make sense of all the macro-upheavals that are surrounding us. Of course, they'll be dealing with their own issues, ones that to us might be as unfathomable as our current issues would be to that telegraph clerk in the Old West. Again, we can't hold back the tide.

When I wrote the epilogue to the first edition of *Leapfrogging the Competition* back in April 1997, the hot news was about Dolly the cloned sheep. In the wake of the experimental results that rocked the scientific community, social pundits were making sweeping predictions about a cold, sterile, Huxley-like "brave new world" where human beings are manufactured like widgets. Politicians were calling for bans on research. Just like the fears that emerged when organ transplants and artificial hearts became real possibilities, similar anxieties were being raised about cloning.

By now, the hot air and hysteria seem to have subsided. The reason, I believe, is that people intuitively understand that it's not merely that banning inquiry is futile; it's that we really have no idea what the cloning experiments will yield for society. Gutenberg himself simply wanted a more efficient means to print Bibles; he had no idea of the enormous ripple effect that his invention would unleash. Similarly, the ultimate impact of the cloning research is presently unknown. It will emerge from efforts of those who are willing to embrace—not reject—the available knowledge to leapfrog over today's conventional wisdom. Some observers predict that the real impact of this train of investigation might be the eradication of world hunger or perhaps the development of gene chips that will revolutionize the entire field of medicine—for the better, I might add.

I happen to believe that moral discourse and debate about any societal transformation is a good thing. But whether we're talking about movable type, telegraphs, or cloned sheep, we can't deny transformation, nor can we even predict the onslaught of changes that are coming around the corner in every sector of the economy. What we can do is search for them, seize them as they emerge, and shape them toward reinventing our businesses and creating new value for our customers and investors. The five Giant Steps will help us do precisely that.

The five Giant Steps are a blueprint, but it is the fifteen Commitments described in these pages that will make or break the execution of that blueprint. Since you've read this far, I suspect that you are quite excited about embarking on this new journey. Let me reassure you that there is every reason for optimism. The terrain of the emerging economy is wide open, available to anyone. The playing field is leveled. It's a great time to be in business.

Keep in mind also that organizational renewal and success do not occur serendipitously. What's required in chaotic times like these are real leaders—people like you—to mold the future, sustain efforts, and keep promises alive. I believe this book will greatly assist you in that quest.

General Colin Powell has correctly argued that in both commercial and military endeavors, "optimism is a force multiplier." Hopefully, these five Giant Steps have provided you with the information and ammunition to set forth optimistically in a direction that can only be described as thrilling, a path that will lead your organization to soar and your own career to attain new heights that your competitors (see them way down below?) can only dream about.

INDEX

A

Aaker, David, 128
ABC, 30, 173
Acer, 89
Acquisitions. *See* Mergers and acquisitions
Advertising industry, 26–27
Akers, John, 39
Allaire, Paul, 121
Allen, Bob, 216–217, 218
AlliedSignal, 199
    stock plans, 84, 85
All in the Family, 42
All Nippon Airways, 151
Alsop, Stewart, 175
Altman, Robert, 42
Amazon.com, 2, 15–16, 32, 69
    cybermarket, 171
Amelio, Gilbert, 28
American Economic Review, 48
American Express, 38
American Home Products, 215
American Income Life Insurance, 185
American Management Association, 147, 174–175
    M2 conference, 188
American Standard, 14
America Online, xxi
    business impact, 70
    Netscape and, 34, 173
Ameritech, 215, 218, 220
AMR, 59
Andersen Consulting, 95, 155
Andersen Windows, 118
    product customization, 143
Anderson, Kris, 177
Andreesen, Marc, 156
Apple Computer, 26, 27–28, 31, 200
    iMac, 28
Appreciation of employees, 237

Arbitron survey data, 41
Arizona Tea, 172
Arnault, Ron, 79, 90–91
Arthur D. Little, 207, 211
Aspen Leadership Institute, 187
Astra, 152
A.T. Kearney, 207
AtlantiCare, 204
Atlantic City Medical Center, 197
    PACE (Patients Are the Center of Everything), 200–201, 203–204
AT&T, 15, 152, 215, 240
    Cemex and, 67
    McCaw Cellular and, 36–37
    NCR and, 218
    Wells Fargo and, 38
Autodesk, 108
Automobile industry, 40–41
AutoNation, 189

B

Baby Bell lines, 36–37
Banking industry, 38–39
    mergers and acquisitions in, 219–220
Bank of America, 158–159, 215, 222
Barksdale, Jim, 138
Barnes and Noble, 15–16
Barron's, 216
Bartz, Carol, 108
Baxter, 113
Beckham, J. Daniel, 128
Bell, Chip, 56, 178
Benetton, 44–45
Ben & Jerry's, 43, 48
Bennis, Warren, 199
Bergsteinsson, Bryan, 189
Berkshire Hathaway, 216
Bezos, Jeff, 2, 15, 32, 46

245

Bifocal vision, 8–9, 56–61
Big body/little brain pyramid, 71–73
Biggs, Barton, xxi–xxii
Bill Graham Presents, 195–196
Billington, Jim, 222–223
Biogen, 152
Biotechnology, 47
Blockbuster, 216
Bloomberg, Michael, 4, 9, 87
Bloomberg LP, 4
    as permeable organization, 86, 87
Bochco, Steven, 42
Body Shop, 4, 6, 124
Boeing, 70, 150, 151, 162, 215, 218
Bonsignore, Michael, 225
Booz, Allen, & Hamilton
    report, 116
Borders, 15, 16
Borland's WordPerfect, 170–171
Bossidy, Lawrence, 48, 85, 199
Boston Consulting Group, 109
Boundary-less organizations, 86–87
Brain-based economy, 73–74, 148
    responsibility of employees,
    83–84
Brand, Steward, 40
Brand image, 142
Bravo! division, Cablevision, 40
Breakthroughs, 104
Brinker, Norman, 225–226
Brinker International, 225
Brinkley, David, 30
British Airways, 151
British Telecom, 149
Brown, Tom, 8
Buckman Labs, 73, 229
Budgets, 236
Buffet, Warren, 216
Bureaucracy, 71, 104–105
    computers and, 105–106
    Total Quality Management
    (TQM) and, 208
Burnout, 237
Business Week, 161, 216, 218, 233

C

Cablevision, 40
CAD-CAM, 138
Cadence Design Systems, 142–143
    expertise, selling, 116–117
Cadillac, 226–227

Calipers, 8–9
Canadian Pacific Hotels, 115,
    116, 156
Candor and team work, 164
Carey, William, 61
Caring and teamwork, 165–166
Car Max, 189
Case, John, 18–19
Casio, 59
Cathay Pacific, 151
CBS, 30, 33, 173, 214
CBS Cable, xxi
CCC Information Services, 26, 39
CDnow, xx
CDs (compact disks), xix–xxi
Celanese, 24
Cemex, 66–68, 73, 104
    customers and, 114
Century Plaza Hotel, Los
    Angeles, 14
Champy, James, 19, 84, 211, 212
Change, xxix–xxxi, 185–240
    direction of, 199–202
    discipline and, 203–205
    fads and, 206–224
    honesty and, 195–205
    managing change, 188
    understanding change, 196–197
    urgency and, 197–199
Chaparral Steel, 73
    curiosity, culture of, 99
    educational sabbaticals, 89
    gain sharing, 84
    as permeable organization, 86
Charles Schwab, 2, 140, 154
    discount brokerage services, 171
Chase Manhattan, xix
Cheers, 42
Chen, Winston, 113
Chrysler, 41–42, 215
CIA, 151
Cincinnati Milacron. See Milacron
CIO magazine, 65
Circuit City, xx
Cisco Systems, 16, 140–141, 154
    acquisitions by, 217
    customers and, 177
Citicorp, 215
Citigroup, 38
Citysearch, 217
Closed door policies, 93

CNN, 2, 5–6, 30, 32, 35
  customer needs and, 13
Cocooning trend, 32
Codependency, 165
Cohen, Paul, 210–211
Coke, 43
Collaboration, 166
  with customers, 229
Comdex convention, Las Vegas, 138
Commodity pricing, 117
Communication
  barriers to, 95
  improving, 18–19
Compaq, 31, 48, 215, 239
Competing for the Future
  (Hamel), 48
Competition
  inviting, 169–176
  new sources of, 37
  overemphasis on, 172–176
  squashing competitors, 169–170
Competitor analysis, 38
Complaining customers, 160,
  177–184
  approach to, 182
  education and, 182–183
  quality and, 182–183
  responding to, 180–181
  rewards for, 183
  team work and, 183–184
  toll-free phone lines for, 179–180
  Web sites, posting complaints
    on, 182
Consensus of team, 163
Construction Calculators, 64
Conventional wisdom, xxvi
Corporate culture
  changing, 20–21
  curiosity, culture of, 87–89
  sacred cows, challenging, 82–86
  secrecy and, 76
  Total Quality Management
    (TQM) and, 209–210
Cost-cutting frenzies, 125
Costello, Joe, 142–143
Costello, John, 142
Cotsakos, Christos, 5
Countrywide Credit Industries,
  xix, 140
Cronkite, Walter, 30
Cross-functional teams, 74

CRSS, 113
CSC Index, 213
CTI, 146, 162
Cultivating relationships, 159
Curiosity, culture of, 87–89
Customers. *See also* Complaining
  customers
  buying customers,
    126–127
  collaboration with, 229
  external customers, 228
  feedback, 44–45
  foresight of, 44
  intangibles, interest in, 132–133
  listening to, 133–134
  meeting needs, 12–15
  naive listening to, 45
  obsession with, 113
  over profits, 121–129
  quality defined by, 114
  satisfying, 3
  unique needs of, 137
  wrapping organization around,
    111–144
Customer service, 118–119
Custom Foot, 139
Custom Publishing, McGraw-
  Hill, 139
Cutler, Wayne, 116
Cynicism, 237

D

Daimler, 215
Daiwa bank, 223
Das, T. K., 161–162
Davenport, Thomas, 211, 214
David, Larry, 42
Davis, Stan, 68
Dayton Hudson Corporation, ii,
  86, 198
  customer and, 142
Dealmaking. *See* Mergers and
  acquisitions
Dean Witter, 215
De Bono, Edward, 38
DEC, 215
Decision-making authority models,
  71–73
De Geus, Arie, 54, 90
Delegation of authority, 236–237
Dell, Michael, 221, 225

Dell Computer, 2, 6, 16, 104,
    118, 154
    complaining customers, 181
    deal-making and, 221
    direct-mail ordering of PCs,
        16–17
    no-intermediary distribution
        system, 171
    stock plans, 84
Deming, W. Edwards, 44
Dent, Harry, 105
DePree, Max, 211
Deregulation, xxii
Dewey, John, 193
Dickinson, Wood, 89
Dickinson Theatre chain, 89
Digital Equipment, 37, 41
Digital Media Association
    (DiMA), xxi
Diller, Barry, 217
Direction of change, 199–202
Discipline and change, 203–206
Discount brokers, 4–5
Disintermediation, 38
Disney Co., 58, 181
Dorothy Lane grocery chain, 141
Dow-Jones, 138
Downsizing, 69
DRAM memory chip, 7
DreamWorks, 173
Drucker, Peter, 29, 99, 122,
    146–147, 188, 223, 226
Dumping, 237
Du Pont, 24

E

Eastern Airlines, 127, 128
Eastman Kodak, 27, 33, 232
Ebbers, Bernard, 58
Economies of scale, 104, 216
Economist, 232
The Economist, 41
EDA Today, 117
EDS, 113, 153–154, 162
    customers and, 177
Education
    on complaining customers,
        182–183
    of employees, 88–89
    perpetual learning culture, 90
Educational forums, 229

Eisner, Michael, 121, 122
ElectricVillage, xx
Electronic Data Interchange
    (EDI), xxiii
El Nuevo Herald, 46
E-Loan, xviii
Employees
    in brain-based organizations,
        73–75
    curios employees, hiring, 88
    liberating employees,
        97–103
    recognition of, 237
    stock plans, 84–85
    work environment for, 234
Empowerment, 94, 99
The End of Work (Rifkin), 107
Enron, 124
Entrepreneurship, 42
    Total Quality Management
        (TQM) and, 209–210
Erickson, Tamara, 211
Ernst & Young, 207
Error, educational element of, 89
ESPN, 58, 124
E*Trade, 5, 6, 140
    customer needs and, 13
EveryCD, xx
Excel, 107–108
Excellent companies, 233
Excite, xxi
    individualized programs, 138
Expansion magazine, 68
Expertise, selling,
    116–117
Exploration, 104
External customers, 228
Exxon, 215

F

Fads. See also Mergers and
        acquisitions; Total Quality
        Management (TQM)
    and change, 206–224
    reengineering, 212–213
Fast Company magazine, 49,
    140, 211
Fax technology, 26
FedEx, 6, 8–9, 16, 169
    Amazon.com and, 32
    customer needs, 13

Fujitsu and, 145–146, 162
Power Ship software system, 13
Service Quality Index, 182
Smith, Fred, 33
Feedback
change and, 193
from customers, 45
importance of, 238
Fidelity Investments, 152
Film photography business, 27
First Auction, 217
First Direct, 13, 149
First-to-market, 17
Fisher, George, 27
Five giant steps, xxv–xxx
Flexibility, 104–105
Foote, Cone & Belding, 161, 168
Forbes, 226
Forbes ASAP, 219
Ford, 41
Forecasting, 48
Fortune 500 list, 147
Foster, Richard, 23–24, 34
401(k) plans, 85
Friedman, Thomas, 70
Fuji, 149
Heavy Industries, 151
Fujitsu, 145–146, 162
customers and, 177
Fuller, Mark, 49–50
Functional barriers, reducing, 19–20

G
Gadamer, Hans, 32
Gain sharing, 84
Gammill, Lee, Jr., 20
Gandhi, Mohandas, 205
Gap stores, 16
Gates, Bill, 33–34, 35, 191, 197
bifocal vision of, 61
membership to Microsoft, 154
on Murdoch, Rupert, 35
Schmidt, Eric and, 172
strategic priorities, 71
Teledesic, 150
Gateway, 117–118
Yahoo! and, 149
General Electric, 48, 59, 233
expertise, selling, 116, 117
Pratt Whitney and, 173–174
stock plans, 84

General Motors, 33, 38, 41, 232
Cadillac, 226–227
Milacron and, 154, 155
profit motive and, 125
Saturn, 153
General Nutrition Centers
(GNC), 139
Geopolitics, 151
Gerstner, Lou, 28–29, 137–138, 202
Giant steps, xxv–xxx
Gilder, George, 108
Gillette, xxii, 16, 124, 153
Glaxo Wellcome, 222
Globalization, xxii, 70
Glover, Rita, 117
Gluck, Frederick, 50
GMAC financing division, 38
Goal-setting, 82–86
GoodNoise, xx, xxi
Graham, Bill, 195–196, 204
Granite Rock, 63–65, 73
education of employees, 89
GraniteXpress, 64–65
Gretzky, Wayne, 61
Grove, Andrew, 7, 28, 57, 98, 191
GTE, 44
Guarantees, 66

H
Hamel, Gary, 21, 44, 48, 60–61, 215
Hammer, Michael, 19, 90, 211
Handlery, Paul, xxv
Handlery hotel chain, xxv
Harari, Oren, i, ii
Hard Candy, 17
Harley Davidson, 124, 154
Hartford Insurance, 38
Harvard Business Review, 117,
124, 199
Harvard Management Update,
222–223
Hayek, Frederich, 48
Headspace, xx
Heineken, 172
Herman Miller, 211
Heskett, James, 13
Hewlett-Packard, xxiii, 95
acquisitions by, 217
distribution organization,
213–214
laser jet printers, 171

Hewlett-Packard, *continued*
   planned obsolescence, 7
Hierarchical model, 104–105
Hill Street Blues, 42
Home Advisor, Microsoft, xviii, 140
Home Depot, 6, 22
HomeShark, viii
Home Shopping Network, 217
Honesty and change, 195–205
Honeywell, 151, 225
Hotel business
   customers and, 115–116
   reservation process, 116

I

IBM, 28–29, 33, 37–38, 59, 151
   change and, 202
   competitors of, 39
   federal systems division, 137–138
   mainframe technology, 31
   Solectron Corporation and,
      112–113
   Sun Microsystems and, 173
Ideas
   barriers to, 79–96
   curiosity, culture of, 87–89
IKEA, 13–14
iMac, 28
Imagination, 104–105
Imparato, Nicholas, xxiv, 56, 71
Imus, Don, 173
Information-spreading, 80–82
InfoSeek, xxi
   individualized programs, 138
Ingram, 32
Iniguez, Gelacio, 68
Ink, 173
*Innovation: The Attacker's
   Advantage* (Foster), 23–24
In Search of Excellence (Peters &
   Waterman), 233
Insider organizations, 93
Insight, 191
Institute for the Future, 108
Intangibles, 68–69
   customer's interest in,
      132–133
   economy of, 104
Intel, xxii, 7, 28, 57, 98, 191
   planned obsolescence, 7

Intellectual Capital (Stewart), 70
Interim Services, 45, 113
Intermountain Health Care, 182
Internal customers, 228
Internal Revenue Service
   (IRS), 137
International Paper/Federal
   Paper, 70
Internet. *See also* Web sites
   third wave of, 138
Intuit, 45
   disintermediation, 38
   QuickenMortgage, viii
Intuition, use of, 45–46
Inventory, just-in-time, 118
Involvement of management, 50
Irvine Sensors, 151

J

Japan Airlines, 151
Java programming, 138, 151
Jenkins, Homan, xxi
Jensen, Torkild, 202
Job descriptions, 76, 108
Jobs, Steve, 28, 31–32, 33
Johnson & Johnson, 152, 153
   acquisitions by, 217
Johnson SC, 16
Johnsonville Foods, 74, 83
Jones, Brian, 190
*The Journal of General
   Management,* 161–162
*Jumping the Curve: Innovation and
   Strategic Choice in an Age of
   Transition* (Imparato &
   Harari), xxiv, 56, 71, 203
Jurassic Park, 152
Just-in-time inventory
   management, 118

K

Kahl, Jack, 89
Kai-zen, 189
Karlgaard, Rich, 219
Kawasaki Heavy Industries, 151
Kelleher, Herb, 88, 197
Kelley, Kevin, 33
Kelley, Tom, 43–44
Kelly, Pat, 88
KFC, 216

KGB, 151
Kinko's Copiers, 13, 225
Kirin, 172
Kmart, 41
K'Netix system, Buckman
    Labs, 229
Knight, Phil, 36, 46–47
Knowledge, 63–109
    barriers to flow of, 76
Koch, Ed, 230
Kolesar, Peter, 116
Kolind, Lars, 94–96, 190
Kroc, Ray, 33
Kuhn, Thomas, 31, 34

L

L. L. Bean, 180
Lankton, Gordon, 75, 142, 155
Larkin, Ray, 197, 199
Latin Finance magazine, 68
Lawrence, Paul, 174–175
Leadership, 98–99
Leader to Leader, 146–147
Leapfrogging organization,
    defined, x
Lear, Norman, 42
Le Duc, Bob, 228
Lego's Mindstorms Robotics
    Invention System, 13, 150, 162
Leonard, Stew, 180, 181
Letting go, 101–102
Level 3, 218
Levering, Robert, 233
Levi Strauss, 59
    custom-built jeans, 138
Levitt, Ted, 122
Liberating people, 83
Life expectancy of
    companies, 232–233
Lipton Tea, 172
Liquid Audio, xx
Listening
    to customers, 133–134
    management and, 231,
        235–236
    naive listening, 225
Live Well stores, 139
Lorenzo, Frank, 128
Lotus, 48
Lucas Arts & Entertainment, 152

Lucent Technologies, 217, 218
Lycos, 217
Lynn, George, 197, 200, 202,
    203–204

M

McCabe, Edward, 121
McCaw, Craig, 15, 150
McCaw Cellular, 15
    AT&T and, 36–37
McColl, Hugh, 222
McDermott, Robert, 121
McDonald's, 33
McDonnell Douglas, 70, 215, 218
McGowan, Bill, 190
McGraw-Hill, Custom
    Publishing, 139
McGuirk, Jim, 137–138
McKenna, Regis, 3
McKinsey & Co., 207
McNealy, Scott, 200
Mahoney, Richard, 47
Management
    failure and, 234
    layers of, 76
    listening and, 231, 235–236
    profit motive and, 123–126
    realities, ignorance of, 238
    trust in, 100–101
Management Review, 20, 77, 147,
    211
Manco, 19
    curiosity, culture of, 87–88
    education of employees, 89
Mandela, Nelson, 205
M & I Data Systems, 158–159
Maney, Kevin, 220
Manker, Faye, 76
Marcar Consulting, 173
Marcus, Bernard, 22, 121
Market research, 42–43
    Pepsi-Cola and, 45
    as tool, 47
Market units of one, 120, 130–144
Markpoint, 202
Marks, James, 5
M*A*S*H, 42
Mass customization, 138
Mass markets, 141
    web relations in, 154

Matra Marconi, 150, 162
Matsushita, 139
Maybelline, 17
MCA Music, 45
MCI, 149–150
MCI/WorldCom, 57–58
Media Lab, 150
Media Metrix, 5
Meeting customer needs, 12–15
Mercedes-Benz, 40–41, 169
Merck, 59, 139, 151–152, 154
    partnering by, 150
Mergers and acquisitions, 126,
    215–216
    in banking industry, 219–220
    ease of financing, 221
    megalomania and, 222
    as panacea, 221–222
    payoff to management and, 222
    rules for, 217–218
    Thomas Lawson Syndrome and,
    219
Merrill Lynch, 38, 171
Meyer, Herbert, 49
Miami Herald, 46
Microsoft, xviii, xxii, 31, 59,
    169, 200
    acquisitions by, 217
    Explorer, 172
    Home Advisor, xviii
    Justice Department action, 34
    market value of, 69
    membership to, 154
    NBC and, 33–34
    Novell and, 170–171
    stock plans, 84
Midland Banks, 149
Milacron, 60, 154, 220
    acquisitions by, 217
    customers and, 177
    General Motors and, 155
Milliken, 180
Mintzberg, Henry, 49
Mitsubishi Heavy Industries, 151
Mobil, 215
Mondex electronic purse card, 38
Monsanto, 47, 215
    bifocal vision of, 60
Moody, William, 157–158
Morgan Stanley, 214

Mortgage Bankers Association of
    America, viii
Moskowitz, Milton, 233
Motorola, 83, 150, 152, 153, 162
MP3 data format, x–xi
Mpath Interactive, 13
MSNBC, 173
Murdoch, Rupert, 35

N

Naive listening, 225
Nardelli, Robert, 117
National Aeronautics and Space
    Administration (NASA), 151
NationsBank, 159, 215, 222
NBC, 30
    Microsoft and, 33–34
NCR, 218, 240
Nellcor Puritan Bennett, 83, 197,
    199
Netscape, xxi, 6, 34, 138, 156
    America Online and, 34, 173
    business impact, 70
    Navigator, 172
NetWare, 171, 172
Newsletters, 229
New York Bankers Association, 152
New York Life Insurance, 20
New York Times, 172–173
Nielson survey data, 41
Nike, 2, 6, 36, 46–47
Nokia, 16, 17
Noorda, Ray, 170
No-rework efficiency, 208
Northrop Grumman, 151
Northwest Airlines, 169
Northwest Mutual Life, 180
Novell, xiii, 170–171
N2K, xx, xxi
NUMMI (New United Motor
    Manufacturing), 20–21
Nyberg, Lars, 240
Nypro, 20, 75, 152–153, 190
    customer and, 142
    customers and, 177
    Vistakon and, 155

O

Obsolescence, 23–35
    mergers and acquisitions and, 222

OEMs (original equipment
    manufacturers), 111
Olevson, Ken, 155
On Achieving Excellence, 190, 210
The 101 Best Companies to Work
    for in America (Levering &
    Moskowitz), 233
Only the Paranoid Survive
    (Grove), 191
The Open Book Experience
    (Case), 18
Open-book management, 80
Oracle, 150, 151
Orfalea, Paul, 225
Organizational pyramid, 71–73
Osteoporosis Centers of
    America, 150
Oticon, 19, 73, 94–96
O'Toole, Jim, 187
Out of Control (Kelley), 33
Outsourcing, 69, 148

P

PACE (Patients Are the Center of
    Everything), 200–201
Paradigm creation, 7–8
Paris Miki, 139
Partnering, 69. See also Teamwork
    difficulties in, 161–162
    relationships, building, 145–184
    trust and, 157–158
Peapod, 14
PE Biosystems, 74–75
People Express, 233
Pepsi-Cola, 43, 216
    market research and, 45
    Performance Research
        Association, 177, 178
Performance reviews, 230
Perkin Elmer, 74
Permeable organizations, 86–87
Perpetual learning culture, 90–91
Peters, Tom, 45–46, 147, 162, 190,
    210, 226, 233
Philips, 169
Physician Sales & Service, 73
    curiosity, culture of, 88
    stock plans, 84
Pizza Hut, 216
Planet Hollywood, 17

Planned obsolescence, 7
Plastics News Processor
    of the Year, 152–153
Platt, Lew, xxiii
Policy manuals, 108
Porter, Bill, 5
Porter, Michael, 126, 169
Post-It notepads, 6, 42
Powell, Colin, 48, 151, 152
PowerPoint, 107–108
Prahalad, C. K., 21, 44, 215
Pratt Whitney, 173–174
Prejudgments, 32
Price Waterhouse, 109
ProAir, 13
Proctor & Gamble, 174, 233
Products
    improving, 7–8
    zero-defects products, 208
Profits, 119–120, 121–129
    as indices, 122–123
Publicis, 161, 168
Purpose of company, 52

Q

Quad/Graphics, xix, 48, 73
    capital budgets, 186
    classroom education for
        employees, 89
    curiosity, culture of, 99
    sacred cows, challenging,
        82–83
Quadracchi, Harry, 48, 82,
    186, 190
Quaker Oats, 107–108
Quality
    complaining customers and,
        182–183
    customers defining, 114
    market unit of one, 120
QuattroPro spreadsheet
    software, 171
QuickenMortgage, Intuit, xviii
Quinn, Brian, 48
Qwest, 218

R

Rand, Barry, 73–74
Raphael, David, 173, 175
Rapoport, Bernard, 185–186

Real Estate Finance Today, xviii
Recognition
    of employees, 237
    of team members, 166–167
Reducing time to market, 15–18
Reeingineering, 212–213
    Total Quality Management
        (TQM) and, 212
Reengineering the Corporation
    (Hammer & Champy), 19, 84
Reich, Robert, 119, 135, 142
Reichheld, Frederick, 13
Relationships in business, xviii–xix,
    145–184
Respect and teamwork, 164–165
Reuters, 223
Revlon, 17
Rewards
    for complaining customers, 183
    for team members, 166–167
Rhone-Poulenc, 152
Rifkin, Jeremy, 107
RIO PMP300 portable
    music player, xxi
Risk-taking, 125–126
Ritz-Carlton Hotel Company,
    115–116, 200
    complaining customers, 181
Rockwell, 151
Roddick, Anita, 4, 124
Rolls Royce Aerospace Group,
    153–154, 162, 174
Rosen, Larry, xxi
Rosenbluth International, 57
Rosenbluth Travel, 23, 140
Rouhana, Bill, 220
Royal Dutch/Shell, 54, 90,
    232–233
Rubbermaid, 45
Russian Space Agency, 151
Ryan, Buddy, xxi

S

Saatchi & Saatchi, 216
Sabre Group, 14
Sacred cows, challenging,
    82–86
Saffo, Paul, 108
Salaries, 83–84
Sales data, 236
Salespeople, 126–127

Sandelin, Martin, 48
SAS Airlines, 91–93
SBC, 215, 218, 220
Schmidt, Eric, xxiii, 171
    Gates, Bill and, 172
Schultz, Howard, 22, 85, 121,
    122, 172
Schwarzenegger, Arnold, 80
ScrubaDub Auto Wash Centers, 13
Sculley, John, 27–28, 45–46
Seagrams, 214
Search engines, 138, 149
Sears, 142
Secrecy in corporate culture, 76
Seiko, 45
Seinfeld, 42
Self-confidence, 191
Senge, Peter, 44
Sermatch Klock, 155–156
Seven-Up/RC Bottling
    Company, 172
Shadowing, 61
Shaffer, Alan, 154
Shapiro, Bob, 47
Shih, Stan, 89
Short-term financials, 125
Silicon Graphics, 152
Sirower, Mark, 126, 216
Smart organizations, 73
Smith, Fred, 33
Smith-Corona, 31
Smith/Kline, 222
Snapple, 107–108
Software, individualized, 138
SOHO, 13
Solectron Corporation, 20,
    111–113, 142
Solvik, Peter, 140–141
Sony, 6, 169
    Walkmans, 6
Southwest Airlines, 23, 197
    curiosity, culture of, 87–88
Spectrum, 117
Sperlich, Hal, 41–42
Spindler, Michael, 28
Spreading information, 80–82
Springfield Remanufacturing
    Corporation, 19, 73, 81, 197
    curiosity, culture of, 88–89
Sprint, 75–76
Stability, 187

Stack, Jack, 81, 197
Staples, 180
Starbucks, 22, 124
stock plans, 84
Starcke, Ebbe, 92–93, 94, 96
Steel Service Center Institute, 158
Stewart, Thomas, 70
Stew Leonard's, 180
Stock plans, 84–85
Stock values, 122–123
Strategy, 47–51
    as conversation, 51
    execution of, 49
    formulation of, 37
    traditional strategy, 6–7
*The Structure of Scientific
    Revolutions* (Kuhn), 31
Success, danger of, 232–240
Sundance Channel, 40
Sun Microsystems, 20, 26, 34, 73,
    151, 169, 200
    IBM and, 173
    Java programming, 138
    as permeable organization, 86
    spreading information at, 81
Swatch, 124
Sweeney, Dan, 187–188
Sykes, Richard, 222
Synergy, 215, 216
The Synergy Trap (Sirower), 216

T

Taco Bell, 216
Target Stores, 198
TCI, 44, 215
Teamwork, 94
    authority of team, 167–168
    building teams, 161–168
    candor and, 164
    caring and, 165–166
    collaboration, 166
    complaining customers and,
        183–184
    connectedness of team,
        167–168
    consensus of team, 163
    influence of team, 167–168
    recognition and rewards,
        166–167
    respect and, 164–165
    trust and, 163–164

Technology, xii–xiii
    comfort levels, 25
    information technology, 16
Teledesic, 150, 162
Teleflex, 155–156
Television networks, 30
Teng, Bing-Sheng, 161–162
Terminator 2, 152
Thomas Lawson Syndrome,
    10, 24–27
    mergers and acquisitions
        and, 219
Thomas W. Lawson, 23–24
Thompson, Jim, 189–190
Thos. Moser, 210–211
3Com, 14
3M
    acquisitions by, 217
    complaining customers, 181
    customer satisfaction
        and, 141–142
    Post-It notepads, 42
Ticketmaster Online, xxi, 217
Time, Inc., 25, 138
Time magazine, 138, 223
Time to market, reducing, 15–18
Time Warner, 25
    CNN and, 35
Tire industry, 24, 36
Toffler, Alvin, 190
Toll-free phone lines, 179–180
Total Quality Management
    (TQM), 189, 206–210
    egotism and, 209
    entrepreneurship and,
        209–210
    minimum standards and, 208
    reeingineering and, 212
    service and, 211
Total Recall, 80
Tower Records, xix–xx, 15
Townsend, Lynn, 125
Toyota, 169, 189
    General Motors and, 20–21
Traditional strategies, 36–46
Traveller's, 215
Travelocity, 139
Trend sniffing, 229
Trust, 157–158
    teamwork and, 163–164
Tullman, Glen, 39

Turner, Ted, 5–6, 30, 32, 33, 35, 46
TWA, 232

U
Ulrich, Bob, i–ii, 86, 142, 143, 198
Understanding change, 196–197
Uniqueness of company, 52
Unisys Federal Systems, 137, 143
United Airlines, 151, 169
Universal, 214
University of San Francisco,
    157–158
UPS, 8
    strike, 1997, 169
Urgency and change, 197–199
U.S. Postal Service, 8, 33
USA Networks, 217
USA Today, 220, 222
Utterback, Jim, 24
U2D2, 107

V
Vallen Corporation, 189–190
Values of company, 53
Van Rysin, Garrett, 116
VeriFone, 19, 73
    Oracle and, 150
    as permeable organization, 86
Viacom, 216
Viller, Philipe, 42
Visa International, 152
Vistakon, 153, 155

W
Walgreens, 150
Walkmans, Sony, 6
Wall Street Journal, 75–76, 135,
    169, 216
    individually tailored on-line
        edition, 138
Wal-Mart, xx, 2, 4, 16
Walton, Sam, 4, 231
Wanniski, Jude, 43
Waterman, Bob, 233
Weaver, 45
Web delivery, 26

Web sites
    complaints, posting, 182
    Dell Computer, 118
    mortgage application sites,
        xviii–xix
Welch, Jack, 85, 117, 174,
    200, 225
Wells Fargo, 38
West, Douglas, 189
Westinghouse, 214, 232
Wherehouse, xix–xx
White Paper, World Gold
    Council, 106
Williams Company, 37
Wilms, Wellford, 20
Windows NT, 170, 172
WinStar, 218, 220
Win-win solutions, 166
Wired magazine, 33
Woolpert, Bruce, 64
Work environment, 234
Work teams, 81
    at Solectron, 112
WorldCom, 149–150, 217,
    218, 220
Worth magazine, 134–135
Wozniak, Steve, 31–32

X
Xerox, 32
    Fuji and, 149
    Palo Alto Research Center, 31

Y
Yahoo!, 9–70
    Gateway and, 149
    individualized programs, 138
Y2K, 137

Z
Zambrano, Lorenzo, 66
Zanuck, Richard, 42
Zeien, Alfred, 191
Zemke, Ron, 178, 180–181
Zero-defects products, 208
Zyban, 139